TWENTIETH CENTURY VIEWS

The aim of this series is to present the best in contemporary critical opinion on major authors, providing a twentieth century perspective on their changing status in an era of profound revaluation.

Maynard Mack, *Series Editor*
Yale University

EZRA POUND

A COLLECTION OF CRITICAL ESSAYS

Edited by

Walter Sutton

Prentice-Hall, Inc., *Englewood Cliffs, N. J.*

The editor is grateful to New Directions for permission to reprint quotations from Ezra Pound's published poems, essays, and letters and from *The Poetry of Ezra Pound* by Hugh Kenner.

Current printing (last digit):

12 11 10 9 8 7 6 5

Table of Contents

Introduction

by Walter Sutton

I

In 1908 a youthful American poet and student of romance literature arrived in Italy, a cultural refugee from the "half savage country" of his birth. At twenty-two, Ezra Pound had just been dismissed from his first and only academic position, an instructorship at Wabash College. To the eastern bred Pound, Crawfordsville, Indiana, had seemed the sixth circle of desolation in "the most Godforsakenest area of the Middle West." In contrast, Europe impressed him as an artist's paradise. After a brief stay in Venice, where he commissioned the printing of a small edition of his poems under the title *A Lume Spento,* he made his way to London, which was to be his home for more than a decade. Here, in the spring of 1909, Elkin Mathews brought out his first commercially published book of verse.

The title, *Personae,* held a special importance for Pound, who later adopted it for his collected poems exclusive of *The Cantos.* Its meaning is a necessary key to an understanding of the motive and method of all his work. In the early essay "Vorticism" (1914), Pound describes his quest for selfhood and "sincere self-expression" in the flux of modern life: "I began this search for the real in a book called *Personae,* casting off, as it were, complete masks of the self in each poem. I continued in long series of translations, which were but more elaborate masks."

All of Pound's early poems, from his first renderings of the Provençal poets through his translations from Anglo-Saxon, Latin, and Japanese poetry to *Hugh Selwyn Mauberley* (1920), gain a common perspective through the idea of the mask. It is a device which carries over into *The Cantos,* where, by the use of a shifting sequence of masks, the poet attempts to establish his identity in a world in which the great cultures of the past survive only in discrete fragments without meaning for most of mankind. It is Pound's mission as a "culture poet" to conserve the best of the past and to renew lost principles of order.

The persona or mask represents the poet's identity in the broadest possible sense: it embraces his choice of subject and language, the very rhythm of his speech, and his distinctive point of view. In surveying earlier literatures and adapting their conventions to his own ends as he speaks in the person of the troubadour, the Anglo-Saxon seafarer, the exiled Chinese warrior and intellectual, the modern aesthete, and the Odyssean wanderer who came to comprehend all these roles and more, Pound combines the Confucian principle of "making it new" with a demonstration of the interaction of tradition and the individual talent.

Pound's early work was favorably received. English reviewers and critics recognized in his poems an authentic new lyric voice and an active and virile spirit, expressed with a "brusque intensity of effect" not to be found in most contemporary verse. For readers accustomed to the Victorian and Georgian poets, *Personae, Exultations,* and the volumes that followed came as a refreshment of the sensibility.

During the productive early years in London, Pound did not confine his abundant energies to the writing of poetry. He gave generous encouragement and practical aid to other as yet unestablished writers, including Robert Frost, James Joyce, and T. S. Eliot. He was active in such revolutionary movements as Imagism and Vorticism. He edited the first Imagist anthology and served as foreign editor and chief talent scout for *Poetry,* Harriet Monroe's Chicago magazine of verse. He also kept up a copious correspondence, maintaining contact with old friends like William Carlos Williams and giving advice to the first of several generations of younger writers.

Hugh Selwyn Mauberley (1920) marks a turning point in Pound's career as a poet and in the criticism of his work. As he moved from a series of shorter individual poems and translations, through *Mauberley,* to the more "engaged" and structurally complex verse of the evolving *Cantos,* Pound shared the experience of numerous artists (Joyce is one) whose later work alienated some early admirers. For some of Pound's critics, *Mauberley* stands as a masterpiece crowning the years of youthful promise, while the less coherent *Cantos* seem a long decline from this early achievement. For others, Pound's poetry is a progression of unbroken development from the minor poems of his early years, through the transitional *Mauberley,* an admirable though limited work, to the more mature vision and technical mastery of *The Cantos.*

In the years following the publication of *Mauberley,* Pound became an increasingly controversial figure. The political and economic ideas of the man, who found a home in Mussolini's Italy during the 1920's, affected the reputation of the poet. Criticism reached its height during his arrest and imprisonment and immediately following the award of the Bollingen Prize for 1948 to *The Pisan Cantos.* Although much of the discussion was concerned with Pound's moral, legal, and psychological status, this period also saw a renewed and mounting interest in his creative work and his contribution to modern literature. As a consequence, much of the most informed and enlightening twentieth century criticism of Ezra Pound has appeared during the past ten or fifteen years. It is the purpose of this volume not to reopen and reconsider the Pound "case," a subject that has been largely exhausted, but rather to illuminate his work by a representative collection of the best available criticism. This is not to say that the ideas and attitudes of "the man" are irrelevant to the achievement of "the poet"—nor to ignore the fact that the question of Pound's poetic achievement has itself remained highly controversial.

II

Differences of opinion about Pound's work have existed even among other poets with whom he has been closely associated. William Butler Yeats, who respected Pound's critical judgment and prized his friendship, was disturbed by the apparent lack of unity in *The Cantos*. In the selection from the introduction to *The Oxford Book of Modern Verse* reprinted here, Yeats remarks that he finds "more style than form" in the work of Pound. For Yeats, who feels that form must be "full, sphere-like, single," the fragmentation and discontinuity of *The Cantos* are serious weaknesses. His reaction is typical of many British readers and writers, who have tended to distrust free verse patterns and experimental techniques. It is perhaps for this reason that more English than American critics have preferred Pound's earlier to his later work.

The American poet William Carlos Williams, who shares a number of Pound's ideas about poetry, admires the open form of his verse. His essay on Pound, like Pound's own prose, proceeds through a series of apparently discontinuous but thematically related abrupt paragraphs that often break through to sudden insights. In "Excerpts from a Critical Sketch," Williams, a defender of the American idiom, approves Pound's efforts to base the rhythms of poetry on those of speech. He notes that Pound, unlike many of his contemporaries who are in the symbolist tradition, has strained to move "away from the word as symbol toward the word as reality" (a nominalist tendency to which a later critic, Harold H. Watts, gives considerable attention). Although in general approving of Pound's language, Williams recognizes a paradoxical quality in his verse: while his words often "affect modernity with too much violence," his versification reflects the attraction of the models of the past, toward which he leans "overmuch."

T. S. Eliot has written about his fellow expatriate and long-time friend on several occasions. Of these, the retrospective essay published in *Poetry* in 1946 provides the most balanced estimate of Pound's importance as a poet, critic, and "force" in modern literature. Eliot likens Pound to Irving Babbitt, pointing out that both men—students and "teachers" of comparative literature—were "dominating directors" of their followers and propagandists for their own special views. Observing that Pound must finally be judged on his "total work for literature," Eliot recapitulates his earlier opinions in a manner that gives greater prominence to Pound as critic than as poet ("I have already said that Pound's criticism would not have the great value it has, without his poetry; and in his poetry there is, for the analytical reader, a great deal of criticism exemplified"). He sums up Pound's achievement in terms of what he has "stood for" as a champion of a new poetry at a time when "some abrupt mutation of poetic form and idiom" was urgently needed.

Hugh Selwyn Mauberley has usually been praised by both those who admire and those who dislike *The Cantos*—sometimes for differing reasons. An early promoter of modern poetry in the English university, F. R. Leavis discusses both Eliot and Pound in *New Bearings in English Poetry*. In his chapter on Pound, Leavis agrees with Eliot's estimate of *Mauberley* as a "great poem," but disagrees with his opinion that *The Cantos* represent an advance from it. *Mauberley* has a representative value as "the summing-up of an individual life," that of the aesthete Pound (of whom the central figure of the poem is a projection), but for Leavis it lacks T. S. Eliot's "complex intensities of concern about soul and body: the moral, religious, and anthropological preoccupations are absent." Still, *Mauberley* is a "whole," upon which Pound's reputation rests, while *The Cantos* (of which, in 1932, thirty had been published) appear to be little more than a pedant's game in which the counters lack "definition and salience."

The American critic Hugh Kenner agrees to the importance of *Mauberley*, but objects to Leavis's simplistic dismissal of Pound as a man of one poem. For Kenner, *Mauberley* is a complex poem that can easily be misread by "men of a certain training" who seize upon elements that "reverberate to an Eliotic tuning fork"—an inadequate instrument for testing Pound. It is wrong to identify Pound with the figure of Mauberley, who is simply "a parody of Pound the poet with which Mr. Pound is anxious not to be confounded." Relating *Mauberley* to the earlier *Homage to Sextus Propertius* and the Cantos that came after, Kenner explicates the poem not as an expression of the hurt disillusionment of an aesthete but as an objective and ironic anatomy of the decadent literary and social culture of England at the close of the First World War. On these grounds the poem has a technical interest beyond that allowed by Leavis. With the advantage of his later and fuller perspective, Kenner does not assign the work the special prominence that Leavis does.

The poetic record of one episode in a long career, *Mauberley* is obviously slight in comparison with Pound's total output as a poet. For better or worse, his reputation is staked to a great extent on *The Cantos*, the "tale of the tribe," the historically oriented poem already under way when he wrote, in *Mauberley*, the coda to one phase of his career. With this task accomplished, Pound turned to the larger problem of assimilating, in a major poem, heterogeneous traditions and literary conventions, Oriental as well as Western—of shaping a modern epic to take its place beside the great poems of earlier and more unified cultures.

Although Pound has cited his classical models, discovering and defining the formal organization of *The Cantos* has been a persistent problem for critics. Certain Homeric and Dantean parallels are traceable, but many critics have complained of a general impression of discontinuity and incoherence. One has even said that, although the mode of expression in *The Cantos* is conversational, the conversation is about "nothing." Another has seized upon a comparison once thrown off by the poet himself and described the work as a "rag bag." Such extreme judgments, which attempt to dismiss rather than to understand and explain the poem, surely fail to do it justice. Despite Pound's stress on a few simplifying ideas (*usura*, for example), the world of *The Cantos*, like the real world, appears complex and often confusing, without clearly established guide lines and standards of value. Yet it represents a largely consistent point of view and is formally organized according to principles which have become more apparent with the addition of successive groups of cantos.

The scrutiny of recent critics has illuminated both original and emergent patterns of organization in *The Cantos*. It has also shown a number of the ways in which the individualistic Pound can be identified with established literary traditions. The brief survey provided by M. L. Rosenthal in *A Primer of Ezra Pound* gives an over-all view of the emphases of the various groups of cantos and their relation to the developing poem. It is followed here by several essays dealing more intensively with special aspects of the work.

Although some of the cantos have a direct relationship to Dante's *Divine Comedy*, from which Pound derived the title of his poem, the pre-Christian Homeric world, with its dark trackless sea and its colorless land of the dead, is closer to the twentieth century writer than the neatly ordered universe of the medieval Christian poet. In "A Man of No Fortune," Forrest Read interprets *The Cantos* as a modern Odyssey in which four of the main characters of the Homeric poem represent alternative and competing ways of life in Pound's Odyssean search for values. The Homeric legend serves to order the experience of the poet, who comes out of the land of the dead a different man and finally emerges into the suffering of the real world in *The Pisan Cantos*.

A number of critics have judged *The Pisan Cantos*, which record Pound's military prison-camp experience, the most effective group because of their intensity and unity of tone. In "Ezra Pound as Prison Poet," David W. Evans interprets them as a modern "prison poem" representing a long established genre.

W. M. Frohock places Pound's work in a more recent tradition. "The Revolt of Ezra Pound" describes the subject of *The Cantos* as "the rejection of life as it is now lived" and identifies the poet with the modern European *révolté* like Céline or Malraux—a perspective that helps to explain apparent incoherence and discontinuity of expression as a calculated and appropriate technique. Frohock points out that the revulsion and violent protest of the rebel, so offensive to complacent ears, are forcible reminders of inhumanities that the modern intellectual and artist—and their readers—cannot afford to ignore.

In "Reckoning," Harold H. Watts relates *The Cantos* to a much older tradition. The ancient realist-nominalist controversy, he believes, lies behind Pound's social and economic ideas and his conception of the nature of poetry. The problem of the concreteness or abstractness of poetic language has implications that go beyond the work of Pound as an individual poet—that bear upon basic questions about the role of literature, and of language, in our culture.

The whole body of Pound's work reveals an unusual breadth of interest in such other arts as music, painting, and sculpture and in other literatures, European and Oriental—supported by a long continuing concern for translation, both as a necessary training for the poet and as a mode of creative expression. Pound has been described by Eliot as the inventor of Chinese poetry for our time. An interest in Chinese and Japanese literature appears, even before the poems of *Cathay* (1915) and *Lustra* (1916), in the principles of Imagism and Vorticism, and it continues through *The Cantos* and the translations of Confucius. In "Pound, *Haiku,* and the Image," Earl Miner demonstrates the pervasive influence of Japanese poetry on Pound's work. An equally long standing enthusiasm for music and belief in its necessary interrelationship with poetry can be seen in Pound's early discussions of the Provençal poets and in *Antheil and the Treatise on Harmony* and the opera *The Testament of François Villon.* Music has affected both Pound's methods of composition and his ideas about the nature and function of poetry. In "Ezra Pound and Music," Murray Schafer discusses this largely neglected influence from the point of view of a composer and musicologist. Long a subject of acrid debate between historical scholars and modernist critics, Pound's competence as a translator is now being more justly and capably assessed by a younger generation of scholar critics familiar with modern art and modern criticism. One of these is J. P. Sullivan, whose essay on the *Homage to Sextus Propertius* as a mask considers Pound's accomplishments as a creative translator, aware of the necessary interaction of past and present.

For many years, beginning long before the Bollingen award controversy, Pound has inspired extreme and often antithetical judgments by detractors who have considered him a crackbrain if not a charlatan and denied him status as a major poet and by admirers who have regarded him as a pioneer in a new mode of creative expression and as one of the great "inventors" in the epic tradition. In "Poet of Many Voices," a representative statement of the negative view, George P. Elliott considers *The Cantos* hopelessly disfigured by obscurity of reference and incoherence of structure —defects which attest the madness of the author. In contrast, Roy Harvey Pearce, in "Pound, Whitman, and the American Epic," relates the poet to Whitman in the American bardic tradition and describes *The Cantos* as an attempt to create an epic in which the poet will "make new" a culture in which he and the modern man he envisages can be at home. In addition to such conflicting summary judgments, the full spectrum of Pound criticism, represented by the essays collected here, embraces differences of opinion on a variety of questions: the respective importance of Pound and Eliot as leaders of modern poetry, the relation of *Mauberley* to Pound's later work, the effectiveness of Pound's poetic language, the soundness of his theory of the ideogram, the relation of music to his verse and to poetry generally, and the extent to which Pound can be judged as an innovator or a traditionalist.

III

Although it is usually agreed that Pound's sensibility is secular and humanistic, rather than religious and mystical, his status as a humanist has been disputed. Liberal and Marxist critics, conscious of the implications of Pound's fascist attitudes and sympathies, have sometimes branded him an "anti-humanist." But in several respects Pound is profoundly a humanist, for better or for worse, according to the viewpoints of differing readers. Highly conscious of his role as an unacknowledged legislator for a decadent (as he sees it) Western society, he has attempted single-handedly to "create" a culture and to order the chaos of his world. Despite the pessimism of many of his comments and the violence of his protest, there is in his work, especially in *The Cantos*, a visionary (though not otherworldly) and even Utopian strain, prophetic of a cultural New Jerusalem that might be realized if the prophet's message were heeded.

His "tradition," unlike that of the followers of Eliot, is a strangely eclectic one. He has drawn upon a great variety of past cultures for spokesmen and examples of the values he wishes to promote. The dramatis personae of *The Cantos* include—besides Odysseus—Confucius, Sigismondo Malatesta, Thomas Jefferson, John Adams, Robert Browning, Gustave Flaubert, Silvio Gesell, Ford Madox Ford, Benito Mussolini, and others.

Like the academic New Humanists, Pound attempts to derive standards for the present from the cultures of the past. Eliot's linking of Pound and Irving Babbitt is acute. Despite differences in temperament and conditioning, both men were essentially aristocratic and anti-democratic in attitude. Both also sought support for their views, not from a religion of revelation, but from a pre-Christian ethical system (Buddhism for Babbitt; Confucianism for Pound). Like Babbitt, Pound is a pedagogue who holds dogmatic opinions and who, unlike the best teachers, has sought to force his opinions and judgments on his followers.

Fortunately there are kinds of humanism other than those represented by Irving Babbitt and Ezra Pound. To the democratic humanist a number of Pound's attitudes are offensive. The poet's long standing aristocratic bias, his fascist ideals of order, and his crass anti-Semitism are obtrusive faults and limiting features of his poetry and cannot be thought of as simply the aberrations and personal opinions of Pound the man. The meanings of literature are among its most conspicuous formal aspects, and an analysis of the ideas and values in a poem cannot be set apart, as a function distinct in kind, from criticism concerned with its patterns of sound, syntax, and imagery. To attempt to do so, as the Bollingen committee did in awarding a prize to *The Pisan Cantos* for aesthetic or technical considerations, apart from the opinions expressed, is to assume an untenable form-content distinction. A writer's work is assessed for the quality of its ideas and values, as well as for the quality of the other formal elements with which they are interrelated.

To say this is not to damn Pound or deny his achievement. It is too easy to do so self-righteously. The image of the alienated artist which he projected as the caged poet of *The Pisan Cantos* stands as a counter-indictment of the world against which he had recoiled in so extreme a fashion—a world which has in many ways been inimical to the human values (for Pound *has* his humanities) and the creative freedom he has championed for half a century.

All things considered, Pound's accomplishments as a poet and a force in modern literature are impressive. Besides serving as a leader and a liberator in the development of new poetic techniques, Pound has through his work as a creative translator established a living relationship between present writing and neglected traditions of the past. Most important, he is a lyric and dramatic poet with a mastery of technique in both traditional and free verse. Through his poems, especially *The Cantos*, he speaks as a writer who has been immersed in the stream of life of his time—who gives us an immediate sense of what it has been like for one perceptive and cultured man to have lived through the first half of the twentieth century, amid so much violence and wreckage, with so little support for principles of social order and community life. He has also given us valuable negative criticism of the kind that the creative writer can best provide.

Admitting the flaws of Ezra Pound's poetic vision and expression (they cannot be glossed over or explained away), one must recognize the compensating excellences of the great body of his work as well as the unquestioned importance of his influence on modern literature.

Ezra Pound

by *William Butler Yeats*

Ezra Pound has made flux his theme; plot, characterization, logical discourse, seem to him abstractions unsuitable to a man of his generation. He is mid-way in an immense poem in *vers libre* called for the moment *The Cantos,* where the metamorphosis of Dionysus, the descent of Odysseus into Hades, repeat themselves in various disguises, always in association with some third that is not repeated. Hades may become the hell where whatever modern men he most disapproves of suffer damnation, the metamorphosis petty frauds practised by Jews at Gibraltar. The relation of all the elements to one another, repeated or unrepeated, is to become apparent when the whole is finished. There is no transmission through time, we pass without comment from ancient Greece to modern England, from modern England to medieval China; the symphony, the pattern, is timeless, flux eternal and therefore without movement. Like other readers I discover at present merely exquisite or grotesque fragments. He hopes to give the impression that all is living, that there are no edges, no convexities, nothing to check the flow; but can such a poem have a mathematical structure? Can impressions that are in part visual, in part metrical, be related like the notes of a symphony; has the author been carried beyond reason by a theoretical conception? His belief in his own conception is so great that since the appearance of the first Canto I have tried to suspend judgement.

When I consider his work as a whole I find more style than form; at moments more style, more deliberate nobility and the means to convey it than in any contemporary poet known to me, but it is constantly interrupted, broken, twisted into nothing by its direct opposite, nervous obsession, nightmare, stammering confusion; he is an economist, poet, politician, raging at malignants with inexplicable characters and motives, grotesque figures out of a child's book of beasts. This loss of self-control, common among uneducated revolutionists, is rare—Shelley had it in

some degree—among men of Ezra Pound's culture and erudition. Style
and its opposite can alternate, but form must be full, sphere-like, single.
Even where there is no interruption he is often content, if certain verses
and lines have style, to leave unbridged transitions, unexplained ejacula-
tions, that make his meaning unintelligible. He has great influence, more
perhaps than any contemporary except Eliot, is probably the source of
that lack of form and consequent obscurity which is the main defect of
Auden, Day Lewis, and their school, a school which, as will presently
be seen, I greatly admire. Even where the style is sustained throughout
one gets an impression, especially when he is writing in *vers libre,* that
he has not got all the wine into the bowl, that he is a brilliant improvisa-
tor translating at sight from an unknown Greek masterpiece:

> See, they return; ah, see the tentative
> Movements, and the slow feet,
> The trouble in the pace and the uncertain
> Wavering!
>
> See, they return, one, and by one,
> With fear, as half-awakened;
> As if the snow should hesitate
> And murmur in the wind,
>   and half turn back;
>
> These were the Wing'd-with-awe,
>   Inviolable.
> Gods of the winged shoe!
> With them the silver hounds,
>   sniffing the trace of air!

Excerpts from a Critical Sketch:
A Draft of XXX Cantos by Ezra Pound

by William Carlos Williams

Poetry? Words: figments of the mind, of no real substance.
What more then is light? It is precisely a figment of the mind if the
apprehension of it be our consideration.
But it is an emanation consequent on microscopic action in the sun.
Then words are the same, call the microscopic action which is their
source "Socrates" or what you will.

The *Cantos* have been in Pound's mind since 1908, at least: "that
forty year epic"—(*Personae,* etc., etc.)

The poem begins after an image much resorted to by modern writers:
the *Odyssey,* ever more pat to the times as time passes— (But it was Virgil
who led Dante through the Inferno.)

The first *Canto* has to do with Odysseus' descent to the world of
shadows. The effect in this case being qualified by Pound's use of a
translation into our tongue of a sixteenth century translation from the
original Greek—thus making the *Odyssey* itself a link with which to hold
together his theme. He uses a poem, words, modes that have been modified by use—not an idea. He uses the poem objectively.

The now hackneyed theme of the appearance of the aged Tiresias comes
up as in the original text (probably) but is not stressed.

The thing that is felt is that the quick are moving among the dead—
and the oarsmen "placed," the oarsmen who went down in the whirlpool
chained to their rowing benches and were not saved.

It is the gone world of "history."

(Canto II)
Now the poet takes his place: hallucination or genius. The ship is
stopped in mid-career, in mid-ocean. The youth beaten by the sailors

into the ship's stern feels the God beside him (Acoetes' story). He chron-
icles the arrest of the vessel's onrush:——

"Ship stock fast in seaswirl, . . ." etc., etc., etc.

As to the Greek quotations—knowing no Greek—I presume they mean
something, probably something pertinent to the text—and that the author
knows what they mean. . . . But in all salient places—Pound has clarified
his out-land insertions with reasonable consistency. They are no particular
matter save that they say, There were other times like ours—at the back
of it all.

Pound has had the discernment to descry and the mind to grasp that
the difficulties in which humanity finds itself need no phenomenal insight
for their solution. Their cure is another matter, but that is no reason for
a belief in a complicated mystery of approach fostered by those who wish
nothing done, as it is no reason for a failure of the mind to function
simply when dangerously confronted. Here is a theme: a closed mind
which clings to its power—about which the intelligence beats seeking
entrance. This is the basic theme of the *XXX Cantos.*

Reading them through consecutively, at one sitting (four hours)
Pound's "faults" as a poet all center around his rancor against the ma-
lignant stupidity of a generation which polluted our rivers and would
then, brightly, give ten or twenty or any imaginable number of millions
of dollars as a fund toward the perpetuation of *Beauty*—in the form of
a bequest to the New York Metropolitan Museum of Art.

"In America this crime has not been spread over a period of centuries,
it has been done in the last twenty or twenty-five years, by the single
generation, from fifteen to twenty-five years older than I am, who have
held power through that slobbery period."

His versification has not as its objective (apparently) that of some contemporary verse of the best quality. It is patterned *still* after classic meters
and so does often deform the natural order—though little and to a
modified degree only (nor is his practice without advantages as a method).
Pound does very definitely intend a modern speech—but wishes to save
the excellences (well-worked-out forms) of the old, so leans to it overmuch.

A criticism of Pound's *Cantos* could not be better concerned, I think,
than in considering them in relation to the principal move in imaginative
writing today—that away from the word as a symbol toward the word as
reality.

1) His words affect modernity with too much violence (at times)—a
straining after slang effects, engendered by their effort to escape that
which is their instinctive quality, a taking character from classic similes
and modes. You cannot *easily* switch from Orteum to Peoria without violence (to the language). These images too greatly infest the *Cantos,* the
words *cannot* escape being colored by them: 2) so too the form of the

phrase—it affects a modern turn but is really bent to a classical beauty of image, so that in effect it often (though not always) mars the normal accent of speech. But not always: sometimes it is superbly done and Pound is always trying to overcome the difficulty.

Pound is humane in a like sense to that of the writer of the great cantos —without being in the least sentimental. He has been able to do this by paying attention first to his art, its difficulties, its opportunities: to language—as did Dante: to popular language—It is sheer stupidity to forget the primarily humane aspect of Dante's work in the rhapsodic swoon induced by his blinding technical, aesthetic, and philosophic qualities.

All the thought and implications of thought are there in the words (in the minute character and relationships of the words—destroyed, avoided by . . .)—it is *that* I wish to say again and again—it is there in the technique and it is that that is the making or breaking of the work. It is that that one sees, feels. It is that that *is* the work of art—to be observed.

The means Pound has used for the realization of his effects—the poetry itself——:

It is beside the question to my mind to speak of Pound's versification as carefully and accurately measured—beyond all comparison——

Perhaps it is and if so, what of it?

That has nothing in it of value to recommend it. It is deeper than that. His excellence is that of the maker, not the measurer—I say he *is* a poet. This is in effect to have stepped beyond measure.

It is that the material is so molded that it is changed in *kind* from other statement. It is a *sort* beyond measure.

The measure is an inevitability, an unavoidable accessory after the fact. If one move, if one run, if one seize up a material—it cannot avoid having a measure, it cannot avoid a movement which clings to it—as the movement of a horse becomes a part of the rider also——

That is the way Pound's verse impresses me and why he can include pieces of prose and have them still part of a *poem*. It is incorporated in a movement of the intelligence which is special, beyond usual thought and action——

It partakes of a quality which makes the meter, the movement peculiar —unmeasurable (without a prior change of mind)——

It is that which is the evidence of invention. Pound's line is the movement of his thought, his concept of the whole——

As such, it has measure but not first to be picked at: certain realizable characteristics which may be looked at, evaluated more pointedly, then measured and "beautifully," "ideally," "correctly" pointed.

They (the lines) have a character that is parcel of the poem itself. (It is in the small make-up of the lines that the character of the poem definitely comes—and beyond which it cannot go.)

It is (in this case) a master meter that wishes to come of the classic but at the same time to be bent to and to incorporate the rhythm of modern speech.

This is or would be the height of excellence—the efflorescence of a rare mind—turned *to* the world.

It succeeds and not—it does and fails.

It is in the minutiae—in the minute organization of the words and their relationships in a composition that the seriousness and value of a work of writing exist—*not* in the sentiments, ideas, schemes portrayed.

It is here, furthermore, that creation takes place. It is not a plaster of thought applied.

The seriousness of a work of art, the belief the author has in it, is that he does generate in it—a solution in some sense of the continuous confusion and barrenness which life imposes in its mutations—(on him who will not create).

It is always necessary to create, to generate, or life, any "life," the life of art, stales and dies—it dies out from under, it ceases to exist—it is not captured merely by studied excellence——

We seek a language which will not be at least a deformation of speech as we know it—but will embody all the advantageous jumps, swiftnesses, colors, movements of the day——

—that will, at least, not exclude language as spoken—all language (present) as spoken.

Pound has attempted an ambitious use of language for serious thought without sequestration (the cloistering of words)—an acceptance—and by his fine ear attempted to tune them—excluding nothing.

He has by intention avoided (quite as much as if he had announced it) the camphorated words of what passes today for classical usage. And also the cracked up—the cracking up of words and natural word sequences in an effort toward synthesis—"synthesis," that is—and—

Pound finds the problem of new word use more difficult than that—and correctly so, I believe; that generation is subtler, that such writers are "seeking in the wrong garbage can."

He is seeking to demonstrate the intelligence—as he believes a poet must—by laboring with the material as it exists in speech and history. Doing that, he is attempting the true difficulty (though I am not here attacking the other slant on the theme).

It is not by a huge cracking up of language that you will build new work, he postulates (that is a confusion even when skillful—a true babel—onomatopoeia, a reversion, its most signal triumph), nor by use of an embalmed language, on the other hand. But by poetry—that will strike through words whipping them into a shape—clarity and motion: analysis: be they what they may.

Analysis. It is what all poets have done with the language about them.

> *Button up your overcoat*
> *When the wind blows free*
> *Take good care of yourself*
> *You belong to me.*

There's speech—fairly accurately. Caught alive, no doubt, and written down, put to a tune.

Pound has wanted to do the same to a heightened and profounder degree. He has chosen flawlessly where and what he will create.

How far has he succeeded? Generation, he says, as I interpret him, is analytical, it is not a mass fusion. Only superficially do the *Cantos* fuse the various temporal phases of the material Pound has chosen, into a synthesis. It is important to stress this for it is Pound's chief distinction in the *Cantos*—his personal point of departure from most that the modern is attempting. It is not by any means a synthesis, but a shot through all material—a true and somewhat old-fashioned analysis of his world.

It is still a Lenin striking through the mass, whipping it about, that engages his attention. That is the force Pound believes in. It is not a proletarian art——

He has succeeded against himself. He has had difficulties of training to overcome which he will not completely undo—in himself at least—if that were all.

But the words reveal it: white-gathered, sun-dazzle, rock-pool, god-sleight, sea-swirl, sea-break, vine-trunk, vine-must, pin-rack, glass-glint, wave-runs, salmon-pink, dew-haze, blue-shot, green-gold, green-ruddy, eye-glitter, blue-deep, wine-red, water-shift, rose-paleness, wave-cords, churn-stick.

We have, examining the work, successes—great ones—the first molds—clear cut, never turgid, not following the heated trivial—staying cold, "classical" but swift with a movement of thought.

It stands out from almost all other verse by a faceted quality that is not muzzy, painty, wet. It is a dry, clean use of words. Yet look at the words. They are themselves not dead. They have not been violated by "thinking." They have been used willingly by thought.

Imagistic use has entirely passed out of them, there is almost no use of simile, no allegory—the word has been used in its plain sense to represent a thing—remaining thus loose in its context—not gummy—(when at its best)—an objective unit in the design—but alive.

Pound has taken them up—if it may be risked—alertly, swiftly, but with feeling for the delicate living quality in them—not disinfecting, scraping them, but careful of the life. The result is that they stay living—and discreet.

Or almost. For beside living passages, there are places where he wrenches the words about for what "ought to be" their conformation.

That's no matter. He has taken up language and raised it to a height where it may stand—beside Artemis——

If that is not a purpose worthy of a poet and if Pound has not done it— then——

It isn't all, it's even (in a sense) a defect to want so much the Artemis thing. But Pound has lifted the language up as no one else has done—wherever he has lifted it—or whatever done to it in the lifting.

His defects (dey's good too) are due to his inability to surmount the American thing—or his ability to do so without physical success—if that be preferred.

Ezra Pound

by T. S. Eliot

Whatever may have been the literary scene in America between the beginning of the century and the year 1914, it remains in my mind a complete blank. I cannot remember the name of a single poet of that period whose work I read: it was only in 1915, after I came to England, that I heard the name of Robert Frost. Undergraduates at Harvard in my time read the English poets of the '90s, who were dead: that was as near as we could get to any living tradition. Nor can I remember any English poet then alive who contributed to my own education. Yeats was well known, of course; but to me, at least, Yeats did not appear, until after 1917, to be anything but a minor survivor of the '90s. (After that date, I saw him very differently. I remember well the impression of the first performance of *The Hawk's Well*, in a London drawing room, with a celebrated Japanese dancer in the role of the hawk, to which Pound took me. And thereafter one saw Yeats rather as a more eminent contemporary than as an elder from whom one could learn.) There were, in the early years of the century, a few good poets writing in England, but I did not know of their existence until later; and it was often Pound (whose appreciation was much more comprehensive than most people realize) who directed my attention to them. But I do not think it is too sweeping to say that there was no poet, in either country, who could have been of use to a beginner in 1908. The only recourse was to poetry of another age and to poetry of another language. Browning was more of a hindrance than a help, for he had gone some way, but not far enough, in discovering a contemporary idiom. And at that stage, Poe and Whitman had to be seen through French eyes. The question was still: where do we go from Swinburne? and the answer appeared to be, nowhere.

It is as well, in writing at the present moment about Pound, to acknowledge one's greatest personal debt at once. I had kept my early poems (including *Prufrock* and others eventually published) in my desk from 1911 to 1915—with the exception of a period when Conrad Aiken

"Ezra Pound" by T. S. Eliot. From *Poetry*, LXVIII (September 1946), 326-338. Copyright 1946 by Modern Poetry Association; © 1958 by T. S. Eliot. Reprinted by permission of the author and the editor of *Poetry*.

endeavored, without success, to peddle them for me in London. In 1915 (and through Aiken) I met Pound. The result was that *Prufrock* appeared in *Poetry* in the summer of that year; and through Pound's efforts, my first volume was published by the Egoist Press in 1917.

Pound was then living in a small dark flat in Kensington. In the largest room he cooked, by artificial light; in the lightest but smallest room, which was inconveniently triangular, he did his work and received his visitors. There he lived until he moved, in 1922 I think, to Paris: but he seemed always to be only a temporary squatter. This appearance was due, not only to his restless energy—in which it was difficult to distinguish the energy from the restlessness and fidgets, so that every room, even a big one, seemed too small for him—but to a kind of resistance against growing into any environment. In America, he would no doubt have always seemed on the point of going abroad; in London, he always seemed on the point of crossing the Channel. I have never known a man, of any nationality, to live so long out of his native country without seeming to settle anywhere else. For a time, he found London, and then Paris, the best center for his attempts to revitalize poetry. But though young English writers, and young writers of any nationality, could count on his support if they excited his interest, the future of American letters was what concerned him most.

No one could have been kinder to younger men, or to writers who, whether younger or not, seemed to him worthy and unrecognized. No poet, furthermore, was, without self-depreciation, more unassuming about his own achievement in poetry. The arrogance which some people have found in him is really something else; and whatever it is, it has not expressed itself in an undue emphasis on the value of his own poems. He liked to be the impresario for younger men, as well as the animator of artistic activity in any milieu in which he found himself. In this role he would go to any lengths of generosity and kindness; from inviting constantly to dinner a struggling author whom he suspected of being underfed, or giving away clothing (though his shoes and underwear were almost the only garments which resembled those of other men sufficiently to be worn by them), to trying to find jobs, collect subsidies, get work published and then get it criticized and praised. Indeed, he was ready to lay out the whole of life for anyone in whose work he was interested—a degree of direction which not all the beneficiaries deserved and which was sometimes embarrassing. Yet, though the object of his beneficence might come to chafe against it, only a man of the meanest spirit could have come to resent it. He was so passionately concerned about the works of art which he expected his protégés to produce that he sometimes tended to regard them almost impersonally, as art or literature machines to be carefully tended and oiled, for the sake of their potential output.

Pound was, in fact, a dominating director. He has always had a passion to teach. In some ways, I can think of no one whom he resembled more than Irving Babbitt—a comparison which neither man would have relished. Perhaps the backgrounds were not unlike; perhaps if Pound had stopped at home, and become, as he might have become, a professor of comparative literature, the resemblance might have been closer still. Babbitt had been my teacher: and by "teacher" I do not mean merely a tutor, or a man whose lectures I attended, but a man who directed my interests, at a particular moment, in such a way that the marks of that direction are still evident. Babbitt's closest friend was Paul More: many years later, More became my friend also. But, once having been a pupil of Babbitt, one did not later become his "friend" in quite that sense; one retained, certainly, not only admiration but warm affection—the affection of the ex-disciple. For when one had come to hold a conviction, religious, social or political, contrary to one of Babbitt's, the status of ex-disciple was the highest to which one could aspire. Some men are so devoted to their ideas that they cannot engage in profitable discussion with those whose ideas differ from their own.

I do not know how good a judge of men Babbitt may have been: when I was his pupil I was too immature to know. But I suspect that he was more inclined to judge men by the ideas they held, than to judge ideas by his understanding of the men who held them. This difference distinguishes two types of intelligence. Pound was always a masterly judge of poetry; a more fallible judge, I think, of men; and he was not at all interested in those who did not strike him as eligible for the ideal intellectual and artistic milieu which he was always trying to find or to found. I think also that sometimes he not only judged too favorably those who shared his views, but was deceived, in judging men by the ideas which they professed to share with him, rather than by their personality and character.

I have been writing mainly in the past tense; for I have been writing of a particular period, that between 1910 and 1922—or, with reference to myself, between 1915 and 1922. (It was in 1922 that I placed before him in Paris the manuscript of a sprawling, chaotic poem called *The Waste Land* which left his hands, reduced to about half its size, in the form in which it appears in print. I should like to think that the manuscript, with the suppressed passages, had disappeared irrecoverably: yet on the other hand, I should wish the blue penciling on it to be preserved as irrefutable evidence of Pound's critical genius.) This is the period which ended with *Mauberley* and *Propertius* and the first drafts of the early cantos. It is also the period in which he exercised a vital influence upon English and American poetry, although this influence has been largely felt by a younger generation, many of whom never knew him personally, and some of whom may be unaware of the extent of the influence upon them. I am not in this statement taking account of "imagism." Whether the name and the principles of imagism were Pound's invention or Hulme's, I do not know, and I am not very much interested. Imagism produced a few good poems—notably those of H.D.—but it was quickly absorbed into more comprehensive influences, including Pound's. Then, in *The Catholic Anthology, The Egoist, The Little Review,* Pound accomplished more than any other man could have done with anthologies and periodicals of such limited circulation. (To Pound, and to Miss Weaver, we owe the publication of Joyce's *Portrait of the Artist* and Lewis's *Tarr.*) Pound did not create the poets: but he created a situation in which, for the first time, there was a "modern movement in poetry" in which English and American poets collaborated, knew each other's works, and influenced each other. Who, I wonder, in England (to say nothing of the rest of Europe) read any American poetry written between Whitman and Robert Frost? If it had not been for the work that Pound did in the years of which I have been talking, the isolation of American poetry, and the isolation of individual American poets, might have continued for a long time. I am not forgetting Miss Lowell, but it seems to me that the work she did, in putting over American poetry upon an American public, was on a lower level. She was a kind of demon saleswoman; and unless my memory of her methods is at fault (for it is a great many years since I read her *Six American Poets*) they were more enthusiastic than critical. If today it is a matter of course that London should take an interest in poetry published in New York, and that New York should be interested in poetry published in London—not simply in the decorated reputations, but in the new verse —this is largely due to what Pound achieved for poetry in a decade.

I cannot say what Pound's critical writing will mean to those who have not known the man, because to me it is inextricably woven with his conversation. I still consider it to be almost the only contemporary writing on the Art of Poetry that a young poet can study with profit. It forms a corpus of poetic doctrine: it has thus a particular relation to poetry in a particular age; and it is moreover addressed primarily to the poet. The opinion has been voiced that Pound's eventual reputation will rest upon his criticism and not upon his poetry. (I have been paid the same compliment myself.) I disagree. It is on his total work for literature that he must be judged: on his poetry, *and* his criticism, *and* his influence on men and on events at a turning point in literature. In any case, his criticism takes its significance from the fact that it is the writing of a poet about poetry; it must be read in the light of his own poetry, as well as of poetry by other men whom he championed. Criticism like Pound's is advocacy of a certain kind of poetry; it is an assertion that poetry written in the immediate future must, if it is to be good poetry, observe certain methods and take certain directions. The important question is, whether the critic is right in his judgment of the situation: if so, his criticism will be permanent, as Dryden's and Wordsworth's are. Only it will have to be read, in the more distant future, with an understanding of the situation for which the critic wrote. You cannot wholly understand Aristotle's doctrine of tragedy without reference to the remains of the Attic drama upon which Aristotle's generalizations are founded. To readers in the future who do not trouble to put Pound's criticism in its proper setting, as to many contemporary readers to whom "literary criticism" means something quite different from the notes of a poet on his craft, Pound will seem irritatingly biased. Such readers will be annoyed, as some have already been annoyed, by his irreverence for reputations which they have been educated to regard as above dispute, and by his affirmation of the importance of writers whom they have never read. To those, however, who appreciate the necessity of some abrupt mutation of poetic form and idiom in the period of which I have been speaking, and who concede that Pound not only grasped the situation but saw the direction which poetry ought to take, these exaggerations and depreciations will appear in their proper setting, and find their justification.

On the whole, I prefer the collected papers as one finds them in the two volumes published in New York, to the later book, *Make It New*, published in London. For me, at least, the former volumes recall the first appearance of several items, in periodicals, and so have a savor of their original timeliness which they cannot have for those who know only the collected criticism. Of the essays in *Make It New*, the essay (which is also a small anthology) on French Poets of the Symbolist Movement does not wear so well as some of the others. Certainly, a different approach would be appropriate now; some of the poets included may now be ignored; Mallarmé is not discussed; and Valéry's finest work was not known. The essay reads like the report of a tourist in French poetry, rather than like the conclusions of a reader who has digested the matter slowly and over a long period of time. The essay on Henry James remains of value, though the study of the subject has now reached a different phase. On the other hand, Rémy de Gourmont does not now appear to have the importance which Pound attributes to him. The observations on the troubadours, on Arnaut Daniel, and on the Elizabethan and other early translators, are as good as they ever were. And the short papers at the beginning and end, *Date Line* and *A Stray Document*, are just as necessary for the beginner in the art of verse as they were when they were written. The most important principle of Pound's criticism is contained in the following paragraphs:

> Theoretically [criticism] tries to forerun composition, to serve as gun-sight, though there is, I believe, no recorded instance of this foresight having ever been of the slightest use except to actual composers. I mean the man who formulates any forward reach of coordinating principle is the man who produces the demonstration.
>
> The others who use the principle learn usually from the example, and in most cases merely dim and dilute it.

I think it will usually be found that the work outruns the formulated or at any rate the published equation, or at most they proceed as two feet of one biped.

A Stray Document is advice to poets. I had not read it for a long time; and in re-reading it for my present purpose, I found that some of the advice in it is advice that I must have given since to many young poets. For instance:

> Let the candidate fill his mind with the finest cadences he can discover, preferably in a foreign language so that the meaning of the words may be less likely to divert his attention from the movement; e.g. Saxon charms, Hebridean folk songs, the verse of Dante, and the lyrics of Shakespeare— if he can dissociate the vocabulary from the cadence. Let him dissect the lyrics of Goethe coldly into their component sound values, syllables long and short, stressed and unstressed, into vowels and consonants.

The only qualification this precept needs is the warning that one is not likely to get a full appreciation of the way poetry in a foreign language should sound until one knows that language very well indeed—at which stage the danger that the meaning of the words will divert attention will appear. But the advice is nevertheless valuable: for instance, I myself have got a good deal of stimulation from Carmichael's *Carmina Gadelica,* a collection of Highland folk poetry.

As for the errors against which Pound warns the beginner, I find them turning up, week after week, in verse submitted for my opinion.

> Be influenced by as many great artists as you can, but have the decency either to acknowledge the debt outright, or to try to conceal it.

The weakness of the greater amount of verse I have to read—apart from that class, abundantly represented, in which the authors do not appear to have read *any* poetry—is that the authors have indeed been influenced, but not by enough, or by enough variety, of first-rate poetry. Often they appear to have read the shorter poems of Donne, several pieces by Gerard Hopkins, and some of the work of their own elder contemporaries. Some poems submitted suggest that the author has opened a volume of Whitman and noted how the lines look on the printed page. What most of the "free verse" derives from (except from the rumor that verse has been liberated) I cannot tell.

Half of the work that Pound did as a critic can be known only from the testimony of those who have benefited from his conversation or correspondence. At a certain moment, my debt to him was for his advice to read Gautier's *Emaux et Camées,* to which I had not before paid any close attention. I have already spoken of his operation upon *The Waste Land.*

I have sometimes tried to perform the same sort of maieutic task; and I know that one of the temptations against which I have to be on guard, is trying to re-write somebody's poem in the way in which I should have written it myself if I had wanted to write that poem. Pound never did that: he tried first to understand what one was attempting to do, and then tried to help one do it in one's own way. There did come a point, of course, at which difference of outlook and belief became too wide; or it may have been distance and different environment; or it may have been both.

I have already said that Pound's criticism would not have the great value it has, without his poetry; and in his poetry there is, for the analytical reader, a great deal of criticism exemplified. I find nothing to abate in my introduction to a volume of Pound's *Selected Poems,* published in London in 1928, except that I should now speak more respectfully of Whitman—a matter irrelevant to my present theme. In that introduction I said nothing about the *Propertius,* which I rate very high indeed. (I am aware of the censure of those who have treated it as a translation; and if it is treated as a translation, they are of course right.) If I am doubtful about some of the *Cantos,* it is not that I find any poetic decline in them. I am doubtful on somewhat the same ground as that on which I once complained to him about an article on the monetary theory of Gesell, which he had written at my suggestion for *The Criterion.* I said (as nearly as I can remember): "I asked you to write an article which would explain this subject to people who had never heard of it; yet you write as if your readers knew about it already, but had failed to understand it." In the *Cantos* there is an increasing defect of communication, not apparent when he is concerned with Sigismondo Malatesta, or with Chinese dynasties, but, for instance, whenever he mentions Martin Van Buren. Such passages are very opaque: they read as if the author was so irritated with his readers for not knowing all about anybody so important as Van Buren, that he refused to enlighten them. I am incidentally annoyed, myself, by occasional use of the peculiar orthography which characterizes Pound's correspondence, and by lines written in what he supposes to be a Yankee dialect. But the craftsman up to this moment—and I have in mind certain recent and unpublished cantos—has never failed. There is nobody living who can write like this: how many can be named, who can write half so well?

I have before now expressed the opinion, that the "greatness" of a poet is not a question for critics of his own age to raise: it is only after he has been dead for a couple of generations that the term begins to have meaning. "Greatness," when the term means anything at all, is an attribute conferred by time. The question of "genuineness" is the first question for contemporary criticism to raise. But there is a third aspect, under which it is proper to consider a poet, a third kind of judgment which may be passed upon him in his later years, the material for which is not only his poetry, but the principle of writing which he has exemplified and defended. I avoid the word *influence,* for there are dangers in estimating a poet by his influence. It takes at least two to make an influence: the man who exerts it and the man who experiences it. The latter may be a writer whose verse would have been bad, whatever influences had gone to form it; or he may have been influenced in the wrong way, or by the wrong things in the work of the poet under whose influence he has come; or he may be born into a period less favorable to the creation of art—though this is a subject we cannot know very much about. So I am not speaking of influence, but of the things for which a man like Pound has stood, in his own time. To appreciate these, we need first, as I suggested at the beginning, some understanding of the state of poetry when the poet began writing. And that is soon forgotten, for each generation tends to accept the situation it finds, as if that situation had always prevailed. I think that Pound was original in insisting that poetry is an art, an art which demands the most arduous application and study; and in seeing that in our time it had to be a highly conscious art. He also saw that a poet who knows only the poetry of his own language is as poorly equipped as the painter or musician who knows only the painting or the music of his own country. The business of the poet is to be more conscious of his own language than other men, to be more sensitive to the feeling, more aware of the meaning of every word he uses, more aware of the history of the language and of every word he uses, than other men. He needs, however, to know as much as he can of several other languages: because one advantage of a knowledge of other languages is that it makes us understand our own language better. Pound's "erudition" has been both exaggerated and irrelevantly under-estimated: for it has been judged chiefly by scholars who did not understand poetry, and by poets who have had little scholarship. Pound's great contribution to the work of other poets (if they choose to accept what he offers) is his insistence upon the immensity of the amount of *conscious* labor to be performed by the poet; and his invaluable suggestions for the kind of training the poet should give himself— study of form, metric and vocabulary in the poetry of divers literature, and study of good prose. Poets should continue to study—and if poetry survives they no doubt will—Pound's poetry, which bridges the gap separating Browning and Swinburne from the present day, and his writings about poetry. He also provides an example of devotion to "the art of poetry" which I can only parallel in our time by the example of Valéry, and to some extent that of Yeats: and to mention these names is to give some impression of Pound's importance as an exponent of the art of poetry in a time when

The "age demanded" chiefly a mould in plaster,
Made with no loss of time,
A prose kinema, not, not assuredly, alabaster
Or the "sculpture" of rhyme.

Ezra Pound

by F. R. Leavis

Mr. Pound has been closely associated with Mr. Eliot. Indeed, Mr. Eliot acknowledges a debt to him:

> A man who devises new rhythms is a man who extends and refines our sensibility; and that is not merely a matter of "technique." I have, in recent years, cursed Mr. Pound often enough; for I am never sure that I can call my verse my own; just when I am most pleased with myself, I find that I have caught up some echo from a verse of Pound's.[1]

And more generally:

> He has enabled a few other persons, including myself, to improve their verse sense; so that he has improved poetry through other men as well as by himself. I cannot think of any one writing verse, of our generation and the next, whose verse (if any good) has not been improved by the study of Pound's.[2]

—*The Waste Land,* we note, is inscribed to Ezra Pound, *il miglior fabbro.* Mr. Eliot's witness carries authority. It is nevertheless plain that when the history of the present phase of English poetry comes to be written, Mr. Eliot will be adjudged to have made the decisive impact and to have opened the way: whatever he and others may owe to Mr. Pound, the influence of Mr. Pound that can be observed from outside is secondary to Mr. Eliot's. The sponsoring by Mr. Eliot of the volume of *Selected Poems* is symbolic; it does not misrepresent their relations, in spite of the consciousness of a debt to Mr. Pound that has, not altogether happily, inspired Mr. Eliot's *Introduction.* Not altogether happily, because this consciousness, together with a generous concern to obtain for Mr. Pound the

---

[1] *The Dial,* January 1928, in an article entitled "Isolated Superiority."

[2] *Ibid.*

recognition due to him, seems accountable for a certain uncritical deflection in Mr. Eliot. No one interested in poetry is quick to dissent from Mr. Eliot's judgment; but the *Introduction* does not represent his criticism at its best. The manner itself sometimes makes us uneasy: it would before have seemed impossible that Mr. Eliot could ever remind us, even remotely, of Mr. G. K. Chesterton. And there are places that pull us up short:

> It may give surprise that I attach so much importance to *Hugh Selwyn Mauberley*. This seems to me a great poem. . . . I know very well that the apparent roughness and *naïveté* of the verse and rhyming of *Mauberley* are inevitably the result of many years of hard work: if you cannot appreciate the dexterity of *Altaforte* you cannot appreciate the simplicity of *Mauberley*.[3]

It does not at all surprise me (in such a matter it is best to speak in the first person) that Mr. Eliot should find *Hugh Selwyn Mauberley* a great poem; but the last assertion does surprise me: it conflicts with my experience, and with the experience of those with whom I discuss modern poetry. Any one capable of profiting by Mr. Eliot's *Introduction* is, I should say, likely to find *Mauberley* immediately convincing: the difficulty is to be interested in the earlier work. One can see, of course, that this was in a sense a necessary part of Mr. Pound's development, but I do not find it (and I have been much corroborated here) a necessary, or even helpful, approach to *Mauberley*.

Once, however, *Mauberley* has been accepted, the earlier work offers some interest (again I report my own experience). It shows what looks like a representative start from the Nineties: "his versification," says Mr. Eliot,[4] "is a *logical* development of the verse of his English predecessors"; and his substance is "poetical." Morris, Swinburne, Yeats make themselves felt, *Cynara*—

> But for all that, I am homesick after mine own kind—

and the Nineties generally. It is a Victorian "romanticism," a response (explicit in the poem[5] just quoted) to the Victorian situation of the artist:

> And I am homesick
> After mine own kind that know, and feel
> And have some breath for beauty and the arts.

[3] *Introduction* to *Selected Poems*, p. xxiii.
[4] *Introduction*, p. xi.
[5] *Selected Poems*, p. 20 (*In Durance*).

But the poet is not content with dreaming

how
"Beyond, beyond, beyond, there lies . . ." ;

another influence, not yet mentioned, manifests itself strongly in his verse
—that of Browning. Browning has much to do with the way in which
the Provençal themes of *Personae* are handled: the poetic world is to be
a "real" world. But Mr. Pound's Provence is none the less a form of
romantic evasion: his Browning consorts quite happily with Mr. Yeats.

It is, however, the versification that Mr. Eliot stresses in his *Introduction.* Elsewhere (in the article in *The Dial* already quoted from) he says
of Mr. Pound:

> What is curious is his complete and isolated superiority as a master of
> verse form. No one living has practised the art of verse with such austerity
> and devotion; and no one living has practised it with more success.

Mr. Eliot's judgment in such a matter is authoritative. But in the
same article (which reads much more like single-minded criticism than
the *Introduction*) he also says:

> I confess that I am seldom interested in what he is saying, but only in the
> way he says it.

He may add: "That does not mean that he is saying nothing; for
ways of saying nothing are not interesting"; but the interest has nevertheless been drastically limited. It is, perhaps, an interest that can be very
significant only to a poet whom chance brought into early association
with Mr. Pound. At any rate, apart from some such happy chance, it
seems improbable that a way of saying that can be so sharply distinguished from the thing said could do much towards re-orientating
English poetry.

The distinction, as a matter of fact, seems to imply a criticism of the
quality of Mr. Pound's own interest in what he says. His various addic-
tions—Provençal, Italian, Chinese—speak the amateur: one cannot doubt
his seriousness or his enthusiasm, but something else, surely, was needed
to impel significant innovations in poetry—and something more than a
devotion to the art of verse. Even when, as in *Lustra* and after, he finds
his themes in the contemporary world and writes consciously modern
poems—

> Here they stand without quaint devices,
> Here they stand with nothing archaic about them

—his modern interests, one feels, are for him mainly opportunities, taken
or made, for verse practice: his partiality for the epigram has its significance (this is not to condemn his epigrams by comparing them with the
Ode to a Nightingale).[6] However, there are some memorable pieces, and
we have to recognize a growing subtlety in his verse. His dropping of
archaisms and poeticisms, and his use of modern speech-idiom, are particularly interesting. But however remarkable the achievement in verse
may be, it is not such that one could have foreseen *Mauberley* in it. Not
to insist on this is to be unfair to Mr. Pound: it might be urged against
Mr. Eliot that his generous concern for justice has led him to minify the
pre-eminence of *Mauberley* when insistence on that pre-eminence is
needed to secure for Mr. Pound the attention he merits.

In *Mauberley* we feel a pressure of experience, an impulsion from deep
within. The verse is extraordinarily subtle, and its subtlety is the subtlety
of the sensibility that it expresses. No one would think here of distinguishing the way of saying from the thing said. It is significant that the pressure seems to derive (we are reminded of Mr. Yeats) from a recognition
of bankruptcy, of a devoted life summed up in futility. A study of the
earlier work, then, does at least help the commentary on *Mauberley*: it
helps to bring out the significance of the poem for the inquiry in hand.

Mauberley is in the first place (the description suggests itself readily)
the summing-up of an individual life. It has also a representative value,
reflecting as it does the miscellaneousness of modern culture, the absence
of direction, of an alphabet of forms or of any one predominant idiom;
the uncongeniality of the modern world to the artist; and his dubious
status there. It offers, more particularly, a representative experience of
the phase of English poetry in which it became plain that the Romantic
tradition was exhausted. One might, at the risk of impertinence, call it
quintessential autobiography, taking care, however, to add that it has the
impersonality of great poetry: its technical perfection means a complete
detachment and control.

To enforce this account some kind of running commentary is needed.
But the more one appreciates *Mauberley* the less happily does one em-
bark upon exposition: it seems impertinent to explain what so incom-
parably explains itself, and all elucidation looks crude. Yet *Mauberley*
has almost wholly escaped recognition, and one may perhaps be too much

---

[6] "The reader who does not like Pound's epigrams should make very sure that he is
not comparing them with the *Ode to a Nightingale* before he condemns them."—
Introduction, p. xix.

afraid of dealing in the obvious. At any rate, courage seems here the better part of discretion.

The opening of the first poem of *Mauberley* (which is more than a sequence) reminds us in movement of certain things of Mr. Eliot's:

> For three years, out of key with his time,
> He strove to resuscitate the dead art
> Of poetry; to maintain "the sublime"
> In the old sense. Wrong from the start—
>
> No, hardly, but seeing he had been born
> In a half savage country, out of date;
> Bent resolutely on wringing lilies from the acorn;
> Capaneus; trout for factitious bait;

—the rhythm of this is curiously like that of the opening of *A Song fo: Simeon*:

> Lord, the Roman hyacinths are blooming in bowls and
> The winter sun creeps by the snow hills;
> The stubborn season has made stand.
> My life is light, waiting for the death wind,
> Like a feather on the back of my hand.
> Dust in sunlight and memory in corners
> Wait for the wind that chills towards the dead land.

This may be an instance of the indebtedness to Mr. Pound that Mr. Eliot acknowledges (it is not often that we find an excuse for the conjecture). Less dubiously it illustrates a certain community of experience: it is not surprising that two poets, in the age that has been described, should have learnt to express so subtly by rhythmic means the break-down of rhythm.

But in essentials Mr. Pound's poetry is very different from Mr. Eliot's. There are in it none of Mr. Eliot's complex intensities of concern about soul and body: the moral, religious, and anthropological preoccupations are absent. Mr. Pound's main concern has always been art: he is, in the most serious sense of the word, an aesthete. It is this that makes the peculiar nature of Mr. Eliot's plea for the earlier work necessary. But here, in *Mauberley*, there is the pressure of personal experience. The title of the first poem, with its ironical allusion to Ronsard—*E. P. Ode Pour L'Election de son Sepulchre*—is explicitly personal: it indicates what is to follow. The poet is looking back on a life devoted to the cultivation of aesthetic fastidiousness, technical perfection, exquisite eclecticism. He is no longer trying to resuscitate the dead art of poetry, or observing the elegance of Circe's hair; he is taking stock, and what has it all amounted to? What is the outcome? He touches various notes, plays on various themes, and recalls various representative memories in the different constituent poems. The poems together form one poem, a representative experience of life—tragedy, comedy, pathos, and irony. And throughout there is a subtlety of tone, a complexity of attitude, such as we associate with seventeenth-century wit.

In this first poem he conveys, with masterly compression, the nature of the interests and attitudes that have occupied his life. The ironically sublime comparison of himself to Capaneus, the hero who defied the gods and paid the penalty, has its comment in the contemptuous contrasting image: "trout for factitious bait"—the stake a mere gaudy fly, and a faked one at that. The Homeric quotation suggests his romantic addiction to the classics and the past: his ear has been unstopped to too many Sirens.

> His true Penelope was Flaubert

—In all his romantic excursions he has remained constant to one faith, the aesthetic: his main concern has been art, art as represented by Flaubert, saint and martyr of the artistic conscience.

> He fished by obstinate isles

suggests his inveterate eclecticism, his interest in various periods and cultures, Provençal, Italian, Chinese, classical, and so on. He has always

> Observed the elegance of Circe's hair
> Rather than the mottoes on sun-dials.

He has devoted his life to aesthetic discrimination and technical perfection while life slipped by. Life now has, it seems, slipped by, and what has come of it all? The last stanza answers with an oblique reference to Villon, the unfastidious blackguard whose "wasted" life produced so rich a harvest of poetry. His own industrious career, on the contrary, our poet sees as yielding

> No adjunct to the Muses' diadem.

Nevertheless, this disillusioned summing-up is itself great poetry, "criticism of life" in the best sense of the phrase, as Mr. Eliot says. For Mr. Pound has not been unaffected by the march of all events. However uncongenial one may find his eclectic aestheticism, his devotion to the

elegance of Circe's hair, it has been accompanied by intense seriousness:
Mr. Pound is not an American for nothing. What we have in *Mauberley*
is a representative sensibility, that of a poet who found his starting point
in the Nineties, lived through the heavy late-Victorian years of Edward
VII, saw his friends disappear in the war, and now knows that the past
holds more for him than the future.

His technical skill is now a matter of bringing to precise definition a
mature and complex sensibility. The rhythms, in their apparent loose-
ness and carelessness, are marvels of subtlety: "out of key with his time" is
being said everywhere by strict rhythmic means. What looks like the free
run of contemporary speech achieves effects of a greater precision than
can be found very often in *The Oxford Book*. And the verse has extraordinary variety. The subtlety of movement is associated with subtlety of
mood and attitude. "Wit" is present. Critical activity accompanies feeling
and remembering. Mr. Pound can be, as the seventeenth century poets
were, serious and light at the same time, sardonic and poignant, flippant
and intense.

Devices that might easily degenerate into tricks ("stunts") remain under
perfect control. Take, for example, the use of inverted commas:

> Unaffected by "the march of events,"

> .   .   .   .   .

> The "age demanded" chiefly a mould in plaster,
> Made with no loss of time,
> A prose kinema, not, not assuredly, alabaster
> Or the "sculpture" of rhyme.

> .   .   .   .   .

> The tea-rose tea-gown, etc.
> Supplants the mousseline of Cos,
> The pianola "replaces"
> Sappho's barbitos.

> .   .   .   .   .

> Incapable of the least utterance or composition,
> Emendation, conservation of the "better tradition,"
> Refinement of medium, elimination of superfluities,
> August attraction or concentration.

To be able to use such a device as freely as Mr. Pound does without
prejudice to subtlety of tone and emphasis is to pass a severe test. His
poise, though so varied, and for all his audacities, is sure; how sure,
nothing can show better than the pun in the last stanza of the third poem:

> O bright Apollo,
> τίν' ἄνδρα, τίν' ἥρωα, τίνα θεὸν,

> What god, man, or hero
> Shall I place a tin wreath upon!

In what poet, after the seventeenth century, can we find anything like
this contributing to a completely serious effect (the poem is not only
tragically serious but solemn).

The second and third poems introduce the modern world of mass-
production and levelling-down, a world that has destroyed the traditions
and is hostile, not only to the artist, but to all distinction of spirit. The
fourth and fifth poems bring in the war. They are a more remarkable
achievement than they may perhaps at first appear to be.

> Died some, pro patria,
>   non "dulce" non "et decor" . . .
> walked eye-deep in hell
> believing in old men's lies, then unbelieving
> came home, home to a lie,
> home to many deceits,
> home to old lies and new infamy;
> usury age-old and age-thick
> and liars in public places.

—That is a dangerous note, and only the completest integrity and the
surest touch could safely venture it. But we have no uneasiness. The poet
has realized the war with the completely adult (and very uncommon)
awareness that makes it impossible to nurse indignation and horror.
Mauberley came out in 1920. The presence of the war in it, we feel, is
not confined to these two small poems: they are not mere detachable
items. They represent a criterion of seriousness and purity of intention
that is implicit in the whole. To say this is to indicate the gulf between
any of the earlier work, archaizing or modernizing, and *Mauberley*.

In *Yeux Glauques,* the next piece, we hark back to the age of peace
and prosperity that prepared the war; the phase of English culture out
of which the poets of the Nineties started. Pre-Raphaelite art with, for
setting, Gladstone, Ruskin, and Victorian morality on the one hand,
and Swinburne, Rossetti, and Victorian immorality on the other. Next,
in *"Siena mi fe'; disfecemi Maremma,"* we have the Nineties themselves
with their blend of religion, religiosity, aestheticism, and dissipation:

> For two hours he talked of Gallifet;
> Of Dowson; of the Rhymers' Club;
> Told me how Johnson (Lionel) died
> By falling from a high stool in a pub . . .
> But showed no trace of alcohol

> At the autopsy, privately performed—
> Tissue preserved—the pure mind
> Arose toward Newman as the whiskey warmed.

The irony of this might be called flippant: if so, it is a flippancy that subserves a tragic effect. Nothing could illustrate more forcibly Mr. Pound's sureness of touch, his subtle mastery of tone and accent. The poem is one of the most daring things in the sequence—though "daring" might suggest a possible qualm about it: it is justified by complete success. Rhythmically it is consummate; but that must be said of *Mauberley* as a whole, in all its rich variety. Mr. Pound's rhythmic suppleness continually surprises.

In *Mr. Nixon* he gets new effects out of colloquial speech. It is sardonic comedy; the theme, Success in modern letters. Mr. Pound's earlier satiric verse is always technically adroit and often amusing; but no one would have thought the author capable of a satiric note that should be in keeping with tragic seriousness. *Mr. Nixon* is. That is enough to say by way of emphasizing the distinction of the achievement.

Numbers X and XI might have appeared in *Lustra*, though they have their place here in the context of the whole. But XII exhibits again technical mastery functioning at the highest level. It is another marvel of tone and poise. The movement is extraordinarily varied, and the tempo and modulation are exquisitely controlled. The theme is another aspect of modern letters: elegant patronage, modish dilettantism.—

> Conduct, on the other hand, the soul
> "Which the highest cultures have nourished"
> To Fleet St. where
> Dr. Johnson flourished;
>
> Beside this thoroughfare
> The sale of half-hose has
> Long since superseded the cultivation
> Of Pierian roses.

—For the author, what is the actuality, what does it all come to, but journalism, the all-absorbing, which hardly any talent nowadays escapes? The trade of writing could once support a Johnson. It is now commercial in senses and at levels inconceivable in Johnson's time.

The *Envoi* that follows sets off the subtlety of Mr. Pound's rhythmic inventions by a masterly handling of canorous lyric measures that can be chanted at sight. This lovely little poem, which will hardly escape the anthologist when he discovers it, I have found useful in convincing the classically trained that Mr. Pound's metrical irregularities are not the result of incompetence.

The section called *Mauberley,* which occupies the remaining five pages of the fifteen, brings the personal focus of the whole to sharp definition.

"Qu'est ce qu'ils savent de l'amour, et qu'est ce qu'ils peuvent comprendre?

"S'ils ne comprennent pas la poésie, s'ils ne sentent pas la musique, qu'est ce qu'ils peuvent comprendre de cette passion en comparaison avec laquelle la rose est grossière et le parfum des violettes un tonnerre?"

—So, with implicit irony, runs the epigraph to the second poem of the section. The habit of disinterested aesthetic contemplation, of observing the elegance of Circe's hair rather than the mottoes on sun-dials, takes on a tragic significance. The poem is poignantly personal, and yet, in its technical perfection, its ironical economy, impersonal and detached. Consider, for instance, the consummate reserve of this:

> Unable in the supervening blankness
> To sift TO AGATHON from the chaff
> Until he found his sieve . . .
> Ultimately, his seismograph:

—With what subtle force the shift of image in the last line registers the realization that the "orchid" was something more, the impact more than aesthetic! And with what inevitability the "seismograph" and the scientific terminology and manner of what follows convey the bitter irony of realization in retrospect! Mr. Pound's regeneration of poetic idiom is more than a matter of using modern colloquial speech:

> He had passed, inconscient, full gaze,
> The wide-banded irides
> And botticellian sprays implied
> In their diastasis;

> Which anaesthesis, noted a year late,
> And weighed, revealed his great affect,
> (Orchid), mandate
> Of Eros, a retrospect.

It is a contemporary sensibility that expresses the futile bitterness of this recognition in this air of scientific detachment, of disinterested scrutiny.

The last stanza evokes directly the sense of frustrate emptiness in a
reference to Ovid (Metamorphoses VII), the image of the dogs turned to
stone in the act of seizing the quarry.

The next poem, *"The Age Demanded,"* has much the same theme,
more generalized: the penalty for absorption in aesthetic contemplation,
for too much concern with fineness of living; the unfitness for survival
of the artist in the modern world, the world of Lady Valentine, and the
world which follows

> The discouraging doctrine of chances

preached by Mr. Nixon. The poem is not difficult, unless rhythmically
(the state of education in poetry being what it is), and comment will
serve no purpose. Along with the preceding one it represents the summit
of Mr. Pound's superbly supple and varied art.

But *Hugh Selwyn Mauberley,* it must be repeated, is a whole. The
whole is great poetry, at once traditional and original. Mr. Pound's
standing as a poet rests upon it, and rests securely. The earlier poems have
a minor kind of interest, and (to revert to the first person of modesty) I
do not think that it is a service to the poet or the reader to insist upon
them. They have the kind of bearing upon *Mauberley* that has been
indicated: they help the commentator. And in them, clearly, Mr. Pound
developed his technique. It is interesting to follow this development, but
not in the least necessary. If the earlier poems are read at all with profit
it is likely to be because of *Mauberley,* which will convince, if at all, by
itself, and is in itself capable of being a decisive influence.

Since *Mauberley* the *Cantos* have, at various times, appeared, the latest
collection being *A Draft of XXX Cantos.*[7] Again I find myself embarrassed
by the necessity of disagreeing with Mr. Eliot. One gathers from the
Introduction[8] to *Selected Poems* that he regards the *Cantos* as being an
advance upon *Mauberley:*

> The closest approximation—I mean the most nearly continuous identifica-
> tion—of form and feeling in Pound's poetry, I find in his *Cantos,* of which
> I can say but little, as I am not permitted to print them in this book. (At
> least, they are the only "poem of some length" by any of my contemporaries
> that I can read with enjoyment and admiration; at most, they are more than
> I could deal with anyway in this essay; in any case, they are a mine for
> juvenile poets to quarry; and in any case, my disagreement with their
> "philosophy" is another affair.)

[7] Hours Press, Paris, 1930.
[8] See p. xxii.

It is to be regretted that Mr. Eliot has not found time to deal with them somewhere. In the article "Isolated Superiority" already referred to, he is indeed more explicit about the "philosophy":

> As for the meaning of the *Cantos,* that never worries me, and I do not believe that I care. I know that Pound has a scheme and a kind of philosophy behind it; it is quite enough for me that he thinks he knows what he is doing; I am glad that the philosophy is there, but I am not interested in it.

This hardly leaves the commentary at a more satisfactory point. Mr. Eliot's pronouncement on the value of Mr. Pound's work to juvenile poets, its value as "an inexhaustible reference book of verse form," [9] it is not for me to question. But he does seem to have limited very drastically the kind of importance that can be attributed to the *Cantos*—more drastically than comports with the effect of his allusions to them in the *Introduction.* It is possible to understand that a poet already strongly impelled, and already definitely orientated, might profit by studying verse form as such. But the influence of verse form so abstracted can hardly be of the order of significance represented by *Mauberley,* which might very well launch a young poet. In any case, it is a kind of influence that I do not know how to take account of.

The possible interest in verse form so distinguishable from interesting communication seems extremely limited. "I confess that I am seldom interested in what he is saying, but only in the way he says it. That does not mean that he is saying nothing; for ways of saying nothing are not interesting." And surely, one may add, the interestingness of ways of saying depends a great deal upon the quality of what is said. "Swinburne's form," goes on Mr. Eliot, "is uninteresting, because he is literally saying next to nothing. . . ."—I am afraid that often in reading the *Cantos* I feel as if what is being said were not much better than nothing.

I am the more emboldened to report my experience and publish my conclusion since, while Mr. Eliot has not been more explicit, other critics who have written on the *Cantos* seem to have adopted his assurance as to their value without being able to say why. The critic whose essay was printed in *The Criterion* for April 1931, does indeed tell us, among a great deal that does not appear to mean very much, that Mr. Pound "is closely related in method and spirit to the kind of ideation found in Dante's *Divine Comedy.*" ["As are: T. S. Eliot in *The Waste Land*; E. E.

[9] "I cannot think of any one writing verse, of our generation and the next, whose verse (if any good) has not been improved by a study of Pound's. His poetry is an inexhaustible reference book of verse form. There is, in fact, no one else to study."— "Isolated Superiority."

Cummings in *Him*; and perhaps one other American, at least in intention."—Footnote.] It does not seem likely that Mr. Eliot would endorse
this account.

The reviewer in *The Hound and Horn* (Winter, 1931) appears more
concerned to be intelligible; but again it is hard to believe that the
various "contrapuntal" and "harmonic" effects that he analyses are what
chiefly interests Mr. Eliot in the *Cantos*. It is not that one finds any
difficulty in seeing what Mr. Pound is at: it is fairly obvious. The
reviewer just mentioned [10] puts it in this way:

> Mr. Pound's documentation is a device, a technic. History and literature
> are for him a mine of images, and his purpose is to fix certain of these
> images in a lasting, orderly design, without reference to a philosophy or to
> any system of teleological principles. Now whether the historical fact, the
> Image, be the blowing of apricot blossoms from east to west, or a narcotic
> charge preferred against Frank Robert Iriquois of Oklahoma City, or the
> departure of Anchises from Troy, it is a detail of supreme importance to the
> frieze, a note of supreme importance to the mélos, which is the poem as a
> whole. The poet, as I have observed, uses images precisely as another poet
> would use metaphors or, even more simply, chromatic words. These images
> have no "hidden" meaning. Malatesta, Frank Robert Iriquois, the apricot
> blossoms, are no more "puzzling" than Shakespeare's "encarnadine" in the
> verse about the multitudinous seas. It is true that if you have enough Latin
> to be able to associate "encarnadine" with "flesh," "carnation," and the
> other rich, warm *carn* words, you will derive more enjoyment from the verse
> than will X, who knows only that "encarnadine" is a euphemism for
> "redden"; but you will "understand" the verse not a whit better than your
> less informed friend. Therefore, the criticism that *XXX Cantos* is incompre-
> hensible is a false criticism; and I have gone into it at some length simply
> because it seems to be the objection that is being most strongly urged against
> the poem. The *Cantos* will baffle persons who are willing to be baffled; but
> this is so in the case of any considerable poem.
>   The *Cantos* may be described as an epic of timelessness. That is to say, the
> poem represents Mr. Pound's endeavour to manage an arrest of time.
> Roughly the method is that of identification or fusion of image. . . .

Without any willingness to be baffled one may reply that while one
"understands" readily enough, the "understanding" one has of a very
large part of the *Cantos* amounts to a good deal less than knowing that
"encarnadine" means "redden." When Mr. Eliot in *The Waste Land* has
recourse to allusion, the intrinsic power of his verse is commonly such
as to affect even a reader who does not recognize what is being alluded
to. But even when one is fully informed about Mr. Pound's allusions one's
recognition has no significant effect: the value remains private to the

[10] Dudley Fitts (W. S.).

author. The methods of association and contrast employed in *The Waste Land* subserve an urgency pressing from below: only an austere and deep seriousness could have controlled them into significance. But the *Cantos* appear to be little more than a game—a game serious with the seriousness of pedantry. We may recognize what Mr. Pound's counters stand for, but they remain counters; and his patterns are not very interesting, even as schematic design, since, in the nature of the game, which hasn't much in the way of rules ("without reference to a philosophy or to any system of teleological principles"), they lack definition and salience.

The radical criticism is made, oddly enough, by this same reviewer in the end of his review, as a kind of unimportant afterthought:

> . . . But he has failed to convey these associations to the reader. For the moment he is indulging in pure pedantry—and not very accurate pedantry at that. Again he has ceased to assert; he has substituted something unconvincingly dead for something convincingly alive. And I would suggest that this tendency is fundamental. Mr. Pound's attitude *is* the pedantic, unreal attitude. Throughout the book he has substituted book-living for actual living.

The judgment seems to me just and damning. The *Cantos* are the kind of "poem of some length" to which, looking back, we can see that the early work (apart from *Mauberley*) points. They are Mr. Pound's *The Ring and the Book.* In so far as they have a representative significance it is as reflecting the contemporary plight that has already been discussed— the lack of form, grammar, principle, and direction. To compel significant art out of that plight needed the seriousness, the spiritual and moral intensity, and the resolute intelligence that are behind *The Waste Land.* Mr. Pound's kind of seriousness is not enough. The very nature of the recognition that (deepened by the war[11]) turned him into a major poet in *Mauberley* seems to constitute a presumption against success in such an undertaking as the *Cantos.*

All this insistence must appear ungracious. But it seems to me the only way of being just to Mr. Pound—to put the stress in a still more important place, the most hopeful way of getting *Mauberley* recognized for the great poem it is.

From Retrospect 1950

Of the major figures dealt with in the book, Pound, though he has written much since (and is still writing), is the one of whom my general sense has been least modified. Of *Hugh Selwyn Mauberley* I think as

---

[11] See especially, *"There died a myriad"* (V).

highly as ever: it seems to me a great poem, and a weightier achievement than any single thing—for *Mauberley* does form a whole—to be found in Yeats. As for the *Cantos,* there are more of them than there were when I first wrote about Pound, and the more of them there are, the plainer does it become that they tend to obscure rather than to strengthen Pound's real claims. I am not at all impressed when I am told by enthusiasts that I ought in consistency to admire them, since they merely employ on a larger scale the methods of *Mauberley.*

I think that Mr. Eliot did Pound and criticism an ill service when he threw out that tip about the superiority of the *Cantos* and their great technical value; a value he defined for himself by saying that he was not interested in what Pound had to say, but only in his way of saying it. Today it is assumed that if one withholds one's admiration from the *Pisan Cantos,* it must be because one's dislike of the Fascism and anti-Semitism in what Pound says (and my own dislike is intense) prevents one from recognizing the beauty and genius of the saying. But how boring that famous versification actually is—boring with the emptiness of the egotism it thrusts on us. A poet's creativity can hardly be a matter of mere versification; there is no profound creative impulse at all for Pound's technical skill to serve. He has no real creative theme. His versification and his *procédés* are servants of wilful ideas and platform vehemences. His moral attitudes and absolutisms are bullying assertions, and have the uncreative blatancy of one whose Social Credit consorts naturally with Fascism and anti-Semitism. It still remains true that only in *Mauberley* has he achieved the impersonality, substance, and depth of great poetry. The classical status of *Mauberley,* however, hasn't anything like general recognition—a fact that throws a depressing light on the supposed liveliness of current interest in contemporary verse.

Mauberley

by Hugh Kenner

With the partial exception of the *Cathay* sequence, the *Personae* volume up to page 183 may be said to be implicit in the *Cantos*. The early poems are deficient in finality; they supplement and correct one another; they stand up individually as renderings of moods, but not as manifestations of mature self-knowledge; they try out poses. They are leading their author somewhere; the reader may be excused if his interests are not wholly engaged, if he finds himself separating the technique from the value of the presented state. This may be said without unsaying anything in the preceding survey, the object of which has been to suggest considerable profit in what may not appear of compelling interest at first glance in 1951. Not only is the history of the purification of our post-Victorian speech contained in those pages, but a right perception of the kinds of achievement there contained will make the *Cantos* easier reading. And in isolating principles of apprehension it has been an advantage to have relatively uncomplicated texts to explicate.

The volume ends, however, with two great self-justifying poems. *Homage to Sextus Propertius* (1917) and *Hugh Selwyn Mauberley* (1920) would, had not a single Canto been finished, dispel any doubt of Pound's being a major poet.

It will be convenient to shorten our discussion by referring the reader to Dr. Leavis' tributes to *Mauberley* in *New Bearings in English Poetry*. That the poem moves him as it does, and that he registers his admiration so adequately and with such economical power of inciting others to comprehension, may, considering the intrinsic resistance of the Bloomsbury-Cambridge milieu to all but certain types of subtly discriminated moral fervors, be taken as some gauge of the emotional weight, the momentum of essential seriousness, massed in these seventeen pages of disrupted quatrains.

Yet the reader will infer correctly from this way of describing Dr.

Leavis' dealings with *Mauberley* that the highly selective vision of that
honest and irascible critic has screened out certain essential elements.
Pound emerges from his account as a man of one poem; the early work
is uninteresting, the *Cantos* a monument of elegant dilettantism. In
Mauberley, for a few pages, under urgent and unhappily transient personal pressures, he found himself with precision and sincerity. Dr. Leavis'
view of Pound's career is introduced here as representative of the most
respectable critical thought. Setting aside journalistic opportunism of the
kind that has no real concern for letters, attacks on Pound are generally
attacks on the *Cantos*. The isolated success of *Mauberley* is generally
conceded. The dispraise even of Mr. Winters is qualified somewhat at this
point.

Mauberley, that is, is a tricky poem. It is difficult for men of a certain
training not to misread it subtly, to select from its elements certain strings
that reverberate to an Eliotic tuning fork. A taste for contemporary poetry
that has shaped itself almost entirely on Mr. Eliot's resonant introspec-
tions has no difficulty in catching what it has come to regard as the sole
note of contemporary poetic sincerity in:

> For three years, out of key with his time,
> He strove to resuscitate the dead art
> Of poetry: to maintain "the sublime"
> In the old sense. Wrong from the start—

It is easy to see how this chimes with such passages as:

> So here I am, in the middle way, having had twenty years—
> Twenty years largely wasted, the years of *l'entre deux guerres*—
> Trying to learn to use words, and every attempt
> Is a wholly new start, and a different kind of failure
> Because one has only learnt to get the better of words
> For the thing one no longer has to say, or the way in which
> One is no longer disposed to say it . . .
>
> *East Coker*, V.

It may briefly be said that there has been a muddle about "impersonality." Mr. Eliot's impersonality is Augustinian; a dispassionate contemplation of the self which permits without romantic impurities a poetic
corpus of metamorphosed personae. Pound's impersonality is Flaubertian: an effacement of the personal accidents of the perceiving medium
in the interests of accurate registration of *mœurs contemporaines*. As we
have said, the adoption of various personae is for such an artist merely
a means to ultimate depersonalization, ancillary and not substantial to
his major work. J. Alfred Prufrock is not Mr. Eliot, but he speaks with

Mr. Eliot's voice and bears intricate analogical relations with the later
Eliot persona who is the speaker of *Four Quartets*. Hugh Selwyn Mauberley, on the other hand, does not speak with Mr. Pound's voice, and is
more antithetically than intimately related to the poet of the *Cantos*. It
would be misleading to say that he is a portion of Mr. Pound's self whom
Mr. Pound is externalizing in order to get rid of him (like Stephen Dedalus); it would be a more accurate exaggeration to say that he is a parody
of Pound the poet with whom Mr. Pound is anxious not to be confounded.

The sort of critic we have been mentioning, the one who finds the note
of sincerity in *Mauberley* as nowhere else in Pound, pays unconscious
tribute to the accuracy with which Pound, in quest of devices for articulat-
ing this quasi-Prufrockian figure, has echoed the intonations and gestures
of a characteristic Eliot poem.[1] Such a critic has been known to quote in
confirmation of his view of Pound Mr. Eliot's remark, "I am sure of
Mauberley, whatever else I am sure of." Mr. Eliot has not, however, the
perceptive limitations of his disciples; in the same essay he insists that
the entire *Personae* collection is to be read as a process of exploration
leading up to the *Cantos*, "which are wholly himself."

It may be helpful to remark that Joyce is in this respect like Pound, an
artist of the Flaubertian kind; his Stephen Dedalus is a parody of himself,
not an artist but an aesthete, at length mercilessly ridiculed in *Finnegans
Wake*. The analogy is reasonably exact; Stephen is partly an aspect of
Joyce himself which Joyce is trying to purify; his horror of bourgeois
civilization echoes Joyce's much as *Mauberley's* "sense of graduations,"

> Quite out of place amid
> Resistance of current exacerbations,

echoes Pound's. But Joyce refrains from unambiguous sympathy with
Stephen's desire for Shelleyan sunward flight; he involves Stephen in an
Icarian fall into the sea of matter just as Pound reduces Mauberley to

> Nothing, in brief, but maudlin confession,
> Irresponse to human aggression,
> Amid the precipitation, down-float
> Of insubstantial manna,
> Lifting the faint susurrus
> Of his subjective hosannah.

This cannot be taken as an account of the poet of the *Cantos* any more
than Stephen's fastidious shrinking away from common noises can be
regarded as characteristic of the author of *Ulysses*. Both men channelled

[1] The primary echo is as a matter of fact with Corbière.

their disgust into patient sifting of immense sottisiers; Pound has been, significantly, almost alone in perceiving the continuity between *Ulysses* and *Bouvard et Pécuchet*. In *Ulysses* Stephen is the focus of spectacular technical sonorities, sympathized with and rejected; the same is true of the Lotus-eaters in the *Cantos*.

It may be remarked that the critic who thinks of *Mauberley* as Pound's one successful poem commonly sees Stephen Dedalus as the hero of *Ulysses,* perceives in both figures elements of failure, and takes as dim a view of Joyce as of the author of the *Cantos.*

Against what may be mistaken for the drift of the above paragraphs, it should be insisted that the process of creating and disowning Hugh Selwyn Mauberley had not the personal importance for Pound that the purgation of the Dedalian aspects of himself had for Joyce. No such trauma was involved in the Idaho poet's flight from America as in the Irish novelist's disentanglement from Church and Motherland. It is not true, on the other hand, to say that Joyce could do nothing until he had focused and gotten rid of Stephen: the bulk of *Dubliners* was written in 1904, in Joyce's twenty-third year. But even when we have balanced *Dubliners* with the social observations in *Lustra,* and *Chamber Music* with the first volume of *Personae,* the excernment of Stephen Dedalus remains of crucial importance to Joyce's future achievement in a way that the writing of *Mauberley* probably was not to Pound. It was probably necessary that he focus in some such oblique way the tension between popular demands and his earlier poetic activities before embarking on the *Cantos;* but the process need not be thought to have coincided with a spiritual crisis from which, as it suits the critic, he emerged either crippled or annealed.

Mauberley does not mark in that way a hurt awakening from aesthetic playgrounds into thin cruel daylight. Its postures and conflicts continue, as we have indicated, those of *Propertius,* the *robustezza* of which could scarcely be confounded with hurt awakening.[2] If a decisive point of maturation must be found, it is to be found in *Propertius,* the earlier poem, it is not always remembered, by some three years. It is easy, for that matter, to over-estimate the reorientation there involved *vis-à-vis* the earlier work. There need be nothing traumatic about supervening maturity; the bulk of *Personae* is the work of a young man in his twenties. Pound was born in 1885. The earliest *Personae,* dated 1908, belong therefore to *aetat.* 23. He published the *Seafarer* translation at 27; *Lustra* at 30, *Cathay* at 31. The next year saw *Propertius* and the first drafts of the earliest *Cantos.* He published *Mauberley* at 35. The *Pisan Cantos* are the work of a man of 60. Emotional maturation may be seen going on in the *Lustra* volume;

---

[2] Since writing this I find in Pound's recently published *Letters* a reference to *Mauberley* as essentially a popularization of *Propertius;* though the context indicates Pound's awareness that this is not the whole story.

and there is enough difference between the monolinear intensity of "The Needle" (*Ripostes*, 1912):

> Come, or the stellar tide will slip away.
> Eastward avoid the hour of its decline,
> Now! for the needle trembles in my soul! . . .

and the calm detached emotion of "Gentildonna" (*Lustra*, 1915):

> She passed and left no quiver in the veins, who now
> Moving among the trees, and clinging
>   in the air she severed,
> Fanning the grass she walked on then, endures:
> Grey olive leaves beneath a rain-cold sky.

to preclude any suggestion of a cataclysmic reorientation a few years later.

These pages will have performed their function if they can arm the reader against the too-easy supposition that Pound found in *Mauberley* an eloquence of disillusion. The subtle balance of diverse strong emotions in that poem will be utterly destroyed by too ready a response to one or two elements. We may now look, belatedly, at the text.

The subtitle ("Life and Contacts") and the title-page footnote (". . . distinctly a farewell to London") furnish a perspective on the title of the first of the eighteen poems: "E. P. Ode Pour L'Election de son Sepulchre." [3] This is largely Pound's career in London seen through the eyes of uncomprehending but not unsympathetic conservers of the "better tradition": a strenuous but ineffectual angel, his subtleties of passion "wrong from the start," accorded the patronizing excuse of having been born "in a half savage country, out of date," and given to Yankee intensities ("bent resolutely on wringing lilies from the acorn") of an unclubbable sort. The epitaph modulates into grudging admiration for the pertinacity of this dedicated spirit—

> His true Penelope was Flaubert,
> He fished by obstinate isles;
> Observed the elegance of Circe's hair
> Rather than the mottoes on sun-dials.

[3] A line of Ronsard, connected by Pound with the *Epitaphe* of Corbière, to whose procedures *Mauberley* is related as early Eliot is related to Laforgue. At the time when *Mauberley* was written, Eliot was getting rid of Laforgue and in collaboration with Pound assimilating Corbière and Gautier. The Corbière reverberations are functional in Pound's poem, relating it to still more complex modes of self-knowledge than we have opportunity to go into here. At its deepest levels the poem is still virtually unread.

The first line of this stanza renders with astonishing concision an intricate set of cultural perspectives. Pound's voyages to China, to Tuscany, to Provence, his battles with Polyphemic editors and his dallyings with pre-Raphaelite Sirens, are transformed, as in the *Cantos,* into an Odyssey of discovery and frustration, imposed, for jealous and irrelevant reasons, by the ruler of the seas (a neat fusion of the chaotic state of letters with English mercantile smugness; the "obstinate isles" are both the British Isles and recalcitrant aesthetic objectives). The irony with which the British mortician of reputations is made to utter unambiguous truths about artistic effort (cf. the "Beauty is difficult" motif of the *Pisan Cantos*) at the same time as he vaunts his national obstinacy and imperception, is carried on with the mention of Flaubert, the "true Penelope" of this voyage. For Pound, Flaubert is the true (= faithful) counterpart, entangling crowds of suitors (superficial "realists") in their own self-deceit while she awaits the dedicated partner whose arm can bend the hard bow of the "mot juste." Flaubert represents the ideal of disciplined self-immolation from which English poetry has been too long estranged, only to be rejoined by apparently circuitous voyaging. For the writer of the epitaph, on the other hand, Flaubert is conceded to be E. P.'s "true" (= equivalent) Penelope only in deprecation: Flaubert being for the English literary mind of the first quarter of the present century a foreign, feminine, rather comically earnest indulger in quite un-British preciosity; "wrong from the start," surrounded by mistaken admirers, and very possibly a whore; a suitable Penelope for this energetic American. England was at that time preparing to burn and ban *Ulysses* exactly as France had sixty years before subjected *Madame Bovary* to juridical process; it was the complaint of the tribunal against Flaubert that he had spent pains on the elegance of his Circe's hair that might better have been diverted to honester causes.

The implications of line after line, irony upon irony, might be expanded in this way; the epitaph concludes with a superbly categorical dismissal of this *impetuus juventus* from the cadres of responsible literary position:

> Unaffected by "the march of events,"
> He passed from men's memory in *l'an trentiesme*
> *De son eage;* the case presents
> No adjunct to the Muse's diadem.

The echo of Villon is of course the crowning irony. *His* passage from the memory of his contemporaries has if anything augmented his place in the history of poetry.

As soon as we see that this epitaph is not (except at the level at which

it transposes Corbière) being written by Pound, the entire sequence falls
into focus. The eleven succeeding poems (II-XII) present an ideogrammic
survey of the cultural state of post-war England: of the culture which we
have just heard pronouncing upon the futility of Pound's effort to
"resuscitate the dead art of poetry." The artist who was "unaffected by
the march of events" offers his version of this criterion:

> The age demanded an image
> Of its accelerated grimace;

the third poem, with its audacious closing counterpoint from Pindar's
Second Olympic (of which there is a readily accessible translation in the
Biographia Literaria, ch. xviii), generalizes with a more austere bitterness:

> All things are a flowing,
> Sage Heracleitus says;
> But a tawdry cheapness
> Shall outlast our days.

Poems IV and V are similarly paired. IV surveys with compassion the
moral dilemmas of the war:

> These fought in any case,
> and some believing,
>> pro domo, in any case . . .

poises sacrifice against domestic cheapness:

> walked eye-deep in hell
> believing in old men's lies, then unbelieving
> came home, home to a lie,
> home to many deceits,
> home to old lies and new infamy;
> usury age-old and age-thick
> and liars in public places.

and closes with a quick evocation of the pullulating new artistic soil,
entrapping the artist in an opportunity for defined and significant
passions that all but swamp his Flaubertian criteria:

> frankness as never before,
> disillusions as never told in the old days,

> hysterias, trench confessions,
> laughter out of dead bellies.

Poem V intensifies the antithesis between sacrifice and gain:

> Charm, smiling at the good mouth,
> Quick eyes gone under earth's lid,
>
> For two gross of broken statues,
> For a few thousand battered books.

The cultural heritage has been reduced to the status of a junkman's inventory by the conservators of tradition mobilized behind the epitaph of poem I; the superimposed tension of the apparent incommensurability, at best, of human lives and civilized achievements brings the sequence to a preliminary climax that prepares for the change of the next six sections into a retrospective key.

"Yeux Glauques" poises the pre-Raphaelite purity,

> Thin like brook water,
> With a vacant gaze

against the bustle of Gladstone and Buchanan (whose attack on "The Fleshly School of Poetry" was answered by Rossetti and Swinburne). The painted woman of the poem contains in her "questing and passive" gaze the complex qualities of passion, between the poles of Swinburne and Burne-Jones, which the aesthetic movement of the nineteenth century mobilized against a world in which "The English Rubaiyat was stillborn." The picturesque reminiscences of the Nineties in the next poem intensify the personal tragedies of the inheritors of that movement; "Dowson found harlots cheaper than hotels." This struggle and rebuttal is, we see, still being carried on; a new dimension of tradition and conflict is added to the efforts of the epitaphed E. P. of the first poem. The success of official literary history in discrediting the vitality of the century of Rossetti, Swinburne, and Fitzgerald and turning it instead into the century of Ruskin, Carlyle, and Tennyson is epitomized in the final stanza:

> M. Verog, out of step with the decade,
> Detached from his contemporaries,
> Neglected by the young,
> Because of these reveries.

M. Verog, "author of *The Dorian Mood*," is a pseudonym for Victor Plarr, who appears in Canto LXXIV "talking of mathematics."

The next three poems are vignettes of three contrasting literary careers. "Brennbaum" (? Max Beerbohm) embodies what passes for the cult of "style":

> The stiffness from spats to collar
> Never relaxing into grace.

This style is neo-classical, not that of the leaping arch; Brennbaum's motive is simply to prepare a face to meet the faces that he meets; such emotional intensity as he knows is not only repressed almost to imperceptibility, its dynamic is private, alien, and accidental to the traditions of Latin Europe: "The heavy memories of Horeb, Sinai and the forty years."

Mr. Nixon, exhibit number two, is the successful public man of letters (? Arnold Bennett). The forced rhymes (reviewer/you are) enact his hearty grimaces; his drawled climactic maxim,

> . . . as for literature
> It gives no man a sinecure,

unites the pretentious popular philosophy of a Wells, a Shaw, a Bennett with the smug generalizations of commercial success and the hard-boiled saws of *Poor Richard's Almanac*.

> "And give up verse, my boy,
> "There's nothing in it."

The third exhibit is the genuine stylist in hiding, an anticlimactic redaction of the Lake Isle of Innisfree:

> The haven from sophistications and contentions
> Leaks through its thatch;
> He offers succulent cooking;
> The door has a creaking latch.

These are not *poèmes à clef*; but the post-war fortunes of Ford Madox Ford are entirely apropos. Ford, the collaborator of Conrad and in the decade pre-war the lone enunciator of the Flaubertian gospel in England, on his discharge from the army retired in disgust to Sussex to raise pigs, and ultimately, at about the same time as Pound, left England. His de-

tailed account of the cultural state of post-war London in the first third
of *It Was the Nightingale* can be made to document *Mauberley* line by
line. The reviewing synod hastened to write his epitaph, so effectively
that his reputation is only beginning to quicken a quarter of a century
after the publication of his best work. Pound has never made a secret of
his respect for Ford, and Ford has testified that Pound alone of the young
writers he could claim to have "discovered" about 1908 did not amid
his later misfortunes disown and castigate him. It pleases at least one
reader to suppose that it is the spectacle of Ford's disillusion that animates
these three extraordinary stanzas.

Poems XI and XII present a post-war contrast to the intricate con-
templative passion of "Yeux Glauques." The twelfth closes the survey of
the London situation with an image of grotesquely effusive aristocratic
patronage; "Daphne with her thighs in bark" dwindles to the Lady Valentine in her stuffed-satin drawing-room, dispensing "well-gowned approbation of literary effort" in sublime assurance of her vocation for a career of
taste and discrimination:

> Poetry, her border of ideas,
> The edge, uncertain, but a means of blending
> With other strata
> Where the lower and higher have ending;
>
> A hook to catch the Lady Jane's attention,
> A modulation toward the theatre,
> Also, in the case of revolution,
> A possible friend and comforter.

Dr. Johnson's letter to Lord Chesterfield stands as the archetypal repudi-
ation of the vague, vain, and irrelevant claims of patronage; but the street
of literary commerce to which Johnson turned has also lost its power to
support the artist:

> Beside this thoroughfare
> The sale of half-hose has
> Long since superseded the cultivation
> Of Pierian roses.

The *Envoi* which follows is a consummate ironic climax; against these
squalors is asserted the audacious Shakespearean vocation of preserving
transient beauty against the tooth of time (cf. the end of the first *Propertius* poem); against the halting and adroitly short-winded quatrains of the
"dumb-born book" is set a magnificently sustained melodic line:

> Go, dumb-born book,
> Tell her that sang me once that song of Lawes:
> Hadst thou but song
> As thou hast subjects known,
> Then were there cause in thee that should condone
> Even my faults that heavy upon me lie,
> And build her glories their longevity. . . .

Seventeenth century music, the union of poetry with song, immortal beauty, vocalic melody, treasure shed on the air, transcend for a single page the fogs and squabbles of the preceding sections in a poem that ironically yearns for the freedom and power which it displays in every turn of phrase, in triumphant vindication of those years of fishing by obstinate isles. The poet who was buried in the first section amid such deprecation rises a Phoenix to confront his immolators, asserting the survival of at least this song

> When our two dusts with Waller's shall be laid,
> Siftings on siftings in oblivion,
> Till change hath broken down
> All things save Beauty alone.

There follows a five-part coda in which the Mauberley *persona* comes to the fore; gathering up the motifs of the earlier sections, the enigmatic stanzas mount from intensity to intensity to chronicle the death of the Jamesian hero who might have been Pound. Part two is practically a précis of the flirtation with passionate illusion of Lambert Strether in *The Ambassadors.* "Of course I moved among miracles," said Strether. "It was all phantasmagoric." The third part contains the essential action; having postulated Mauberley's "fundamental passion":

> This urge to convey the relation
> Of eye-lid and cheek-bone
> By verbal manifestations;
>
> To present the series
> Of curious heads in medallion,

and implied a context of opportunities missed—

> Which anaesthesis, noted a year late,
> And weighed, revealed his great affect,
> (Orchid), mandate
> Of Eros, a retrospect.

—Pound particularizes on the Propertian conflict between the aesthetic martyr and the demands of the age.
Contemplation is weighed against Shavian strenuousness:

> The glow of porcelain
> Brought no reforming sense
> To his perception
> Of the social inconsequence.
>
> Thus, if her colour
> Came against his gaze,
> Tempered as if
> It were through a perfect glaze
>
> He made no immediate application
> Of this to relation of the state
> To the individual, the month was more temperate
> Because this beauty had been.

In Canto XIII Confucius provides a cross-light:

> And Kung raised his cane against Yuan Jang,
>   Yuan Jang being his elder,
> For Yuan Jang sat by the roadside pretending to
>   be receiving wisdom.
> And Kung said
>   "You old fool, come out of it,
> Get up and do something useful."

The serious artist does not "pretend to be receiving wisdom"; we have heard Pound dilating on his quasi-automatic social functions. It is the essence of the artist's cruel dilemma that his just reaction against politicians' and journalists' canons of usefulness drives him so perilously close to

> . . . an Olympian *apathein*
> In the presence of selected perceptions.[4]

[4] It should be noted that the *Pisan Cantos* derive their extraordinary vitality from the fact that an *apathein* among memorably rendered "selected perceptions" is not being crudely opposed, in H. S. Mauberley's fashion, to the "current exacerbations" of the prison-camp. The moon-nymph, the lynxes, the Chinese sages, the healing rain, unite with the gun-roosts and the dialogue of murderers to form new perceptive wholes. Pound's "armor against utter consternation" is not gotten "by constant elimination" but by vigorous fusion. *The Pisan Cantos* comment on *Mauberley* in a way Pound furthered by incorporating plangent scraps of the earlier poem into Canto LXXIV.

The descent into this Nirvana of the fastidious moth with the preciously
cadenced name is chronicled with elaborate subtlety. The validity of his
perceptions is played off against "neo-Nietzschean clatter"; but meanwhile the directness of the opening images, the red-beaked steeds, the
glow of porcelain, is being gradually overlaid by a crescendo of abstractions: "isolation," "examination," "elimination," "consternation," "un-
dulation," "concentration." The tone shifts from the sympathetic to the
clinical:

> Invitation, mere invitation to perceptivity
> Gradually led him to the isolation
> Which these presents place
> Under a more tolerant, perhaps, examination.

The preservation of a critical distance both from the inadequacies of
Mauberley and from the irrelevantly active world of Mr. Nixon, Nie-
tzsche, and Bishop Bloughram, with its "discouraging doctrine of chances,"
the realization of an impersonality that extracts strength from both of the
antithetical cadres of the first twelve poems, is the major achievement of
these final pages. Mauberley's disappearance into his dream-world is related without approbation and without scorn:

> A pale gold, in the aforesaid pattern,
> The unexpected palms
> Destroying, certainly, the artist's urge,
> Left him delighted with the imaginary
> Audition of the phantasmal sea-surge,

and we are warned by inverted commas in the next stanza against adopt-
ing too readily the standpoint of pontifical criticism:

> Incapable of the least utterance or composition,
> Emendation, conservation of the "better tradition,"
> Refinement of medium, elimination of superfluities,
> August attraction or concentration.

That "better tradition" interjects the accent of a Buchanan or an
Edmund Gosse; the other canons are Flaubertian. Mauberley is not simply a failure by Mr. Nixon's standards of success, he is a failure *tout court;*
he is the man to whom that initial epitaph might with justice be applied;
the man for whom the writer of the epitaph has mistaken "E. P." It is the
focusing of this that guarantees the closing irony:

Ultimate affronts to
Human redundancies;

Non-esteem of self-styled "his betters"
Leading, as he well knew,
To his final
Exclusion from the world of letters.

The irrelevancy of the canons of "the world of letters," for once right but
from utterly wrong reasons, very efficient in guillotining the already
defunct, could not be more subtly indicated.

As a technical marvel this poem cannot be too highly praised. Only
Pound's economical means were sufficiently delicate for the discrimina-
tions he sought to effect: "perhaps" and "we admit" belong to one mode
of perception, "the month was more temperate because this beauty had
been" to another, the concessive "certainly" and the clinical "incapable"
and "in brief" to a third. The technique of distinguishing motivations
and qualities of insight solely by scrupulous groupings of notes on the
connotative or etymological keyboard has never been brought to greater
refinement. One cannot think of another poet who could have brought
it off.

The sequence is re-focused by a vignette of hedonistic drift protracting
the coral island imagery that had troubled Mauberley's reverie, ending
with an epitaph scrawled on an oar,

"I was
And I no more exist;
Here drifted
An hedonist."

pathetic echo of the elaborate opening "Ode Pour L'Election de son
Sepulchre." The final "Medallion," to be balanced against the "Envoi" of
the first part, recurs in witty disenchantment to the singing lady. Neither
the Envoi's passion:

Tell her that sheds
Such treasure on the air,
Recking naught else but that her graces give
Life to the moment . . .

nor Mauberley's "porcelain reverie":

Thus if her colour
Came against his gaze,

> Tempered as if
> It were through a perfect glaze

is denied by the paradoxical dispassion of the final picture:

> Luini in porcelain!
> The grand piano
> Utters a profane
> Protest with her clear soprano.

But the tone is "objective" in a way that detaches the "Medallion" from the claims of the various worlds of perception projected in earlier parts of the poem. There are witty echoes of those worlds: the "profane protest" of heavy-fingered clubbably professional letters;[5] an ambrosial Mauberleian dream of braids

> Spun in King Minos' hall
> From metal, or intractable amber;

but the closing stanza is pitched to a key of quasi-scientific meticulousness that delivers with Flaubertian inscrutability a last voiceless verdict of inadequacy on all the human squinting, interpreting, and coloring that has preceded: fact revenging itself on art and the artists—

> The face-oval beneath the glaze,
> Bright in its suave bounding-line, as,
> Beneath half-watt rays,
> The eyes turn topaz.

Beauty? Irony? Geometrical and optical fact?

And this last poem yields a final irony. "To present the series / Of curious heads in medallion" was, we remember, Mauberley's ambition, and this sample Medallion in its very scrupulousness exemplifies his sterility. His imagination falls back upon precedents; his visual particularity comes out of an art-gallery and his Venus Anadyomene out of a book. The "true Penelope" of both poets was Flaubert, but Pound's contrasting Envoi moves with authority of another order. Mauberley cringed before the age's demands; he wrote one poem and collapsed. Pound with sardonic compliance presents the age with its desiderated "image" (poems 3-12); then proves he was *right* from the start by offering as indisputable climax the "sculpture of rhyme" and the "sublime in the old sense" which

---

[5] Cf. "as the young horse whinnies against the tubas" (Canto LXXIX).

the epitaph-writer had dismissed as a foolish quest. And he adds a sympathetic obituary and epitaph of his own for the *alter ego*.

This thin-line tracing of the action of *Mauberley* is offered with no pretense to fullness. It is possible, as we have seen, to spend a page meditating on a line. The writer professes two objectives in proceeding as above. First, it seemed profitable to trace the "intaglio method" through an entire work, with a detail which will be impossible when we come to the *Cantos*. Secondly, it seemed important to guide the reader towards an apprehension of *Mauberley* in terms that will not falsify his notion of Pound's later or earlier work. The poem has commended itself too readily as a memorable confession of failure to those whom it comforts to decide that Pound has failed. Anyone to whom the above pages are persuasive will perhaps agree that a less obvious perspective augments, if anything, the stature of this astonishing poem.

The *Cantos*

by M. L. Rosenthal

Space forbids our going into the *Cantos* in even as much detail as we have into *Mauberley*. We have already, however, noted some of the leading ideas behind this more involved and ambitious work, and though we cannot here trace their handling throughout its winding, Gargantuan progress, a few suggestions concerning its character as a poetic sequence may be useful. First of all, we may take as our point of departure the fact that in motivation and outlook the *Cantos* are a vast proliferation from the same conceptions which underlie *Mauberley*. The difference lies partly in the multiplicity of "voices" and "cross-sections," partly in the vastly greater inclusiveness of historical and cultural scope, and partly in the unique formal quality of the longer sequence; it is by the very nature of its growth over the years a work-in-progress. Even when the author at last brings it to conclusion, reorganizing it, supplying the withheld Cantos 72 and 73, completing his revisions, and even giving his book a definitive title, it will remain such a work. Each group of cantos will be what it is now—a new *phase* of the poem, like each of the annual rings of a living tree. The poet has put his whole creative effort into a mobilization of all levels of his consciousness into the service of the *Cantos;* there has been a driving central continuity, and around it new clusters of knowledge and association linked with the others by interweavings, repetitions, and over-all perspective. Pound has staked most of his adult career as a poet on this most daring of poetic enterprises; literary history gives us few other examples of comparable commitment.

The *Cantos* has been called Pound's "intellectual diary since 1915," and so it is. But the materials of this diary have been so arranged as to subserve the aims of the poem itself. Passage by passage there *is* the fascination of listening in on a learned, passionate, now rowdy, now delicate intelligence, an intelligence peopled by the figures of living tradition but not so possessed by them that it cannot order their appearances and relationships. Beyond the fascination of the surface snatches of song, dialogue,

and description, always stimulating and rhythmically suggestive though
not always intelligible upon first reading, there is the essential overriding
drive of the poem, and the large pattern of its overlapping layers of
thought. The way in which the elements of this pattern swim into the
reader's line of vision is well suggested by Hugh Kenner, one of Pound's
most able and enthusiastic interpreters:

> The word "periplum," which recurs continually throughout the *Pisan
> Cantos* [74-84], is glossed in Canto LIX:
>
> > periplum, not as land looks on a map
> > but as sea bord seen by men sailing.
>
> Victor Brerard discovered that the geography of the *Odyssey*, grotesque when
> referred to a map, was minutely accurate according to the Phoenician
> voyagers' *periploi*. The image of successive discoveries breaking upon the
> consciousness of the voyager is one of Pound's central themes. . . . The
> voyage of Odysseus to hell is the matter of Canto I. The first half of Canto
> XL is a periplum through the financial press; "out of which things seeking an
> exit," we take up in the second half of the Canto the narrative of the
> Carthagenian Hanno's voyage of discovery. Atlantic flights in the same way
> raise the world of epileptic maggots in Canto XXVIII into a sphere of swift
> firm-hearted discovery. . . . The periplum, the voyage of discovery among
> facts, . . . is everywhere contrasted with the conventions and artificialities
> of the bird's eye view afforded by the map. . . .[1]

Thus, the successive cantos and layers of cantos must be viewed not so
much schematically as experientially. Here we see how the early Pound's
developing idealization of the concrete image, the precise phrase, the
organically accurate rhythm are now brought to bear on this vast later
task. The many voices, varied scenes and *personae,* and echoes of other
languages and literatures than English reflect this emphasis on experience
itself: something mysterious, untranslatable, the embodied meaning of
life which we generalize only at peril of losing touch with it. So also with
Pound's emphatic use of Chinese ideograms, whose picture-origins still are
visible enough, he believes, so that to "read" them is to think in images
rather than in abstractions. His use of them is accounted for by the same
desire to present "successive discoveries breaking upon the consciousness
of the voyager." The first effect of all these successive, varied breakings is
not intended to be total intellectual understanding, any more than in real
experience we "understand" situations upon first coming into them. But

---

[1] Hugh Kenner, *The Poetry of Ezra Pound* (Norfolk, Conn.: New Directions, 1951),
pp. 102-103. Kenner's use of Roman numerals follows Pound, but the latest groups of
cantos (*Rock-Drill* and *Thrones*), published after Kenner's book, change to Arabic
numerals. For consistency's sake we have followed the latter usage throughout [this
essay].

by and by the pattern shapes up and the relationships clarify themselves, though always there remains an unresolved residue of potentiality for change, intractable and baffling.

Pound's "voyager," upon whose consciousness the discoveries break, is, we have several times observed, a composite figure derived first of all from the poet-speaker's identification with Odysseus. A hero of myth and epic, he is yet very much of this world. He is both the result of creative imagination and its embodiment. He explores the worlds of the living, of the dead, and of the mythic beings of Hades and Paradise. Lover of mortal women as of female deities, he is like Zagreus a symbol of the life-bringing male force whose mission does not end even with his return to his homeland. Gradually he becomes all poets and all heroes who have somehow vigorously impregnated the culture. He undergoes (as do the female partners of his procreation and the *personae* and locales in time and space of the whole sequence) many metamorphoses. Hence the importance of the Ovidian metamorphosis involving the god Dionysus, the sea (the female element and symbol of change), and the intermingling of contemporary colloquial idiom and the high style of ancient poetry in Canto 2. The first canto had ended with a burst of praise for Aphrodite, goddess of love and beauty, and in language suggesting the multiple allusiveness of the sequence: to the Latin and Renaissance traditions, as well as the Grecian-Homeric, and to the cross-cultural implications suggested by the phrase "golden bough." The second canto takes us swiftly backward in the poetic tradition, through Browning, then Sordello and the other troubadours, and then to the classical poets and the Chinese tradition. All poets are one, as Helen and Eleanor of Aquitaine and Tyro (beloved of Poseidon) and all femininity are one and all heroes are one.

In the first two cantos, then, the "periplum" of the sequence emerges into view. Three main value-referents are established: a sexually and aesthetically creative world-view, in which artistic and mythical tradition provides the main axes; the worship of Bacchus-Dionysus-Zagreus as the best symbol of creativity in action; and the multiple hero—poet, voyager, prophet, observer, thinker. The next four cantos expand the range of allusiveness, introducing for instance the figure of the Cid, a chivalric hero, to add his dimension to the voyager-protagonist's consciousness. Also, various tragic tales are brought to mind, extending the initial horror of Odysseus' vision of the dead and thus contributing to the larger scheme of the poet in the modern wasteland. In absolute contrast, pagan beatitudes are clearly projected in Canto 2 in the pictures of Poseidon and Tyro:

> Twisted arms of the sea-god,
> Lithe sinews of water, gripping her, cross-hold,
> And the blue-gray glass of the wave tents them . . . .

and, at the scene's close, in the phallic "tower like a one-eyed great goose"
craning up above the olive grove while the fauns are heard "chiding
Proteus" and the frogs "singing against the fauns." This pagan ideal
comes in again and again, sharp and stabbing against bleak backgrounds
like the "petals on the wet, black bough" of the "Metro" poem. Thus, in
Canto 3:

> Gods float in the azure air,
> Bright gods and Tuscan, back before dew was shed.

In Canto 4:

> Choros nympharum, goat-foot, with the pale foot alternate;
> Crescent of blue-shot waters, green-gold in the shallows,
> A black cock crows in the sea-foam . . . .

In 4 and 5 both there are deliberate echoes of such poets as have a kindred
vision (Catullus, Sappho, and others), set against the notes of evil and
damnation. The lines from Sordello in 6 serve the same purpose:

> "Winter and Summer I sing of her grace,
> As the rose is fair, so fair is her face,
> Both Summer and Winter I sing of her,
> The snow makyth me to remember her."

The Lady of the troubadours, whose "grace" is a secularized transposition
from that of Deity, is another manifestation of "the body of nymphs, of
nymphs, and Diana" which Actaeon saw, as well as of what Catullus
meant: " 'Nuces!' praise, and Hymenaeus 'brings the girl to her
man. . . .' "

After these archetypal and literary points of reference have been established, Cantos 8-19 move swiftly into a close-up of the origins of the
modern world in the Renaissance, and of the victory of the anticreative
over the active, humanistic values represented by Sigismundo Malatesta
and a few others. (Canto 7 is transitional; in any case we can note only
the larger groupings here.) The relation between the "Renaissance
Cantos" (8-11) and the "Hell Cantos" (14-16), with their scatological pic-
turings of the contemporary Inferno, is organic: the beginning and the
end of the same process of social corruption. The beautiful dialogue on
order in 13 provides a calm, contrasting center for this portion of the
sequence, and is supported by the paradisic glow and serenity of Elysium,
revealed in 16 and 17. The earlier cantos had given momentary attention
to Oriental poetry and myth and, as we have seen, Elysian glimpses also.

Now these motifs are expanded and related to a new context, bringing
the sequence into revised focus but carrying all its earlier associations
along. This leaping, reshuffling, and reordering is the organizational principle behind the growth, the "annual rings," of the *Cantos*.
The next ten cantos interweave the motifs of these first two groups and
prepare us for the next leap (in Cantos 30-41) of perspective. There are
various preparations for this leap, even as early as Canto 20, in which
there is a moment of comment from the "outside" as if to take stock
before hurtling onward. From their remote "shelf," "aerial, cut in the
aether," the disdainful lotus-eaters question all purposeful effort:

> "What gain with Odysseus,
> "They that died in the whirlpool
> "And after many vain labours,
> "Living by stolen meat, chained to the rowingbench,
> "That he should have a great fame
> "And lie by night with the goddess? . . ."

Is the question wisdom or cynicism? No matter. The poem, given the
human condition and the epic tasks that grow out of it, is held in check
but an instant before again plunging ahead. The *Cantos* accepts the
moral meaning and the moral responsibility of human consciousness. The
heroic ideal remains, as on the other hand the evil of our days remains
even after the goddess' song against pity is heard at the beginning of 30.
The new group (30-41) is, like the later Adams cantos (62-71), in the
main a vigorous attempt to present the fundamental social and economic
principles of the Founding Fathers as identical with Pound's own. Adams
and Jefferson are his particular heroes, and there is an effort to show that
Mussolini's program is intended to carry these basic principles, imbedded
in the Constitution but perverted by banking interests, into action. Pound
works letters and other documents, as well as conversations real and
imagined, into his blocks of verse, usually fragmentarily, and gives modern close-ups of business manipulations. The method has the effect of a
powerful exposé, particularly of the glimpsed operations of munitions-
profiteers. The cantos of the early 1930's have, indeed, a direct connection
with the interest in social and historical documentation and rhetoric that
marks much other work of the same period, and at the end of Canto 41
(in which Mussolini is seen) we should not be surprised to find an oratori-
cal climax similar in effect to that of Poem IV in *Mauberley* (1919). As in
the earlier groups, however, we are again given contrasting centers of
value, especially in Canto 36 (which renders Cavalcanti's *A lady asks me*)
and in Canto 39, whose sexually charged interpretation of the spell cast
over Odysseus and his men on Circe's isle is one of Pound's purest successes.

The Chinese cantos (53-61) and the Pisan group (74-84) are the two most important remaining unified clusters within the larger scheme. Again, the practical idealism of Confucianism, like that of Jefferson and Adams, becomes an analogue for Pound's own ideas of order and of secular aestheticism. Canto 13 was a clear precursor, setting the poetic stage for this later extension. "Order" and "brotherly deference" are key words in Confucius' teachings; both princes and ordinary men must have order *within* them, each in his own way, if dominion and family alike are to thrive. These thoughts are not clichés as Pound presents them. We hear a colloquy that has passion, humor, and depth, and what our society would certainly consider unorthodoxy. Kung "said nothing of the 'life after death,' " he considered loyalty to family and friends a prior claim to that of the law, he showed no respect for the aged when they were ignorant through their own fault, and he advocated a return to the times "when the historians left blanks in their writings, / I mean for things they didn't know." The Chinese cantos view Chinese history in the light of these principles of ordered intelligence in action, with the ideogram *ching ming* (name things accurately) at the heart of the identity between Confucian and Poundian attitudes. "The great virtue of the Chinese language," writes Hugh Gordon Porteus, "inheres in its written characters, which so often contrive to suggest by their graphic gestures (as English does by its phonetic gestures) the very essence of what is to be conveyed." [2] The development of Pound's interest in Chinese poetry and thought, as well as his varied translations from the Chinese, is in itself an important subject. This interest, like every other to which he has seriously turned his attention, he has brought directly to bear on his own poetic practice and on his highly activistic thinking in general.

With the *Pisan Cantos* and *Rock-Drill* [3] we are brought, first, into the immediately contemporary world of the poet himself, in Fascist Italy toward the close of World War II, in a concentration camp at Pisa, during the last days of Mussolini; and second, into a great, summarizing recapitulation of root-attitudes developed in all the preceding cantos: in particular the view of the banking system as a scavenger and breeder of corruption, and of ancient Chinese history as an illuminating, often wholesomely contrasting analogue to that of the post-medieval West. Even more than before, we see now how the *Cantos* descend, with some bastardies along the line, from the Enlightenment. They conceive of a world creatively ordered to serve human needs, a largely rationalist conception. Hence the stress on the sanity of Chinese thought, the immediacy

[2] "Ezra Pound and the Chinese Character: A Radical Examination," in *Ezra Pound*, p. 215.

[3] *Section: Rock-Drill: 85-95 de los cantares* (New York: New Directions, 1956). This was the first group of cantos to be published separately since the *Cantos* appeared in 1948.

of the Chinese ideogram, and the hardheaded realism of a certain strain of economic theory. The *Pisan Cantos* show Pound's vivid responsiveness as he approached and passed his sixtieth birthday: his aliveness to people, his Rabelaisian humor, his compassion. The lotus-eaters of Canto 20, aloof and disdainful, have missed out on the main chances. Canto 81 contains the famous "Pull down thy vanity" passage in which the poet, though rebuking his own egotism, yet staunchly insists on the meaningfulness of his accomplishment and ideals. As the sequence approaches conclusion, the fragments are shored together for the moral summing-up. In the *Rock-Drill* section, Cantos 85-95, the stocktaking continues and we are promised, particularly in Canto 90, an even fuller revelation than has yet been vouchsafed us of the Earthly Paradise.

Cantos 96-109[4] begin to carry out this promise, though after so many complexities, overlappings, and interlocking voices it must be nearly impossible to bring the work to an end. It is essentially a self-renewing process rather than a classical structure, and there is no limit to the aspects of history and thought the poet has wished to bring to bear on the poem. Canto 96, for instance, touches on certain developments after the fall of Rome, especially two decrees in the Eastern Empire by Justinian and Leo VI concerning standards of trade, workmanship, and coinage. The special emphasis in this canto on Byzantine civilization is particularly appropriate because of Byzantium's historical and geographical uniting of East and West as well as its mystical associations pointing to a new and dramatic paradisic vision. Although the memory of earlier glimpses of "paradise" and the recapitulative, self-interrupting method militate against an effect of a revelation overwhelmingly new, the pacing of the whole sequence has made this difficulty at the end inevitable. Pound's conclusion must be introduced as emergent from the midst of things, still struggling from all in life and consciousness that makes for disorder.

[4] *Thrones: 96-109 de los cantares* (New York: New Directions, 1959).

A Man of No Fortune

by Forrest Read

Perhaps the most frequently heard complaints against *The Cantos* of Ezra Pound are that it appears to be formless and that it is made unnecessarily difficult because of Pound's apparently unfathomable literary and historical allusions. In addition, it has been said that sections of *The Cantos* are dull and verbose. Particularly is this criticism made of the Chinese history Cantos (LIII-LXI) and, somewhat less often, of the John Adams Cantos (LXII-LXXI). It may well be argued that Pound does not attain in either of these sections the incisiveness and vigor of the Malatesta Cantos (VII-XI). But whether or not these sections detract from the movement of the poem is not at issue here. Accepting the apparent difficulties of *The Cantos,* how is one to read it? How is one to superimpose upon it enough of form to make it seem, at least on one level, intelligible?

I should like to suggest the following conclusion and approach: *The Cantos* can best be read as a modern *Odyssey,* following with varying degrees of exactness the experience of Odysseus as Ezra Pound sees it. The narrator of the poem follows the trail of Homer's wanderer, seeking the way home.

Many critics have explained that *The Cantos* follows a pattern somewhat similar to that of Dante's *Divina Commedia.* They point, justly, to the *Commedia's* division into cantos, and speak of a three-fold separation of *The Cantos* into something much like Dante's *Inferno-Purgatorio-Paradiso* triptych. Further, they note that Pound has spoken of a poem of one hundred cantos, the same number Dante wrote for his *Commedia.*

To offer some bolstering to this thesis, there is the explanation Pound himself made to his father in a letter dated April 11, 1927. There Pound speaks of three fugal components that will wind through *The Cantos:*

A. A. Live man goes down into the world of the Dead

C. B. The "repeat in history"

B. C. The "magic moment" or moment of metamorphosis, bust through from quotidien into "divine or permanent world." Gods, etc.

This tripartite scheme has its parallel in the division Dante constructs. One sees, correspondingly, the underworld (*Inferno*), the mountain (*Purgatorio*), and the heavens (*Paradiso*). And as far as the construction of *The Cantos* is concerned, there is a parallel to be observed and followed in the state of mind of the narrator and observer.

But there is an important difference: in the *Commedia* it is very clear who, what, and where the narrator is. He is Dante, a medieval man, at home in a medieval world ordered by the Christian myth. In *The Cantos* there is no presupposed Christian myth as guide. One must search for another myth. And that myth, set in the first Canto, is the myth of Odysseus, the hero who wishes to return home but cannot return until he has suffered and learned through that suffering. But far more important than the construction is the identification of the person who sees and tells in *The Cantos*. The narrator is Erza Pound as Odysseus, and his Cantos relate the education of Ezra Pound, the modern man, as Homer's poem relates the education of Odysseus.

The window through which this identity becomes clear is Canto XXXIX, which sets forth the core of the *Odyssey* and of *The Cantos*. Canto XXXIX is about four characters, Elpenor, Circe, Eurilochus, and Penelope, who assume vital importance in both the *Odyssey* and *The Cantos* as their significance is understood.

I would suggest that in Canto XXXIX Elpenor and Eurilochus[1] embody alternatives Odysseus may choose as he stands before Circe, who tells him he must go to Hades to seek directions home from the shade Tiresias. Passive Elpenor (man-destroying passion) and aggressive Eurilochus (man-destroying intellect) are shown as aspects of Odysseus' own nature from whom he learns, as in the *Odyssey*, to strike the middle way. Both appear in Canto I, which sets the stage for the listener, Odysseus-Pound, as he stands at the fosse hearing the tales of the dead and awaiting the advice of Tiresias which will lead him home.

Let us consider Canto XXXIX, divided according to the four characters.

Elpenor ("Desolate. . . . vocem," lines 1-36)

Elpenor was the member of Odysseus' crew who fell from the roof of Circe's house, and who met Odysseus when Odysseus and his men entered

---

[1] In Greek Elpenor (ἐλπίς, *hope for* and ἀνήρ, *man*) means the man who hopes the future will turn out all right without his having to act. Eurilochus (εἰρύ, *wide* and λοχος, *snare*) means the man of widespreading snares.

the underworld. Elpenor was "the youngest of us all, one not so very
valiant in war or steady in mind" (*Odyssey* x. 552-53). It is he who speaks
as the Canto opens on a scene of lavish, perverted voluptuousness. We
first see Elpenor lying on the roof of Circe's house, befuddled and dreaming. We then see him as one of the crew approaching the enchantress's
house to be turned into swine. The picture is one of unrestrained passion,
both sexual and of the stomach. Circe is identified as the daughter of the
Sun, whose sister, Pasiphae, became maddened with lust and copulated
with a bull, bringing forth that monster, the Cretan Minotaur. Circe is,
to Elpenor and the men-swine, "Venter venustus, cunni cultrix, of the
velvet marge." The association of Circe with Pasiphae stresses the metamorphosis of passion into degeneration, which results if passion is allowed
to pass beyond its allotted bounds:

> Spring overborne into summer
> late spring in the leafy autumn

"KALON AOIDIAEI" ("the beauty of her singing," *Odyssey* x. 227) is the
bewitching song of Circe, which wooed the crew into her house to be
transformed into swine. The metamorphosis is again pointed up:

> First honey and cheese
> honey at first and then acorns

These lines emphasize the appetite which allowed Circe to change the
crew from men, who ate honey and cheese, to swine, whose diet is acorns.
Elpenor speaks languidly, underscoring the metamorphosis of the "ver
novum" of the *Pervigilium Veneris* into "late spring in the leafy autumn."
The Elpenor section ends with a quotation from Ovid (*Metamorphoses*
XIII. 538-9): "illa dolore obmutuit, pariter vocem." The line refers to
Hecuba as she suffers the final calamity wrought by Paris' unrestrained
passion for Helen, which caused the Trojan War. In Ovid, Hecuba's last
living child, Polydorus, is washed ashore a corpse. The old queen stands
transfixed with grief, and after slaying her son's murderer, gives way to
her hysteria and is metamorphosed to a wolf who goes shrieking over the
plains. Elpenor's overindulgence has brought him to the metamorphosis,
and its extremity does him to death as he tumbles from Circe's roof in a
drunken stupor.

Circe (Greek passage, lines 37-41)

The scene of passion suddenly ends, and there follows the passage from
the *Odyssey* (x. 490-5) in which Odysseus, after a year spent in Circe's

bed, hears the goddess tell him he must, to get home to Ithaca, go to Hades and seek advice of the soothsayer Tiresias. This is the Tiresias who lived both man and woman, and was struck blind by Hera for judging from that experience that in bed a woman's pleasure is greater than a man's. As recompense, Zeus, who won the wager with his fiery wife, gave Tiresias the everlasting power of prophecy. Thus the Greek passage places us at a point just before *The Cantos* opens. In Canto 1 Odysseus and his crew are on the way to Hades, having followed Circe's directions. They sail, under Circe's tutelage:

> Circe's this craft, the trim-coifed goddess

One must realize that Circe is not merely a witch, but part of the scheme of life. She is "cunni cultrix," a goddess. While she turned the crew into swine, Eurilochus balked; fearing danger, he refused to enter her house, thus denying the metamorphosis. She also failed to transform Odysseus, who with the help of moly, withstood her magic and overpowered her. But Odysseus did, of his own free will, lie with her for a whole year. Thus he neither denied nor succumbed to the metamorphosis, but assimilated it.

Circe's advice is here given in Greek, with no translation, signifying that Pound as Odysseus does not comprehend the full import of her advice. It is as though she spoke to deaf ears in this case, the ears of the man who refused to unbend to her, Eurilochus.

Eurilochus ("When Hathor . . . . boat yet?" lines 42-65)

In the Eurilochus section the key lies in the man who refuses to undergo the metamorphosis in any way. Eurilochus' hardness and his bodyless, physically passionless attitude bring destruction on him when he holds stubbornly to them. The section opens with Hathor, Egyptian sun-goddess, bound in a box and afloat on the sea. Here the sun-goddess is enslaved and powerless, in direct opposition to Circe's sway over the passionate Elpenor. In this Eurilochean section we shall find that this parallel with the Elpenor section continues—recurring images are altered to conform with the cautious, aspiring Eurilochus; intelligence is perverted instead of lust.

The Italian—"Che mai da me non si parte il diletto"—comes from Dante's *Paradiso* (XXIII. 129), where the redeemed form a crown of light about Mary, singing "Regina Coeli." This is an entirely different kind of singing from Circe's KALON AOIDIAEI—that of a too intellectual divine love as opposed to the call to a too sensual pleasure. And the Virgin Mary is another type of divinity from "cunni cultrix"; Dante is drawn to redemption through contemplation of an ideal love, Beatrice. "Fulvida di folgore" (*Paradiso* XXX. 62) portrays a river of light "intra due rive / dipinte

di mirabil primavera." This spring and these banks exist quite removed
from "late spring" and "the velvet marge" which holds "Venter venustus."
The "due rive" hold the Church Triumphant, a far cry from Elpenor's
sexual passion.

Then comes the picture of Eurilochus, who enters "with Glaucus
unnoticed." Glaucus (Ovid *Metamorphoses* XIII. 898-XIV. 74) also had his
run-in with Circe. Having eaten a strange grass which made him play-
fellow with the gods, he loved Scylla. But Circe, here an evil enchantress,
turned her thoughts to Glaucus and, jealous of the mortal Scylla, turned
her to a beast from the waist down. Both Glaucus and Eurilochus spurn
Circe and the passion of "cunni cultrix," not recognizing her as the goddess who takes the edge off Odysseus' hubris. Eurilochus refuses to enter
Circe's swinesty—"nec ivi in harum / nec in harum ingressus sum." He
denies her bed, maintaining his overhaughty eminence.

"Eurilochus, Macer" ("Macer" recalls irresistibly Julius Caesar's remark
about Cassius: "Yon Cassius hath a lean and hungry look") would be
better off had he entered the swinesty, where he would have had at least
good acorns. As it is, he becomes the victim of Poseidon, who would have
done in Odysseus too, had "the man of many devices" not attained
reverence from Circe and the journey to Hades.

Circe prepared him for his journey:

> "I think you must be Odysseus. . . .
> feel better when you have eaten. . . .
> Always with your mind on the past. . . .

Circe's words underscore Odysseus' Eurilochus alternative—he is too
cautious to commit himself, to break down and yield to the metamorphosis which can save him. Odysseus has been guilty of hubris, and
Circe lets him know he had better soften a little. He does, but up to this
point he has not "Been to hell in a boat yet."

Eurilochus here is the mirror which reflects the Odysseus who craftily
devised the Wooden Horse to sack Troy; who unreasonably sacked the
Cicones in his warriorlike homeward voyage; who, in his pride, told
Polyphemus his name and address, thus bringing down the wrath of the
Cyclops' father, Poseidon; who reached for his sword to cut off Eurilochus'
head when that worthy tried to keep the rest of the crew from going to
Circe's house after half the men had been turned to swine. This Eurilochus is the destructive side of Odysseus' nature, able in war; he is as much
a perversion of intelligence as Elpenor is a perversion of passion. Both are
"late spring in the leafy autumn," so to speak. It was Eurilochus who
forced Odysseus to put in at Thrinacia, the isle of Circe's father, Helios,
where the sun-god's flock pastured. It was Eurilochus who instigated the

murdering and eating of the sun-god's sacred cattle, thus bringing destruction to the ship and the crew before they reached Ithaca.

Odysseus underwent at Circe's house the experience which altered him, preparing himself for the NEKUIA, or journey to the underworld. Had he refused to enter Circe's bed he would have clung to the Eurilochus alternative and would not have been in the passive mood which opened his heart to the words of Tiresias, thereby to absorb the wisdom of the Land of the Dead. Without that "education," Odysseus would never have reached Ithaca, his home.

Penelope ("Sumus . . . flame," lines 66-105)

The last part of Canto XXXIX shifts to the female and portrays real sexual union between man and woman, with the proper ritual. The music is that of the virgins sacred to Artemis, the "Puellaeque canamus" who dance "To the beat of the measure." "Ver novum" of the Elpenor section no longer is "overborne into summer," but the real spring, "Betuene Aprile and Merche / with sap new in the bough." Spring is "made new" (Pound's favorite Chinese maxim), and the god is made by sexual union with the reverent man. At the end of the Canto, what before appeared metamorphosed into perversion shines now in the blush of its earthy and human perfection.

> His rod hath made god in my belly
> Sic loquitor nupta
> Cantat sic nupta

At the end Penelope, Odysseus' perfect wife, blossoms in full splendor. She sings—not Circe's KALON AOIDIAEI calling men to debauchery, nor the heavenly host's "Regina Coeli"—but as the bride, made new in the flush of youth. One is tempted to think the handmaid who kindled the flame is none other than Circe, who taught Odysseus the glories of passion. It is Penelope who says: "I have eaten the flame."

In Canto XXXIX we have seen the four characters who, taken together, give meaning to the man Odysseus, himself absent from the Canto. Even when Circe seems to speak to him, she directs her words to Eurilochus, who is presented as an alternative to the complete man who can be reborn if he attains the humility toward which Circe and Tiresias are ready to guide him; the man who will return from war to peace and to the perfect union with Penelope. The Canto is like a Chinese ideogram: all the components of Odysseus are set forth, and taken together they produce Odysseus.

To lay the groundwork for this drawing together of threads which mark a path through *The Cantos,* one can point to earlier signposts. The following are only a few of those that recur again and again.

After the stage is set with Odysseus-Pound's journey and the metamorphosis of Acoetes' crew (Cantos I-II), we find in Canto IV:

> Palace in smoky light,
> Troy but a heap of smouldering boundary stones

The Canto recounts the travels of Odysseus[2] the wily one after he brought about the destruction of Priam's city, for it was he, acting his Eurilochean role as the "man of wide snares," who invented the Wooden Horse ruse. And Pound finds himself leaving behind a wrecked modern civilization to find his way home.

The prime cause of Troy's fall was Helen, who kindled Paris' passion. The wave which "runs into the beach grove," the sea of time floating bits of history onto the shore, tells the poet:

> "Eleanor, ἐλέναυς and ἐλέπτολις!"   (Canto II)
>
> Ελέναυς, ἔλανδρος, ἐλέπτολις   (Canto VII)

But Helen, the cause of destruction who winds through the early Cantos, has another aspect. In Canto XX she (woman) is "jungle, / basis of renewal, renewals;" out of which, under the artist's hand, leaps the new born. In Canto XXVII a fragment from a ballata by Guido Cavalcanti shows Helen's creative role, which flowers forth in Canto XXXIX:

> Formando di disio nuova persona
>
> (Canto XXVII)

In Canto XXIX, woman is described:

> Wein, Weib, TAN AOIDAN
> Chiefest of these the second, the female
> Is an element, the female
> Is a chaos
> An octopus
> A biological process
>   and we seek to fulfill . . .

---

[2] Odysseus is the man who "saw many cities of men, and learnt their minds":
        many men's mannirs   videt et urbes   πολύμητις
        ce rusé personnage, Otis   (Canto LXXVIII)

And in Canto xxx, we find woman is by no means evil: "Time is the evil. Evil." Time is the sea which metamorphoses and sends perfection—"the magic moment"—into decay. Thus in Canto xxx again, Artemis complains, "none may seek purity / Having for foulnesse pity"

> Nothing is now clean slayne
> But rotteth away.

And the same is true of the goddess of love, Aphrodite, who "hath pity on a doddering fool,"

> She tendeth his fyre,
> She keepeth his embers warm.

Canto xxxvi prepares for Canto xxxix with its delineation of woman as natural adjunct to the male, providing "Venter venustus" to his flame. In Canto xxxvi Pound has translated Cavalcanti's "Donna mi prega" canzone, as authority as to what thing is love. "Donna mi prega" prepares for the excursion into the *Odyssey* to portray Odysseus as the man of many devices who finds that his craftiness and resourcefulness cannot, alone, get him home to Ithaca. He needs reverence, and a knowledge of the limitations of man. After "Donna mi prega" comes the bridge to Canto xxxix:

> Sacrum, sacrum, inluminatio coitu

With this preparation, the light shines full on Odysseus as the central character of Canto xxxix. The absence of perfection of the Odysseus who fought at Troy is shown as the alternate extremes: passive Elpenor and aggressive Eurilochus. It is only when he has swallowed the essence of Elpenor that Odysseus is prepared to rule in peace at Ithaca. For till then he has been Eurilochus.

If we can accept the myth of Odysseus as the central theme of *The Cantos,* and if we can say that the experience of Odysseus is paralleled by that of Ezra Pound himself, then we shall find that *The Cantos* is not a confused mass of learning, but rather that, like "the rose in the steel dust," the Odysseus myth orders the experience Pound undergoes as he travels through the Land of the Dead and comes forth a different man.

The structure of *The Cantos* is what the narrator sees, as Odysseus before him saw, in Hades. The experience is not Dante's, for Dante began in the *selva oscura* and progressed from the depths of despair to the perfection of the divine world. Pound and Odysseus undergo different experiences. To gain specific ends they withdraw from the everyday world to establish contact with those who have preceded them, so that they can better cope with this world when they return.

Odysseus' purpose is to return home to Ithaca, to Penelope and his son. To do so, he must understand and purify himself after the war at Troy and the affront to Poseidon. Pound's goal is set toward discovering what he is and what his world is. His return home is really his discovery of what his goal as a man is, and home is a settling into some surroundings. Pound is the wanderer, traveling blindly, groping for an answer to the question, "What am I doing in this world? And what kind of world is it, anyway?" Pound is searching for an ethos, as Dante did not have to search because Dante had the Thomistic world laid out for him. Odysseus-Pound has to search, in the absence of a predetermined ethos, his own way.

From the beginning of *The Cantos* the narrator is Odysseus-Pound hearing the speech of those he meets at the fosse in the Land of the Dead. He not only sees men and women in the underworld, but attempts, through metamorphosis, to enter their experiences and understand their spirits. He follows in the wake of an earlier Odysseus; it is to this new Odysseus that Tiresias says in Canto I:

> "A second time? why? man of ill star,
> "Facing the sunless dead and this joyless region? . . ."

The Cantos are the NEKUIA through Canto LI, where Odysseus-Pound reaches the pivot (Ching Ming) and shifts into a history of the world from ancient China, moving to John Adams's America in 1766, and continuing to Adams's death. In Cantos LII-LXXI he considers in action ideas he had found earlier in the poem: those of Confucius and Adams.

The message of Tiresias comes to Odysseus-Pound in Canto XLVII. We have noted that Circe spoke in Canto XXXIX, telling Odysseus he must seek advice from Tiresias before he could return home. We have noted further that Circe spoke in Greek, and was then unintelligible. Now in Canto XLVII the Greek appears translated, signifying that the advice has been digested:

> Who even dead, yet hath his mind entire!
> This sound came in the dark
> First must thou go the road
>
>   to hell
> And to the bower of Ceres' daughter Proserpine,
> Through overhanging dark, to see Tiresias,
> Eyeless that was, a shade, that is in hell

> So full of knowing that the beefy men know less than he,
> Ere thou come to thy road's end.
> > Knowledge the shade of a shade,
> Yet must thou sail after knowledge
> Knowing less than drugged beasts. *phtheggometha*
> *thasson*
> φθεγγώμεθα θᾶσσου

The Greek words re-echo Canto xxxix, where the men first hear Circe singing, and cry: "Let us call to her quickly!"

Tiresias' advice, which follows, expresses an ethos for individual man, related to the hell-traveler Odysseus-Pound as he had related prophecy to Odysseus. Tiresias' advice sums up the drama of Canto xxxix, where opposites were posed and Circe shown as the catalyst which resolved the paradox. Speaking of Odysseus' return home to Penelope, Tiresias says:

> To the cave art thou called, Odysseus,
> By Molü hast thou respite for a little,
> By Molü art thou freed from the one bed
> > that thou may'st return to another

There follows a ritual passage from Hesiod's *Works and Days*, foretelling "the process" which dominates the Pisan Cantos:

> Begin thy plowing
> When the Pleiades go down to their rest,
>
> .   .   .   .   .
>
> When the cranes fly high
> > think of plowing.

This advice, however, is for the moment lost on Ezra Pound. For though he has succeeded in learning the minds of the shades he finds in Hades, he has not yet undergone Odysseus' immediate personal suffering. He understands the ethos Tiresias outlines, but he is not yet ready to put it into action. Pound has not gained the reverence and intimate communion Odysseus established with gods and men after his NEKUIA. One recalls the forbearance Odysseus showed in threading Scylla and Charybdis; his consent to Circe's instruction to allow himself to be tied to the mast while he listened to the song of the Sirens; his giving away to Eurilochus' demand that they put in at Thrinacia; his patience and endurance in preparing for the ritualistic murder of the suitors who were befouling his home. And even more significant: his deference to the unburied Elpenor and the crescendo of his reunion with Penelope.

The Pisan Cantos mark that intense personal suffering as the real world thrusts itself onto Pound. No more is he a traveler in the Land of the Dead, hearing ancient stories. The social world as he knew it has been destroyed, and he is confined in his own home (Italy) by hostile men, as the suitors held Odysseus. Out of this confrontation with stark fact, Pound comes forth in humility.

Pound is in the prison camp, but in his imagination he is ΟΫ ΤΙΣ— no man—or Odysseus afloat on the sea of time. As ΟΫ ΤΙΣ he is also Everyman, and ἄχρονος (freed of "time, the evil" Canto LXXX). As the Pisan Cantos open on destruction, he calls as he called to Polyphemus, revealing himself to the vengeance of Poseidon: "ΟΫ ΤΙΣ, ΟΫ ΤΙΣ? Odysseus/the name of my family" (Canto LXXIV).

The explosion of that overweening pride (which Odysseus-Pound has certainly been guilty of earlier in *The Cantos*) comes as Pound moves away from Eurilochus and becomes Elpenor, lying with the crew in Circe's swinesty:

> ac ego in harum
> so lay men in Circe's swine-sty;
> ivi in harum *ego* ac vidi cadaveres animae
>
> (Canto LXXIV)

The Elpenor identification continues through the Pisan Cantos, as Pound calls himself "a man on whom the sun has gone down" and, as he had called Elpenor in Canto I, "a man of no fortune and with a name to come."

The Pisan Cantos revolve around Pound's memory as he lies in the physical swinesty. Memory orders the bits of reminiscence of what he saw in hell and of the companions he fought with—through his life as Ezra Pound, and at Troy as Odysseus. Pound recalls

> Lordly men are to earth o'ergiven
> these the companions
>
> (Canto LXXIV)

as he remembers the companions of his literary existence. We note correspondingly Odysseus' encounter with Agamemnon and Achilles in Hades.

Pound recalls the past as his imagination floats in "periplum," [3] as

> periplum, not as land looks on a map
> but as a sea bord seen by men sailing.

This type of voyage—"see it for yourself"—is the kind Odysseus made, and the kind the time-traveler Odysseus-Pound, makes.

[3] In Canto LIX Pound defines "periplum," after having described that made by Hanno the Carthaginian in Canto XLV:

Odysseus floated from Ogygia and the goddess Calypso to Phaeacia, the last stop on his way home. His body rests in the Pisan camp, where his eyes receive comfort from the landscape and the soothing winds cool him.[4]

> By no means an orderly Dantescan rising
> but as the winds veer
>
>   .   .   .
>
> as the winds veer and the raft is driven
> and the voices   , Tiro, Alcmene
> with you is Europa nec casta Pasiphaë
>   Eurus, Apeliota as the winds veer in periplum

He lies calm, in tune with "the process":

> How soft the wind under Taishan
> where the sea is remembered

Taishan is the sacred mountain of the oriental sages, where they withdraw to breathe "the process." And there may be a hint here of the final oblation Odysseus makes as he rests in the land where the oar is thought to be a winnowing fan.

The music of Circe (KALON AOIDIAEI) and of the Virgin ("Regina Coeli") are transformed in the Pisan Cantos into "La Canzone de li Uccelli" in Canto LXXV. And in Canto LXXXII music becomes part of "the process" as Pound sees birds writing notes on the wires:

> three solemn half notes
>   their white downy chests black-rimmed
> on the middle wire
>   periplum

Pound's own personal despair weaves through his consciousness:

> dry friable earth going from dust to more dust
>   grass worn from its root-hold
>   is it blacker? was it blacker? Νύξ animae?

[4] Pound at Pisa may also be thought of as lying in the hut of Eumaeus the swineherd, the first person Odysseus spoke to when he returned to Ithaca. Thus the eyes that enter his tent find their correspondence in those of Athena appearing to Odysseus, and the question Pound asks "sorella della pastorella dei suini" (Canto LXXXIV), is the one Odysseus asked Eumaeus about the suitors who sat at the absent Odysseus' table.

is there a blacker or was it merely San Juan with a belly ache
          writing ad posteros
in short shall we look for a deeper or is this the bottom?

                           (Canto LXXIV)

Pound's suffering brings home to him the wisdom of Tiresias' advice:

        J'ai eu pitié des autres
probablement pas assez, and at moments that suited my own
                            convenience

          .   .   .   .

Came Eurus as comforter
and at sunset la pastorella dei suini
      driving the pigs home, benecomata dea

                         (Canto LXXVI)

Here the Pisan landscape blends with Circe, as she appears in her role as "comforter," a part of "the process" as is Eurus, the southeast wind.

Love is stressed throughout by references to Cavalcanti's "Donna mi prega," particularly love's association with memory, "dove sta memoria" (Canto LXXVI). Love is brought full force by "Amo ergo sum" (Canto LXXX), and love is the maintainer of the "magic moment," preventing the slip into metamorphosis and decay:

        What thou lovest well remains,

                     the rest is dross
                     (Canto LXXXI)

Penelope, to Pound, suggests the earth and is referred to in the Pisan Cantos as GEA TERRA, Tellus, Demeter:

      man, earth :   two halves of the tally
      but I will come out of this knowing no one
      neither they me
              connubium terrae ἔφατα πόσις ἐμός
              ΧΘΟΝΙΟΣ, mysterium

                     (Canto LXXXII)

Finally the journey on the raft ends, with a résumé of Odysseus:

      the folly of attacking that island
        and of the force ὑπέρ μόρον

> with a mind like that he is one of us
> Favonus, vento benigno
> Je suis au bout de mes forces/
>
>   .   .   .   .
>
> hast'ou swum in a sea of air strip
>   through an aeon of nothingness,
> when the raft broke and the waters went over me

Prayer follows, and then humility:

> Les larmes que j'ai creées m'inondent
> Tard, très tard je t'ai connue, la Tristesse,
> I have been hard as youth sixty years   (Canto LXXX)

At last Odysseus-Pound has learned, devoured, and digested the wisdom Tiresias spoke in Canto XLVII. In one of the most beautiful passages in *The Cantos* he repeats the core of the blind seer's soothsay, revealed to him as he sits in his tent in the prison camp.

The revelation begins when the famous women appear to Pound in his imagination. They appear to him personally, not as the dead, but they seem to enter his tent "in the timeless air"

> . . . nor is this yet *atasal* [5]
> nor are here souls, nec personae
> neither here in hypostasis, this land is of Dione
>   (Canto LXXVI)

The women and the goddesses, wound into the Pisan landscape with the sun, moon, animals, birds, insects, and winds, form a background of permanence and beauty as the Pisan Cantos unfold. With nature, the women form "the process." Then in Canto LXXXI they reveal to Pound the burden of Tiresias' advice:

> Ed ascoltando al leggier mormorio
>   there came new subtlety of eyes into my tent,
> whether of spirit or hypostasis,
>
>   .   .   .   .
>
>   careless or unaware it had not the
> whole tent's room
> nor was place for the full Εἰδὼς [6]

---

[5] According to Pound, "*atasal*" means union with god, and comes from Avicenna, the Mohammedan physician and philosopher through whose works Aristotle became known in Europe.

[6] "Εἰδὼς" is the full knowing, or revelation, which occurs later.

> interpass, penetrate
> > casting but shade beyond the other lights
> > > sky's clear
> > > night's sea
> > > green of the mountain pool
> > > shone from the unmasked eyes in half-mask's space.
> What thou lovest well remains

The hymn breaks forth, echoing the words of Canto XLVII: "Pull down thy vanity," "Learn of the green world," "Master thyself, then others shall thee beare."

The hymn leads to the calm stillness of Pound's response:

> But to have done instead of not doing
> > this is not vanity
> To have, with decency, knocked
> That a Blunt should open
> > To have gathered from the air a live tradition
> or from a fine old eye the unconquered flame
> This is not vanity.
> > Here error is all in the not done,
> all in the diffidence that faltered

Here is the true Odyssean experience breaking through into revelation. The hardness has been metamorphosed by revelation born of knowledge and suffering. And Pound can answer the question posed in the hymnal response of Tiresias' words:

> Whose world, or mine or theirs
> > or is, it of none?

In the next to the last of the Pisan Cantos, the poet attains *atasal,* or union with the gods whose eyes had entered his tent and revealed to him what he, a man, was. The Canto opens with the resolution of the feud with Poseidon, who becomes part of "the process":

> ὕδωρ
> HUDOR et Pax
>
> .   .   .   .
>
> > the sage
> delighteth in water
> > the humane man has amity with the hills

Then comes the revelation, as the poet unites with "the process":

> A fat moon rises lop-sided over the mountain
> The eyes, this time my world,
>> But pass and look *from* mine
>>> between my lids
>>>> sea, sky, and pool
>>>> alternate
>>>> pool, sky, sea

And the denouement, the calm after the dark night of the soul has passed, is expressed in the final lines of the last Pisan Canto:

> If the hoar frost grip thy tent
> Thou wilt give thanks when night is spent.

Ezra Pound as Prison Poet

by David W. Evans

Any approach to the *Pisan Cantos* of Ezra Pound must be made with a certain amount of caution. Being what they are, political sensibilities may become inflamed at the mere mention of Pound's name, and aesthetic sensibilities are apt to react almost as violently at any effort to separate one part of the *Cantos* from the whole for consideration as an independent entity. The real problem, however, lies not so much in avoiding the political Charybdis while skirting the aesthetic Scylla as it does in trying to establish the fact that the eleven cantos written during his internment in Italy, the *Pisan Cantos,* taken together, constitute Pound's best integrated, most tightly unified, single composition—not excepting even the *Mauberley* cycle. It is a risky business because Pound's critics are almost at one in condemning the disordered structure of the *Cantos* in whole or in part. The word, in short, most frequently associated with Pound's great "poem of some length" is the word "chaos."

The *Cantos,* to be sure, were supposed to have a plan, a grandiose design, which was first outlined in some detail by W. B. Yeats in *A Packet for Ezra Pound.* The trouble with the plan was that it didn't seem to fit the poem very well, and it was not long before R. P. Blackmur, having taken a cue from Pound himself, was referring to the *Cantos* as a "jungle" and cautioning that "what happens when things meet in a form and have ending is rejected for the inchoate, the anecdotal, the deliberately confused. . . ." Blackmur's opinion never has been refuted. Indeed, by implication it has received support from Richard Aldington, for instance, who has expressed the opinion that some of the pages of the *Cantos* "include lapses into lucidity, flashes—alas! too brief—of real beauty, like the haphazard glitterings of a broken mirror."

An organic concept like the Blackmur jungle might seem preferable to the shattered mirror with its connotations of the brittle and the static, but the mirror analogy is apparently here to stay, for it seems to be hinted at

"Ezra Pound as Prison Poet" by David W. Evans. From *The University of Kansas City Review,* XXIII (Spring 1957), 215-220. Copyright © 1957 by *The University of Kansas City Review.* Reprinted by permission of the author and the editor of *The University of Kansas City Review.*

again in Hugh Kenner's lecture before the English Institute in 1953 on "The Broken Mirrors and the Mirror of Memory." In this, as in his book, *The Poetry of Ezra Pound,* Kenner devotes himself tirelessly and sometimes doggedly to further analysis and extenuation of the *Cantos.* Few critics have subsumed more rigorously whole hierarchies of values in Pound's work, have pursued with greater diligence first this and then that correspondence, have graphed and extrapolated at greater length than has Kenner, but in all this discussion the term he usually applies to Pound's "plotless epic" is "flux"—a word with suspicious overtones of euphemism.

One of the most stimulating treatments of the *Cantos* in print is that of D. S. Carne Ross, whose critique appeared in the presentation anthology of essays compiled and published by Peter Russell on the occasion of Pound's sixty-fifth birthday. Carne Ross suggests that Pound's obscurity is purely an obscurity of reference and that a detailed commentary would remove most of the problems presented by the work. Sympathetic and judicious as he is, however, Carne Ross ends by asserting that the "general impression which the *Cantos* give is one of chaos," a lack of coherence, unity, and order which extends even to detail. This "absence of architectonics," coupled with Pound's refusal to make "rigorous use of the binding elements" which might otherwise have unified the work, results in the "impressive failure" of the *Pisan Cantos.* "Would it matter," he asks, "if any incident occurred in a slightly different place?" or if "a careless printer were to transpose a few pages or even alter the order of the entire *Cantos?*"

Amidst so much smoke there must certainly be some fire, but perhaps the deplorable lack of order in the *Cantos* depends somewhat on the point of view. Certainly within the *Pisan Cantos,* at any rate, there is a machinery of organization, although it has very little to do with the crusting of legend, the Confucian ethic, the Homeric enthusiasm, the *Metamorphoses* of Ovid, the Renaissance splendor, the Economic didoes, or even all the talk about "ideas going into action." It owes its existence rather to the peculiar circumstances under which the poem was written. On one level the work even has an argument in the classical sense, and what could be more conducive to order? An egocentric old man who has been "hard as youth" all his life, charged with propagandizing for the enemy in time of war, is taken prisoner by the American troops in Italy in 1945. He is committed to the Army Disciplinary barracks near Pisa, and there, a cultivated Barabbas amongst criminals rather worse than thieves, is allowed to sort out his memories, ponder on life, and out of the turmoil of his mind to achieve whatever kind of compromise he can with the desperation of his plight.

Carne Ross notwithstanding, these cantos could not be transposed without destroying what seems to be a very conscious emotional unity—

an organization not unlike that of Sophoclean tragedy. The work has been inaccurately called a monologue. It is not. Even without the comments of the prisoners and the guards, the "dialog repartee at the drainhole," the conversations recalled in retrospect, Pound's imagination charges the whole with such dramatic intensity that it quivers to life in almost every line. The action, albeit largely an action of the intellect, follows a rising curve in which the struggle against despair is documented, in which incident after incident compounds the knowledge that Pound dwelt very literally in the death cells with "the shadow of the gibbets attendant," that he very literally did not know what the end might be. The note of foreboding is sounded almost at once with the mention of the "twice crucified" Mussolini and again in the query:

> we will see those old roads again,
> question, possibly
> but nothing appears much less likely . . .

It appears whenever the prisoner Till, who "was hung yesterday for murder and rape with trimmings," is mentioned, and whenever the loss of contact with the outside world becomes acute:

> O white-chested martin, God damn it,
> as no one else will carry a message . . .

Against this background of disaster—disaster, nonetheless, although leavened with sharp ironic wit and made bearable through the courage of the "heart indestructible"—a desperate search, a search for some sustaining force, advances, quickening the half-musing daydreams and sharpening the autobiographic memories with a sense of urgency. The process includes a searching of the soul in which Pound habitually lapses into French to disguise what might otherwise seem like self-pity or unseemly emotion. "Tard, très tard je t'ai connue, la Tristesse," he writes, or, in a moment of wry confession: "J'ai eu pitié des autres / probablement pas assez, and at moments that suited my own convenience." He takes an inventory of the things he has "carried to nowhere," the red leather notebook, the eucalyptus pip, and the image of Cassandra whose "eyes are like tigers." And always the questioning goes on, as in: "Shall we look for a deeper or is this the bottom?" or "Will the world ever take up its course again/ very confidentially I ask you: Will it?" And what seem like answers ("Ain committed no federal crime/ jes a slaight misdemeanor" or "No, they will do nothing to you"), when they come, echo with a hollow assurance.

Viewed in this light, the work is not a patchwork coat of many colors.

Pound is a poet of economy, and very little of what he has included in the *Pisan Cantos* is superfluous. The places and the faces and the incidents recalled have a bearing on the matter in hand, the predicament of a man who does care that he has been "untrumpeted" and who, after sixty years, finds that his world has been cut from under him, a man, in short, "on whom the sun has gone down." The accretion of detail, moreover, the piling up of memory on memory, often because of its seemingly slight significance, contributes the more powerfully to the climax when it comes. For the work does build to a point of decision, a point at which Pound seems to resolve the turmoil of his mind and for a moment succeeds in justifying himself to himself—if not to the world. The climax is reached in the glittering pyrotechnics of Canto LXXXI, and it begins with some of Pound's loveliest lines: "What thou lovest well remains/ the rest is dross." It rises with driving intensity to the commanding "Pull down thy vanity/ I say pull down," and it rounds itself off in the proud concluding assertion:

> But to have done instead of not doing
> this is not vanity
>
> .   .   .   .   .
>
> To have gathered from the air a live tradition
> or from a fine old eye the unconquered flame
> This is not vanity.
> Here error is all in the not done,
> all in the diffidence that faltered.

From this emotionally exhausting high point there is a natural falling off. Canto LXXXII, for instance, is marked by the strained casualness of: "the loneliness of death came upon me/ (at 3 P.M., for an instant)." Canto LXXXIII contains a rigidly controlled power of understatement which flickers in a line like "That day I wrote no further" and in the concluding "Down, Derry-down/ Oh let an old man rest." In the last canto a final supplication is made to "the green world" for the hope that "out of all this beauty something must come." In lesser hands the whole work might have sunk into bathos at a dozen places. In Pound's it does not, for out of it, in the last analysis and quite apart from questions of guilt or innocence, emerges the very moving portrait of a human spirit under agonizing duress.

A second mode of organization which can be seen operating actively in the *Pisan Cantos* lies in a rigid adherence to the sequence of time. Canto LXXIV, the first, opens with the grim commentary on the end of Mussolini, and before it is over the reader knows that Pound has seen a copy of *Time* magazine for June 25th, 1945, that Bastille day, the 14th

of July, has come and gone, "with the hill ablaze north of Taishan"
under the summer sun. Canto LXXXIV, the last of the sequence, begins
the 8th of October and closes with the hoar frost descending on the prison
tent. The dates could scarcely have been more firmly fixed. Between this
beginning and this end, moreover, the slow passage of the days and the
hours is established as an important structural element of the individual
cantos. Time is conveyed in subtle, precise, and marvelously varied ways:
"Be welcome, O cricket my grillo, but you must not/ sing after taps."
Or again: "The shadow of the tent's peak treads on its corner peg/ marking the hour." Or: "The moon has a swollen cheek/ and when the morning sun lit up the shelves and battalions of the West, cloud over cloud/
Old Ez folded his blankets . . ." There is even that moment when,
lapsing into French again, "au bout de mes forces," he finds that the
"wind is lighter than swansdown" and "the day moves not at all."

There is movement here, however, and the movement is forward in
time. The war ends in August, and Pound hears about it in the camp
privy. The rains come, marking the end of summer and the beginning of
autumn. Life in the camp goes on, the musters, the sick calls, the activity
around the obstacle fence—its "gibbet-iform posts supporting barbed
wire." The "Hup—two—three—four" of the marching trainees as they
count cadence reaches Pound in his tent and is transmuted into *"Hot
hole hep cat,"* which, in turn, allows him to slip smoothly into a whimsical
and wonderful diversion with the camp cat who has come scavenging
for supper. Dozens of such nimble transitions throughout the *Pisan
Cantos* are intended to demonstrate, and do demonstrate, that "the old
hand as stylist" has lost none of its cunning.

He writes at the "table ex packing box" which is intended to get him
"offn th' groun'" and which was made for him by one of the Negro
prisoners with the stern admonition: " 'doan you tell no one I made it.' "
From the tent and across the ditch, dug about him "lest the damp gnaw
through my bones," he observes the small life of nature around him, the
"bambooiform" grass, the smell of mint after rain, the sky, and the Pisan
hills beyond. The fidelity to beauty and to fact of the descriptions he
records is absolute and a little breathtaking. It seems not to have been
realized that in these particular cantos Pound takes a giant step forward
from the purely literary type of nature, the artificial nature, of his earlier
work. Natural description for Pound before Pisa was apt to resemble on
occasion that which T. S. Eliot so brilliantly caricatured in "East Coker,"
description admirable in itself—a line, for instance, like "Late roses filled
with early snow"—but carrying about it the faint suggestion of contrived
conceit. Perhaps the difference in the *Pisan Cantos* is one of "distinctions
in clarity," at any rate, of authenticity. Pound is convincing. He has lain
in the darkness and heard the wind, "mad as Cassandra," play "hob in
the tent flaps." He has watched the fog rise over the marshland, "bringing

claustrophobia of the mist," and seen the "ants seem to stagger/ as the dawn sun . . . trapped their shadows." He has watched the sky "wet as ocean/ flowing with liquid slate" and watched the sunset—"grand couturier."

He looked then to the small natural phenomena, the lizards and ants, somewhat as the psalmist once looked to the hills, for strength, and some of his perceptions—the little drama, for instance, of the new-born wasp descending from its mother's bottle-shaped nest—are quite unmatched in twentieth century literature. They serve, of course, a subtle purpose, for while they recur throughout the poem with the rhythmical consistency of fine musical phrasing, they are repeatedly interrupted by the jarring counterpoint of the prison background. The line about the mist rising from the marshes, for instance, is followed immediately by reference to "the stockade," beyond which "there is chaos and nothingness."

Pound never forgets that he is "among the slaves learning slavery," that the prison wards are like the decks of a slave ship, and that, remembering Lovelace the cavalier, rather than Bunyan the Puritan, he has no Althea at the grates. It is the familiar trick of contrast, of black against white, of light against darkness, of hope against despair. It was old when Thomas Gray was celebrating the "mute inglorious Milton," the "Cromwell guiltless of his country's blood," and the two poets, both having read their *Odyssey*, are not by any means so far apart as might be supposed if one compares Pound's "Man of no fortune and with a name to come" with the epitaphal line of Gray's *Elegy*: "A Youth to Fortune and to Fame Unknown." The device of contrast, in any event, has never been handled with greater finesse, and in the *Pisan Cantos* it is used to masterful advantage as a means of inducing order. No less important in its own way than the ordering of the emotional context and the treatment of time, contrast functions here as a third and a major unifying element.

The *Pisan Cantos,* of course, have a natural place in Pound's massive uncompleted magnum opus. They are linked to the cantos preceding by continued development of the metamorphic theme, the Odyssean voyage or periplum, the further use of ideogram which, if anything, becomes even more pronounced, and by the descent into a more immediate and personal type of hell. On its own merits, however, and considered as a unit, the *Pisan Cantos* is first of all a prison poem, a genre not without honor in literature since Boethius first wooed philosophy from his cell in Alvanzano not overly far from Pisa. Crimes against state, both real and fancied, bedizen the pages of history, and that of Ezra Pound remains sadly unresolved, but the exigencies of war have made the concentration camp and the prison stockade a rather particular symbol of the twentieth century—the difference between Manzanar and Buchenwald, vast as it is, being after all a difference of degree. Any number of writers, notably for instance Arthur Koestler, have tried to perpetuate the symbol in prose which, if not deathless, is likely to preserve the flavor of the era for later generations. Alone among poets of stature, Ezra Pound has had the unhappy privilege of preserving the symbol and the experience in poetry. Whatever else may be said of them, and there is much yet to be said, the *Pisan Cantos* are a very moving reflection of one aspect of the contemporary human condition.

The Revolt of Ezra Pound

by W. M. Frohock

What we think of Pound's poetry as a whole ultimately adds up to
what we think of *Cantos*. The earlier poetry is too manifestly clever;
constantly peeking out through it is the grinning jackanapes that Pound
too often was. He was always showing the world what he could do if he
really should set his mind to it. And to judge him in the climate his
own work created would be unfair, for Pound was always a more accomplished poet than his work, up to and including the Mauberley poems,
revealed him to be.

He could sound as much like Browning as Browning ever did. He
could parody Housman. He could make himself indistinguishable from
W. B. Yeats playing his fiddle in Dooney. His variations on Bertrans de
Born and other Provençal canzonists demonstrated that it was possible for
a man to be a philologist of parts without necessarily drying up the
springs of his own poetry. His translations, which R. P. Blackmur declared once to be Pound's best poetic work, also revealed talent that
perhaps should be called genius, but even in these there is a touch of the
look-Mom-no-hands: for instance, the rendering of a line of Propertius
about polishing a style, "Look, we have kept our erasers handy," can
only be called the work of a prestidigitator.

The early Pound had learned much from the medieval *jongleurs,* but
a *jongleur* was a juggler as well as a composer of verses, and Pound
learned too well the art of keeping a number of sharp instruments in the
air at once. The stricture does not apply to all of his poems, of course,
but to far too many. He entrances us, but we emerge from the trance
wondering what next he will pull out of his sleeve. The amazing, amusing Smart Aleck of the "Letters" is never far away. The fantastically
acute ear, responsible for introducing no one knows how many new
cadences to English, is too often put to hearing puns where no one
heard them before; the poet of Audiart is the correspondent who turns

"The Revolt of Ezra Pound" by W. M. Frohock. From *Southwest Review,* XLIV
(Summer 1959), 190-199. Copyright © 1959 by Southern Methodist University Press.
Reprinted by permission of the author and the editor of *Southwest Review.*

the name of James Laughlin IV's publishing enterprise into "nude erections."

This is selling Pound short, obviously. But Pound, given the size of his talent, was selling himself short, also. We read the *Personae* today with indulgence, taking what we want ("The Seafarer" and the Mauberley poems, in my case, would be typical instances) and leaving the rest, because we know *Cantos* will be along presently. But if Pound had not at last written *Cantos,* what would he look like now other than a poet who was magnificently equipped to say something if ever he had found what it was he wanted to say? In other words, after the Mauberley poems it was time for Pound to take a subject his own size, just as Eliot had finally done.

But what is the subject of *Cantos*? I mean "subject" in its simplest sense: What does the poem treat? We need to know whether there is a meaning attached to the poem as a whole beyond the sum which the meanings of individual parts may happen to add up to. The poet himself has testified on both sides: at one point he encouraged us to believe that the subjects of individual Cantos were as disparate as the subjects of conversation among intelligent men; but he also assured correspondents, very early in the composition of the work, that he had everything in hand and all would come out all right—he gave us the harassing metaphor of the rag bag which could hold anything he chose to tuck into it, but also the famous story, relayed by Yeats, of the all-inclusive diagram of the disposition of materials. Allen Tate was persuaded at the end of *XXX Cantos* that they were "about nothing." And numerous later critics, like Blackmur, have been satisfied to list the seemingly unrelated subjects of the seemingly unrelated parts. For a long time they had to be, for at first there was no way to distinguish minor themes from major ones or to recognize, from having heard them before, the varied voices in which the poet speaks. Tate was right in what he said . . . at the moment when he said it. But fortunately Eliot was also right, later, in saying that with passing time the Cantos had become much more intelligible.

One might add, "*And* with the publication of additional Cantos." For it is a peculiarity of the Cantos that while one cannot see clearly enough ahead to predict where they are going, one can see much better where they have been. They do not have the kind of schematic structure which would allow us to say, at the end of one section, what kind of section would have to follow it. They have no structural necessity of such a nature. But almost invariably, when we finish the reading of the next section in the series we perceive the connection with what has come previously and find, in fact, that the earlier sections have received illumination from the new one.

There is only one other piece of literature of which this is so thoroughly true, *Remembrance of Things Past.* Doubtless the experience of a naïve first reading of Proust's novel is no longer possible. We know too well, today, how the story turns out. To remember one's puzzlement as to where the story was going next, one's semiperception of the meanings of the thematic repetitions, one's gradual and joyful realization—toward the end—that all the elements were falling together, dates the reader who remembers them. Only the most veteran of Proustians can recall how the significance of the earlier sections grew upon them as they read the later ones—and especially the great flood of illumination which spread back over the whole work as its true subject was finally revealed in *The Past Recaptured.*

It is too much to hope, however, that the present generation will have a similar experience with *Cantos.* There is no verifiable sign that at the beginning Pound had any very clear idea of how the poem would end, and too much had happened to him in the intervening years, anyhow. His personality must have altered too much, and the look of the world must have changed for him at the same time. There is little chance of his giving us the functional equivalent of *The Past Recaptured,* and we shall never talk of *Cantos* with the sureness with which we discuss *Remembrance of Things Past.* But there is, even so, a sense in which it can be said that *Cantos* has revealed its subject as the parts have wound their slow length along.

Presumably we all agree that *Cantos* contains some sort of occult and only incompletely rational discourse. We may not look for a coherently logical argument in the work any more than we may look to Proust for a theorem about the working of time. It proceeds, rather, by the patterned juxtaposition of elements, in the way in which, as a matter of fact, so much interesting modern literature proceeds. We have to note the nature of what is juxtaposed, for it is in the contrasts between the elements that the meaning emerges, and not only from contrasts in sense but from contrasts in tone also. Thus we may get at a sort of inherent dialectic—a meaning conveyed in the structure, for the poem is constructed on these juxtapositions and whatever it is that dictates what elements shall be juxtaposed constitutes the subject of the poem.

For example, Canto LI—the second "Usura Canto"—puts next each other the eloquent enumeration of the paralyzing effects of usury and the precisely detailed directions for tying the Blue Dun and Grannom trout flies. To the reasonably alert reader two questions immediately present themselves: first, why does Pound repeat here what he said so admirably about usury in Canto XLV and, second, what under heaven are the tyings of these two trout flies doing in the poem anyhow? We are far enough along in the poem at this point to be convinced that Pound rarely stuffs such unlikely seeming rags as these in his "rag bag" for the mere hell of it. There must be a reason for even such implausible juxtapositions

as this, and I suspect very strongly that the reason lies in the very strange-
ness of the juxtaposition itself. The usury sequence sounds remarkably
like some parts—say Jeremiah or certain Psalms—of the King James
Version: indignant, full of the wrath to come, and somewhat archaic.
The trout-fly descriptions are in something like the quiet language of
Charles Cotton, the man who completed Walton.

The burden of the usury passage, of course, is that where bad banking
practices prevail all falls apart, the center does not hold, and all endeavor
which satisfies only through its own perfection is ruined. When he has
said this much, Pound shifts into the placid—though again Elizabethan
—tones of Cotton and, sacrificing all other effects to the communication
of precise detail, displays two examples of perfectly disinterested creative
effort. For neither the Blue Dun nor the Grannom is anything but a
lovely piece of work to contemplate. They are both noteworthily useless,
even for catching fish. One ties the Blue Dun, in particular, only because
fly-tying is a traditional craft, because this fly is part of the tradition,
and because one is an incomplete craftsman unless one can tie this pattern. Thus we first hear of what *usura* does, and then see samples of what
it cannot do and of what it ruins. What Pound says about usury in this
passage is, as has been remarked, not new in the poem; *what is new is the
particular juxtaposition into which, this second time, he casts it.* For the
sake of the new juxtaposition he repeats himself.

No one, so far as I can discover, has studied out all the juxtapositions
in *Cantos.* Certainly I have not done so. But almost anyone who has read
the Cantos with attention will agree as to the nature of the juxtapositions
which have claimed his special notice: they place in contrast something
from the past and something from the present, in such a way that the
present is disparaged. And this fact, if I am right, will eventually lead us
to the subject of the poem.

But first, one observation about the poem's nature. The whole thing,
from one end to the other, reposes on the most hackneyed of metaphors,
the familiar equation of life with a journey or voyage. After all, the poem
is called *Cantos* to remind the reader of the *Divine Comedy*; whole
Cantos, like the immensely obscene one about the munitions-makers, are
directly reminiscent of Dante; various reminders, such as the use of
"And I" (Dante's "Ed io") introducing a quotation, are planted about in
other places. Dante's poem, among all the other things it is, is an allegory
of life's journey. And at the same time, in the early Cantos, there is the
constant reference to voyages and voyagers, the returning figure of
Ulysses, the reiterations of "periplus." The nature of *Cantos* as account
of a journey is firmly established. The account, we may add, is to be
accompanied by a commentary, and the burden of the commentary is
that he, the voyager, has looked upon life and not found it good. This
commentary is furnished by the juxtapositions of materials in the poem.

In other words, I am proposing here that the principal subject of *Cantos* as a whole poem, the only one capable of subsuming the subjects of the individual Cantos and of drawing them all into one intelligible system of meanings, is the rejection of life as it is now lived, not merely its politics and its economics but also its art, its religion, and its metaphysics. Pound began, I believe, with a rejection of our corrupt and worn-out language, and has ended by turning his back upon everything else. Those who have recently reread *Make It New* doubtless remember the surprising lines where Pound records his admiration for a writer who, he says, wrote "book after book against oppression, against all the petty sordid personal crushing oppression, the domination of modern life," and who spoke out for "human liberty, personal liberty, the rights of the individual against all sorts of intangible bondage." These lines surprise because their subject is one who usually does not strike his readers as a crusader: Henry James. Possibly Pound's judgment is wrong here; we need not care. What is important is that he is using phrases like "intangible bondage." They date from 1918, and sound as if the process of rejection had begun at that time.

Such phrases would surprise us little if we found them in, say, the *Pisan Cantos,* because *Cantos* rejects the culture which produces the "intangible bondage." We may understand the lines:

> "half dead at the top"
> My dear William B.Y. your ½ was too moderate

to mean that against this bankruptcy of a whole culture it is not enough to be defiant and set a powerful emblem up. Yeats does not really reject; he merely laments and regrets. Something more radical is required, not merely the refusal to play, but *révolte.*

I am using the French word here in place of its English cognate because the English word does not quite convey the idea. *Révolte* is very largely a European product. In America if you call a man a *révolté* you disparage him. We have never got to the point of dissociating the term from the image of the spoiled brat; it smacks of the Greenwich Village of 1913, of unwillingness to recognize routine conventions, and of relaxed sexual behavior. We labor under the conviction that the *révolté* is not quite grown up and that any sign of inability to conform is also a sign of *révolte.*

In Europe *révolte* implies less a kind of conduct than an intellectual position. It is a refusal, both instinctive and reasoned, of life in the conditions under which a man has to live it; it expresses a feeling that somehow humanity merits better than it gets, that the human condition is a sort of cosmic injustice. Without necessarily being satanical it echoes the *non-serviam* of Milton's Satan. It automatically involves the *révolté* in some visible gesture of protest—which often takes the form of a work of art. A man has no means of changing the limitations inherent in being human, but he is free to withhold his acceptance, not to say his approval, of them; he cannot break his human bondage but at least he need not love his bonds. He can take satisfaction in expressing this absence of love. One student of the subject, Malraux, considers the whole history of art to be the history of such gestures.

The French, who have reason to be especially interested in this human phenomenon, tend to recognize the *révolté* as a characterized personality type, marked by a peculiar intensity, easily exacerbated sensibilities, and an acute indisposition to compromise. The prototype would be the Rimbaud of *A Season in Hell*. Prominent among his more recent successors would be Malraux, Louis-Ferdinand Céline, Georges Bernanos (in spite of his Roman Catholicism), and perhaps Albert Camus.

What preoccupies them is something quite different from the protest of the so-called Lost Generation. If there was a *lost* generation at all, if indeed the young men and women who flocked to Europe in the twenties were impelled by their alienation and not by the knowledge that life was pleasant and living cheap in Europe—if, to be brutal, the Lost Generation was not a myth invented by Gertrude Stein and Malcolm Cowley—certainly its protest was specific and limited, directed against conditions specifically American. Besides, Pound was a permanent feature of the European landscape long before the American exodus started. The irony is that the young Americans arrived in France, Italy, and the Balearics at exactly the moment when their European counterparts were beginning to turn their backs upon the old continent in a gesture prefatory to turning them upon the world altogether. Marcel Arland's famous article, from which the movement of *révolte* in Europe may be dated, appeared in the *Nouvelle Revue Française* in 1923.

Cantos belongs in a category of poetry of *révolte*, what is sometimes called *poésie de refus*, by virtue of the deeply underlying principles which determine its style and structure. This kind of work regularly reveals the intention of achieving some sort of statement, some inexplicit expression which is not entirely contained in the materials the work brings together. Almost inevitably the result is a kind of intentional incoherence. Syntax, the articulation of the parts, is lacking; the parts are not conjoined, coordinated, or subordinated in relation to each other. They are just placed side by side.

A novelist like Malraux writes a bitter tale about men who find that they can live satisfactory lives only in the service of an ideal which is bound to destroy them. But to his demonstration that the price of living a significant life is the loss of it, Malraux juxtaposes a magnificent picture of his heroes going to destruction, and the picture is noble enough to remove all the bitterness and leave behind only a feeling of enlightenment and wisdom. In construction, *Man's Fate* is thus incoherent: the logic of the main parable points in one direction—and the picture of the tragic outcome contradicts this logic. Without the incoherence, undoubtedly, there would have been far less power in the novel.

A novelist like Céline puts his story in the mouth of a hero who cannot tell a story well, who blurts instead of talking, and whose adventures come to the reader in discontinuous fragments. Characteristically, Céline assumes that literary art—style, in this case—is a mere lie, and another instance of the universal *saloperie* of life. When he continues the biography of his hero in a second novel, periods at the ends of sentences are replaced by suspension points to show that any continuity between sentences is purely coincidental. Again, incoherence and discontinuity are fundamental to the structure of the book.

Such incoherence, of course, is never complete. We can judge incoherence only by some standard of coherence, discontinuity only by some gauge of continuity. Novels like *Journey to the End of the Night* and *Man's Fate* may *be* incoherent; they *say* something measurably coherent. In other words, their incoherence is part of their method. And if this be method, then there is not necessarily any madness in it. Those who have taken the incoherence of *Cantos* to be the first indications of mental unhealth overlook the considerable number of writers in other countries who have taken the method for their own.

Each of them has written books—prose or poetry—which declare life as they have known it to be impossible. Bernanos, stout Catholic that he was and as such unwilling to commit the sin of despair, finally threw up his hands at the mess his native continent had become. "I can no longer pray for Europe," he told his friends, and he went off to spend his last years in South America and Africa. The central theme of Céline's work is that human decency, the mere ability to treat one's neighbor as if he too were human, is no longer within the competence of the Western personality; the hero of his novels, an obviously autobiographical figure, wanders through Europe, Africa, and America and finds almost nothing but complete nastiness. Malraux, as I have tried to show before now, discovered that the essential condition for producing works of art in our time is complete rupture with the West, followed by a long sojourn elsewhere. Jean Giono, Henri de Montherlant, and a host of others have made similar or parallel discoveries.

Let me be the first to concede that Pound looks somewhat out of place in such distinguished company. In a sense he is indeed out of place in it; he is much more the artist than any of these Frenchmen, with the possible exception of Henri de Montherlant, and he is correspondingly less of an intellectual. He is obviously incapable of recognizing the difference between ideas of general significance and expressions of private and personal like and dislike; his failure to discriminate between his own predicament and the universal condition of mankind has the annoying effect of reducing his most plausible complaints against the cosmos to statements of mere individual gripe. His radical simplifications—such as the famous one which blames all the cheapness and absence of quality in modern life on the institution of usury—will not stand up against the most elementary criticism, and yet it seems obvious that criticism of even such elementary nature is far beyond the range of his capacities. In comparison even the least endowed for conceptual thinking among his French compeers, Giono, whose revulsion from the ugliness and squalor of modern life is, probably, almost as instinctual and uncritical as Pound's, emerges as his intellectual superior. Most of the literature of *révolte,* including even the work of Céline, maintains a kind of dignity, whereas Pound's persistence in putting so much lore and erudition at the service of so few brains keeps his own dignity, and that of his work, in constant peril.

Even so, Pound stands a much better chance of being understood by Europeans than by us. They can at least recognize his type. We lack the *révolté* tradition and, if Riesman is right, the day may come when we are not even capable of imagining it. Our habit of mind works another way, through our inveterate unwillingness to despair over anything gone wrong and our blithe confidence that repair is never impossible. *Révolte* is un-American.

But self-conscious craftsmanship is not un-American, and thus Pound brings something American to the Europeans. His contribution to the *poésie de refus* may add little to the magnitude of the refusal; it achieves something much more impressive as poetry.

Cantos becomes much more intelligible, I think, as soon as we recognize that it belongs in this category. Otherwise one is always plagued by the seeming irrelevance of certain parts of the poem to the rest. We have to deal with the "Chinese" Cantos as well as the "Pisan," and those insufferable ones which Hugh Kenner labels Adamic and Jeffersonian; we have to cope with the problems created by the opening of a bank at Siena and those created by the tales of the exploits of Renaissance plug-uglies like Sigismondo Malatesta; we have to reconcile ourselves to the appeals for an oriental kind of order in the midst of a disorderly poem and discover *some* significance in Jim X's telling the Banker-Deacons of Chicago the Tale of the Honest Sailor. And *Cantos* as poem does not furnish us the help we need.

I find myself unable to work up much agreement with the claim of some Poundians that the reader does not need the help of glosses to get him through *Cantos*: and for the work of the group at the University of Chicago who have been compiling and circulating in mimeograph the requisite supplementary information, I would like my gratefulness on record. Pound has spent a lifetime reading; he knows a lot; and he is no man to leave what he knows out of his poetry. Who but Pound could expect the reader to know, for instance, what he intends in the reference to Shoeney's daughters in Canto II? Unless one has read somewhere about the source, and knows also that the eccentric spelling is Pound's own, the job is hopeless. We may not feel that all Pound's erudition is useful to the poem, and at times we may feel that he is merely parading it; even so, we have to put up with it, and for any relief much thanks. More than we have had to date would be welcome. But I don't see how any amount of it can open the poem completely to us unless we realize also the meaningful discontinuity—or incoherence—of the *révolte*.

So I am arguing that we have to read *Cantos* somewhat as we read that other masterpiece of discontinuity, Céline's *Journey to the End of the Night*. Céline sends his hero down the dark corridor of life, looking anxiously for some glimmer of light. In rare instances he catches a momentary flicker—the sergeant growing a few rachitic flowers in the African wilds and sending home his pay to care for a relative's child; Molly, the honest whore in Detroit, with her instinctive kindliness. But the rest of life is only the *saloperie*, the tangible as well as the intangible bondage. Pound's poet moves along his "periplus," until it becomes finally a "periplus" in a camion full of prisoners. His present is Céline's darkness; the flashes of light are from the past. The integrity of John Adams, the humaneness of Hapsburg-Lorraine, Kung's vision of order, My Cid riding up to Burgos, leave the darkness only deeper after they have flared for a moment and died again. *Donna mi prega* illumines just by being beautiful . . . and inaccessible now that the maid's needle has been blunted. And if the poem is consistently ironic because the method of juxtapositions is inherently an ironic one, and also because after speaking again and again in an assumed voice the poet reveals that the assumed voice is really a deformation of his own, it is also pathetic because the things which might relieve the darkness are so thoroughly lovely and desirable but at the same time thoroughly out of reach.

Taken as an expression of *révolte*, *Cantos* seems to me to be a very great poem, second among its kind only to Rimbaud's *Saison en enfer*. Because of its nature it will rarely be known in its entirety and because of its subject many readers will never be able to take it for anything but a historical document. They will think it a monstrosity, and they will be right; to a certain extent, monstrosity is implied by the subject itself. Other readers will object, so long as the poem has readers at all, to the parts which give evidence of Pound's almost unlimited self-indulgence, his willingness to run on eternally on his favorite subjects, his affectations (including the part of his erudition which is affected), his use of the Chinese characters which he has to clip from a dictionary and stick to his manuscript because he is unable to draw them himself, and other similar annoyances. They will be right, in a degree, also. But so will those who insist that in *Cantos* Pound has done something that is worth doing and that has never been done before.

The year 1958 will go down as the one when Pound went back to Rapallo. There has been no triumph of justice or of injustice. A court found, twelve years earlier, that he was mentally incapable of defending himself; it has now declared that, in the eyes of the law, he will never be able to do so. All the painful ambiguities and uncertainties of the case remain, however. Nothing has really been settled.

Yet it is easier to write about him now than it was while he was shut up in Saint Elizabeth's Hospital. His case had been tried too abundantly in the newspapers. The organs of American Philistinism, led by *Time*, had convinced too many that modern poetry was on trial with him. Especially after the award of the Bollingen Prize, with the attendant outcry from the *Saturday Review* and similar periodicals, anything said about Pound's poetry was bound to be taken either as a plea for setting him loose without further legal formality, or else as a demand that he should be taken forthwith before a firing squad.

Under the strain the situation generated, few managed to write about Pound with anything like appropriate dispassionateness. Hugh Kenner's *Poetry of Ezra Pound* is full of useful information and keen insights, but normally mild reviewers have gone on record as finding it full, also, of bumptious nonsense. Kenner stopped some digestions completely with his declaration that some three hundred years ago English poetry went off on the wrong track and has had to wait out the long interval for Pound to put it right. But his pro-Pound extravagance was matched, as other normally mild reviewers again noted, by the anti-Pound extravagance of Rossell Hope Robbins' *The T. S. Eliot Myth* and the argument that it is impossible to write good poetry if one holds bad political ideas —a thesis which would disqualify much poetry from Hesiod to the present. Anyone else writing about Pound, except for largely factual accounts like the excellent one by Hayden Carruth in *Perspectives USA*,* felt the danger of being forced into one camp or the other, of being taken to line up beside Kenner or beside Robbins. It was hard to find a place to stand alone.

It is good that this condition has changed. Pound had been that rarest phenomenon, a bellwether for a generation of poets who was also a considerable poet in his own right. He was a more genuine leader of movements, for example, than Amy Lowell, and his poetry was better, too. None of it may be so compelling as the best of Eliot's, but for a moment he had been Eliot's master—the *miglior fabbro* of *The Waste Land*—and

* "The Poetry of Ezra Pound," *Perspectives USA*, No. 16 (Summer 1956), 129-159.

he had had the public personality to play the role of the embattled poet among the Philistines as the less flamboyant Eliot never could. Some of his criticism is still good reading, years after the event; and his correspondence, even in the incomplete and defective edition available, is perhaps the liveliest and most revealing since Flaubert's. And in his moments of generosity he was an accomplished chivvier of publishers, a stout rescuer of distressed literary reviews, and a support for men like William Butler Yeats.

If he had not set up, many years ago, as an expert on the subject for which, of all possible subjects, he was the least equipped, economics; if he had not adopted the thoroughly unacceptable politics which was the only one in which his distributist economics could reasonably be expected to work; if he had not allowed his politics to sanction his broadcasting over the Italian radio—if, in other words, he had behaved reasonably in spheres remote from poetry—some of his poetry would be different, of course, but he would be venerated, if not understood, at this writing. From such dilemmas as, in historical fact, Pound forced upon us, there is no pleasant exit. A simpler time than ours might have shot the broadcaster and enshrined the poet without experiencing any uncomfortably contradictory emotions. Ours cannot. At the end of World War II, the French shot Robert Brasillach and imprisoned Charles Maurras for life; neither solution now seems to have been satisfactory. Pound did not even get his day in court.

Neither did we, his readers, although we needed, in a way, the cleansing experience of a verdict more than Pound did. We did not get it—and are permanently denied release from our own ambivalences. The best we can do at this point is to discipline ourselves into becoming a dispassionate, detached audience capable of an effort toward understanding. The fact that the figure of the *révolté* looms so large in modern literature, and that *révolte* has forced itself on us as one of the dominant themes in modern writing, presents us with an obligation. Not to face it would be to surrender a chance to understand ourselves.

Reckoning

by Harold H. Watts

I

The Cantos is a poem that interests in many connections. It is the capital piece of "evidence" in any dispute between Ezra Pound and the United States government. Literarily, it cannot be regarded as a "sport," a willful driving of the language in the direction of obscurity and inconsecutiveness. It is rather—in respect to technique—the investigation of the resources of our language when manipulated in an unusual way: a way that Pound was driven to discover as an alternative to communication that is orderly, logical, and (in Pound's opinion) bootless.

At this point, certain things must be clear. We can know what the poem attempts and what it does not attempt. We can see that there are *different* techniques of confusion in our culture, techniques that the facile reader lumps together. We can see that it is uncritical to identify a technique that is invented and perfected in the interest of renewing our language and culture (Pound's technique in *The Cantos*) with techniques which, at points, it may resemble. These other techniques may prove, on inspection, to be no more than verbal gestures that express despair or cynicism in the face of our cultural crisis. They may record—as readers of much recent poetry know—the poet's sense that he is utterly apart—in himself and in his peculiar and injured sensitivity—from the great panorama of destruction that is our time. At any rate, his poem will be a record—more or less confusing in technique—of what it is for one person to live through a troubled age; his poem may even be a gesture of resignation in the face of what is too great for him to think of mastering. Study of the work would doubtless be complete at such a point; if no more than personal revelation is supposed or guessed to inhere in a poem, "justice" is done it when one has pointed out the probable sources of the malaise and the peculiar use of language which is useful to the poet in registering or alleviating this malaise. One may say that, for such a poet, the writing of a poem is fundamentally expression and only incidentally communication.

It is not so with Pound. The writing of *The Cantos* is at least as much communication as expression. True, it would not have been written save for the deep discomforts, the intense impatiences, that can be identified as the fruit of Pound's immediate and personal contact with capitalist-democracy. He never lets us forget that the times are out of joint. Nor does he let us forget what is more important: that if the times are to be set to rights, it is he and his poem that very likely will do it.

It is because of this optimism—an optimism marked by old wounds but doggedly pursuing success within very constricted limits—that analysis may not stop at this point. Optimistic after its fashion, Pound's poem aims at communication; the effect expected of it is that, by the act of communication, it will modify the "paideuma," the cluster of custom and idea to which we attach ourselves uncritically. Our reckoning of *The Cantos* involves us not only in treatment of the poem itself but also in estimates of its value as an attack on the crucial ailment of our time. The ailment may be phrased thus, in language that is in line with Pound's own angle of approach: there is a great defect in the inner "go" of our culture; and it is a defect that will not be offset by conferences, treaties, and pacts—nor yet by the pulpit exhortations of the frocked and of the non-frocked in "learneries." That Pound has addressed himself to this huge task leads us to execute a further act of judgment that would not be at all necessary were *The Cantos* chiefly a self-gratifying act of skill. This act of judgment involves answering the following questions. Does the method of the ideogram—the striving to put to work in English (and at an exceedingly complex task) a mode of communication that Pound first perceived in Chinese poetry—actually produce the communication that Pound desiderates? Effective or not, to what general tendency in modern culture may Pound's chosen mode of communication be linked? (To be sure, Pound's tone suggests that his chosen mode is unique, a new departure in our culture. Of this claim in particular we need to be skeptical.) Finally, is what Pound does communicate as full of meat as he thinks it is? Does it—this proffered aggregate of insights—actually constitute a really impressive prologomena to the labors of renewing our culture? Does it, by the light it casts on dark reaches of our experience, teach us to walk better than we walk at present?

It is indeed wise to be on one's guard at two related points: reckless and subjective speculation about what a poet's intention might have been, and the uncritical acceptance of the poet's own account of the intention that lay behind the writing of a certain poem. Neither clue should be regarded as the final measure of the worth and the effect of a finished poem. Any judgment of a poem like *The Cantos* must be very

incomplete indeed if it does not run the risk of "the intentional fallacy."
It is apparent that the subject of this essay is not *The Cantos,* the poem
for its own sake, cut free of the ties that link it to the poet and the age
in which both we and the poet live. This study, it is plain, is concerned
throughout with *The Cantos* as an important part of a phenomenon
that is both complex and instructive: a "composed" triad made up of
three terms—Pound, his poem, and us as elements in an age. The meaning of any one of these items is impoverished when it is detached from
the other two. Let us insist that Pound's account of what his poem is supposed to be and how it ought to operate does not constitute a complete
statement of what the poem actually is. In fact, Pound's account must be
"corrected" by answers to the following questions. Is the ideogram-
method actually effective in English? What place does Pound occupy in
the traditional picture of Western thought? What is the actual moral and
political illumination contained in *The Cantos?* Perhaps a useful predic-
tive statement can be made. What Pound says of his rhetoric is apt and
casts light on dark places in the poem. But what Pound claims for the
effect of his poem—that it avoids the sins of abstraction and generates new
volitions in the reader—must be regarded with some suspicion. But the
strongest suspicion must be reserved for Pound's claims to being a social
prophet both novel and worthy of credence.

II

   The concept at the heart of Pound's thought is that of "ideas in
action." Though Pound is quite modest in his frequent acknowledge-
ments of his debt to the studies of Fenollosa which introduced the ideogram to him, his estimate of what the ideogram-method will accomplish
in poetry and later in our culture is not modest. Acting through *The
Cantos,* the "ideas in action" will assault the modern will effectively—
will be the fulcrum to pry the carriage of modern civilization from bad
rails to good ones. This—let us concede—is a far from modest estimate
of an idea. But if events should justify Pound (and he is optimist enough
to expect them to), he would have no reason to be modest. No one pre-
tends that our society does not stand in grim need of renovation. Nor
would anyone deny the word epochal to an idea or set of ideas that really
"delivered"—that did for our culture what Pound believes his concept
can.
   To a point, Pound's development of his central insight into a programme, a basis for action, has a good deal of cogency. We grant that our
civilization languishes; we concede that one of the vitiating forces (not the
only one) is usury as Pound understands it. As students of literature, we
also find it pleasant to agree that it is only the power of language, only

the changes it may induce in our modes of thought, that will take us from the evil paths in which we walk. We can see—both from Pound's theory and his practice—that language as it is manipulated now exerts little pressure on our wills and our thoughts. We grant that its custodians have, consciously or unconsciously, sold out to the usurers (or to whatever group or force that, in our judgment, threatens our culture with disunity and decay). It is true that words, for the most part, have come to stand for nothing at all; it is probably true that words must come to stand for something if the society in which we live is to be the expression of more than clouds of undefined, unsatisfied desires which now surround us.

Pound's vehemence suggests that he is fighting a solitary battle. But there is actually a large area of agreement that we share with him. Indeed, no one who follows the general movements of Western thought can regard as detached or novel Pound's diagnosis of culture and language disintegration; nor will the observer have to think long to remember the names of other writers who seek to renew a lapsed and betrayed language.

Therefore, Pound's inferences from the concept, "ideas in action," must not mislead us. We can make out a large "area of agreement." More important—and by that token more difficult to grasp since more is demanded than facile acquiescence to implement this second perception—is it to see that "ideas in action" is in itself not a novel concept. By framing this concept Pound (whether he wishes to or not) becomes party to a struggle that is not new at all. The struggle is a perennial one, one that is much older than usury itself (at least, as Pound reckons the age of usury).

To be sure, we are likely to be misled by Pound when we seek to identify this struggle, since (for Pound) the crucial stages of this struggle occur in periods when capitalist-democracy is emerging or dominates. Perhaps to confess that the lineage of the struggle is ancient would be distasteful to Pound, for it would limit the validity of the usurious-nonusurious division that runs through Pound's speculation. But since that division need not be basic to ours, we damage nothing dear to us when we perceive that Pound is taking part in the latest round of the old realist-nominalist struggle: the struggle that emerged (not for the first time) in history and embroiled Abelard with Albertus Magnus.

The battle centered on this issue: Have ideas, in some sense, existence apart from or superior to their temporary material realization about which sense-impressions inform us? Or is the only reality which man knows that which keeps making direct assault on his five senses? The medieval realists asserted that ideas are superior in being or essence—without always agreeing on precisely how ideas had won and maintained this superiority. The nominalists—Abelard was one of these—insisted that the successive, separate moments of man's existence were the sources of the only insights worthy of trust. For the nominalists, ideas—at least, ideas as their opponents described their existence and operation—were at best view a deceptive twilight lingering on after the sun—the sense impressions—had vanished over the horizon. In another figure, the world as the nominalist saw it would have slight "tolerance" for the burdens of abstracted concepts that the other party tried to make it bear. To respond truthfully and accurately to the messages which the senses despatch is the whole duty of man; he misreads his destiny when he fancies, when he believes, that there are in addition ideas or concepts curiously self-existent to which he also owes service.

So stated, the twelfth century battle seems somewhat arid and devoid of import in a reckoning of Pound's "ideas in action" as they do indeed work out in action. How the old battle went, who won it (Abelard lost) is matter we expect to encounter in a history of philosophy—matter we dismiss as representative of the sort of busy work men invented when (as Pound tirelessly observes) they had nothing *but* words to work with.

Pound—let us observe immediately—is nowhere so foolish as to assert that idealism (our counterpart of the medieval "realism" that found concepts in themselves more real than what the senses absorbed *seriatim*) is exclusively the associate of usury. But Pound is sure that it is the climate of idealism that is the climate most favorable to usury; it is insidiously enervating—it discourages men from specific survey and study of the evils of our time. Pound notes several times that medieval "realism" was, as an intellectual construct, vastly superior to modern idealistic systems that keep us from having a precise view of our culture. True, the medieval systems Pound reprehends may have no closer touch with the five senses than their present counterpart; but the systems of Aquinas and others can at least provide esthetic pleasure, for the scholastics were able to manipulate their needlessly multiplied entities with grace and precision: both virtues of presentation that usury would rather not encounter, even in the realm of self-existent ideas.

But, praise the medieval "realists" as one will, one must not ever forget that they sponsored habits of thought that detached men from the life of the five senses, the nominalist reality. Abelard's resistance to these habits necessitated a work of destruction to precede the work of construction; he—or any other foe of "realism" ancient or modern—would have to discredit "realist" approaches to crucial problems before he would have any chance of displaying the profits inhering in his way of approach. In exactly the same way, Pound sees his labors beginning with a struggle to discredit the debased, shoddy version of "realism" that usury permits in our culture. Pound must win this battle (by explicit prose argument, by use of the method of the ideogram that is the basis of *The Cantos*) before he can really point to the profit of depending on his version of nominalism, of discovering counsel and motive force in "ideas in action." If we recall what this concept really comes to, we see that it is sheerly nominalist. For the concept is a distillation of Pound's reading of human experi-

ence. Special events in human history and special facets of past human
culture remain potentially sovereign for our current ills so long as our
handling of history and past culture allows the import of a special event
to remain firmly attached to the moment in time at which it first occurred.
The special event must be kept firmly localized, crusted over with all in
the way of the peculiar and the grotesque that being localized offers as
opposition to the facile operations of a generalizing or abstracting "realism." This battle of Pound's, however individualized by his statement of
the grounds on which it may properly be fought, should be seen as part
of a general struggle that animates Western culture at present—or con-
vulses it. We have placed Pound's struggle in the region of ideas (if such
a region may be mentioned in discussion of a person who denies that such
a region exists). It is necessary here to suggest that a capital aspect of the
"crisis" of our culture is the continuation, in our culture, of the realist-
nominalist struggle. In our days, the struggle is fought, naturally, not
with medieval weapons but with the instruments we chance on in contemporary armories. We need to see in what precise ways Pound's "ideas
in action" employ weapons quite familiar to us. When we rehearse, as
here, what the "ideas in action" are—words and acts resolutely undifferentiated from the contingent, condemned to wither the instant they are
detached from the moment—we should hear familiar chimes ringing.

Pound is involved in a conflict deeper than fascist-democratic, a battle
that in the last few generations has been fought not across boundaries but
inside the boundaries of all the nations of which we have much knowledge. What must be condemned or accepted is not Pound the fascist (a
word that tends to lose its precise significance now that it is applied to
anything one happens to dislike); it is Pound the nominalist (as a
thinker, as a poet) that we must approve or censure. He is essentially one
of a company that locates truth and wisdom in the transient moment; he
—like many other persons (many of them highly respected)—denies that
truth exists in a fashion different from that in which the moment exists.
In other words, the crux of the Pound problem is neither a political nor
economic one, though—as we have seen—the problem seems to be stated
in political and economic terms. The crux is, rather, this one: in what
fashion do we read from experience; in what ways are we to lead others
to read experience as we have read it? The poet is a political animal; yes.
But he is a political animal not concerned with politics in any narrow
sense—concerned rather with understanding and "rendering" the inclusive view that alone makes "politics" bearable. Pound would say that
"politics" are bearable only when discussed and manipulated nominal-
istically, only when brought into contact with "ideas in action."

This faith of Pound's—shall we call it the deification of the realized
moment?—generates certain problems, in and out of poetry. The problem
—political, it will be seen—is this: how, from a perception of moments,

of particles of reality, can there emerge a really altered sensitivity, a will whose reorientation can be termed both "better" and "permanent"? To make a brutal stricture, is this not to expect from the impact of the "ideas in action" the very results that "realists" (medieval and modern) used quite emptily to believe came from assiduous exposure of the mind to the proper set of abstract ideas?

Pound, at any rate, is confident that the discipline of *The Cantos,* of the method of the ideogram, re-founded sensitivities; and it will make them harmonious and strong without any nonsensical talk about harmony and strength. It is the duty of a teacher of gymnastics to cultivate "form"; but he usually does so without much talk about form. Indeed, talk *about* form would doubtless confuse the minds attached to the splendid bodies in the teacher's charge. The body—and, with Pound, the will—is instructed by doing. This parallel, though close, is unjust to Pound at one point. He is a nominalist, he believes that the will must be assaulted by "engines" forged in a nominalist workshop; but he is not the ordinary sort of anti-intellectualist. A fair judge must concede that he uses his own mind rigorously; and it is plain that he expects his readers to respond keenly and accurately to the stimuli he offers them in *The Cantos.*

However, the fact remains that salvation by immediate experience is indeed the opposite of salvation by shared and perhaps imposed concepts. Further, one must grant that a trust in "ideas in action" pervades many quarters of modern literature. How else explain the almost mystical attachment to presentation of the thing-in-itself which informs a good deal of literary realism or naturalism? It cannot escape an observer that the naturalistic writer, after denying that his work stands in any relation to "first principles," makes a leech-level survey of his slice of life—almost as if he hoped that the significance he denied elsewhere will emerge here. This being true, the artist does well to exercise all his ingenuity as he stalks each separate moment, each "idea in action." Moreover, each stalking would be a new one, nor would one's present stalking be much aided by what one has learned from other intense forays on the moment in itself. Careless readers of *The Cantos* might think these remarks describe what one finds in Pound's poem; they do not, for reasons that will soon be clear. There is more in *The Cantos* than devout prostration before the object, the moment without filiations.

Pound's treatment of the moment, the only really numenous object in human experience, is qualified by the intensity, the protractedness, of the struggle in which he senses he is immersed. Before the moment can be adored, ideas in the form of general statements or coercive procedures must be driven from our culture. For Pound, this is the step which "costs" —costs in effort, in ingenuity, in courtship of failure even. Involved in taking this step, Pound cannot take one that would otherwise be highly attractive to him: that of maintaining that each moment is utterly detached, utterly devoid of correspondences with other moments. This latter step is an easy one to take; it leads the artist to a series of fervent embraces that can have no consequences, can lead to no entanglements. Furthermore, faith in the uniqueness of each moment forbids one from comparing embraces. Yet Pound, as a political animal, is committed to comparing embraces, to expecting consequences from them. He is intellectually a fervid endorser of the nominalist point of view; but he also hopes fervently for "results." On what basis may a nominalist work for results? Can he so work without diminishing the gulf that he wants to keep between himself and all forms of conceptualism?

By a process, certain semanticists say, which can be called "time-binding." Time-binding differs—that it really does differ depends on an act of faith and cannot be supported by clear experiment—from the process of abstraction in that the person who is time-binding is able to put into one bouquet flowers culled from various gardens *without* causing the flowers which make up the bouquet to lose their separate beauty and aroma.

The Cantos, it seems to me, is the product of a sustained attempt to present—in practice rather than by general description—an actual experiment in time-binding. We have seen that, for Pound, the necessity to act, to will, to reshape an evil world, makes the rapt adoration of the separate moment neither defensible nor tolerable. Here, indeed, is the underlying reason for Pound's detaching himself from the early imagist "programme"; for that "programme" did indeed advocate prostrating oneself before the moment, the object-in-itself. Is not this conflict relative to the proper treatment of what experience, from instant to instant, presents the old conflict between Martha and Mary? Mary sits at the feet of the Lord, the supreme and unique instant, and practices adoration; and Martha works to get the meal on the table. Pound, in mid-career, came to the conclusion that his lot (as a poet) was the task of getting the meal on the table: something that had not been done properly for generations. His was the labor of readying and directing a wide world of the imagination that would serve as a basis for future practical action.

But if Pound chose the activity of Martha, it had to be that activity on terms that do not vitiate such activity; there must be no contact with general concepts, with herbarium ideas. So the path of Pound (in *The Cantos*) is beset with dangers, just as—also of necessity—the path of his readers is beset with obscurities that cannot be removed. For the obscurities are the token that Pound remains on guard against the idealist incursions that would enervate both the writing and the reading of *The Cantos.*

Modern attempts toward such reordering and arrangement are, of course, not limited to Pound, nor are they limited to literature and verbal expression. We are familiar with the celebrated attempts of Cézanne to "do over" Poussin according to nature; we know the bold efforts of the post-impressionists to "correct" the dissolution of nature into points of light and color effected by Monet and others. Such "making things new" in terms of light and color is, however, comparatively easy because of the medium involved; the painter works in color and line and the "vibrations" color and line can set up. Identical effects are, we shall soon see, impossible of achievement in the medium of words and rhythm. In painting meaning and concepts can easily be regarded as secondary. But with written expression, meaning is or tends to become primary. Whatever present theories of poetry may say, words do not have the detachability from context, from the history of their use in the past, that color and line have. Perhaps for those who still seek "purity," a terminus exists: the study of higher mathematics. And perhaps one may even, for painting and music, tolerate such a definition of art as this: Art tends to the conditions of mathematics. One may tolerate the definition, provided one understands that the verb *tends* signalizes an inclination that will not be realized. But the definition is hardly one that casts much light on what literature is; and I say this with unorthodox recent developments in mind. Further, I underline this reservation to suggest that a parallel between post-impressionism and "post-imagism" in poetry as it works out in *The Cantos* was intended to remind us of what the nominalist dilemma is; it was not intended to predict our judgment of the time-binding efforts of Pound's poem. That is, Cézanne may do over Poussin according to nature, and we may be quite willing to concede that he has done something that fulfills his promise, that he has done justice to nature without repeating the idealistic sins of Poussin. We may concede still more—that he has turned from the utter nominalism of Monet without becoming a returned votary at the shrine of the Ideal.

What we have now to ask is whether Pound's retreat from utter nominalism (which is, humanly speaking, quite as productive of inanity as the exact opposite, utter devotion to the undifferentiated One) has been as successful as Cézanne's and others. If it is successful, we should expect to find these two things: first, the creation of a sufficiently directing form, the literary analogue of the slopes of Cézanne's Mont Ste. Victoire; second— and here we bow to Pound's professed programme—exertion of sufficient pressure on the human will to produce a reorientation free of the dangers of idealism or abstractions: an aim, I feel, that is not open to one who works in color and line rather than in words.

The answer to the first question—whether there is, in *The Cantos,* a sufficiently directing form, will have to remain a subjective one. But as for the second point—whether Pound's poem works on the will as he hopes it will work—I think it is possible to be quite objective.

Perhaps the answer to the first question may take this form. We are aware that (in our present terms) a time-binding process is at all points under weigh in *The Cantos*. We are aware of cross-references, of clusters of ideograms that (like bees swarming) mysteriously but demonstrably swarm together. Each cluster of ideograms gets *some* of its cohesion because of its polarity to another cluster. How keenly this cohesion, this polarity, is felt must remain a matter for individual judgment.

But to answer the second query—whether Pound's poem actually makes the impact on the will that he desiderates—we can suggest a fairly objective answer. If the poem exercises coercion on the will, is that coercion effectively explained in nominalistic terms or in terms quite opposite? Does the coercion, if we grant it is in some way exerted, avoid the dangers said to inhere in the activity of professed idealism—such dangers as oversimplification of a problem and delusive separation from the complex reality that is man's only true reality, moment-to-moment experience? If it does not avoid these dangers, what is it that catches up with *The Cantos:* a defect in the poet, or factors of frustration in language itself? In brief, what is the real effect of *The Cantos*—the one Pound confidently predicts or some other?

The coercion, one may begin by saying, is *not* effected along purely nominalistic lines. It is not even effected along the relatively nominalistic lines that provide many a post-impressionist painter some basis for operation. Why is it that what is admittedly a delicate adjustment in painting becomes quite impossible for Pound? Why does the time-binding in *The Cantos* actually come so much nearer the "sins" of abstraction? The answer is this. The artist who works in line and color has a free field for his experiments once he has shattered (as many a painter and his critical sponsors have indeed been able to shatter) the public's habitual expectations as to painting: that pictures have a subject, that they should correspond to what our defective vision reports of reality. To shatter these habitual expectations was not easy (*vide* the critical battles fought over the successive efforts to present, on canvas, a new arrangement); but they have, by now, among the cognoscenti and the semi-cognoscenti, been shattered. The result is that today the knowing approach a new painter or a new "period" of an old artist with no expectations whatever except a hope to discover novelty, to see how this time nature has been rearranged. Perhaps the only objective test now applied to a new picture is whether there is—to a special rearrangement—an inner cohesion, a "go" that the cultivated sensibility may respond to. If this is so in art, why is it not possible in literature? Why may we not become accustomed there to the destruction of old expectations, the creation of new sets of attention? Pound plainly has faith that such a destruction and creation are quite possible.

There is an important difference that this analogy between painting and poetry must not conceal, a simple but a crucial one. Pound, as artist, submits to the bondage not of line and color but to the bondage of words:

a much more onerous bondage. Line and color appeal direct to the sense of sight; and it is fairly easy to detach the sense of sight from the earlier expectations to which it has been—some would say "badly"—habituated. Thus, the "bondage" exercised by past use of line and color really rests lightly on the shoulders of the painter. Words are ineradicable. Their roots are their rhythms, their long-established harmonies with each other, their traditional ways of coming into relation with each other (and I mean more than grammar and syntax here). So the question reshapes itself thus for *The Cantos.* Can nature be rearranged in the medium of language, of an established verbal vehicle, without a reproduction of some of the effects judged (by Pound and others) to be pernicious? I do not think so.

Pound would, I am sure (as would a great many other writers who apply their talents to similar tasks) deny this with all the considerable vehemence at his command. He would maintain that *his* attack on the reader's sensibility, that the entire educative impact of *The Cantos,* reshapes the habitual patterns of our language, redirects its evolutions, arouses new expectations and then satisfies them. There are (he would argue) no abstractions or abstracting in *The Cantos;* rather is there a series of pure sensations, poignant and intense. It is because of lengthy submission to these sensations that the reader rises a changed person, his will urging him to travel in a new direction, his mind purified of those modes of employing words that have been the bane of Western capitalist-democratic culture. We may be willing to grant—as we have done—that a comparable reversal of will and sensibility may well take place in persons responsive to the full effects of (say) Picasso's reorganizations in line and color. But that such a reversal follows upon a careful reading of *The Cantos* is a hope rather than a fact. Such is the compulsion—some will say, "Such is the tyranny"—inherent in our language. We are not, of course, prohibited from depicting for ourselves the results of the cessation of the law of gravity, a shift in the condensing point of vapor. But only the writers of "science fiction" try to follow out fancies about altered laws of nature; and we must observe that Pound comes close to realizing his myth of an altered language very seldom. What he does in *The Cantos* is different from what he judges he is doing. This observation does not deny merit to the poem; it seeks rather to clarify the merit that the poem really has.

What follows—as "proof" of the observations just made, as clarification of Pound's poem—is, naturally, the product of one person's reading of *The Cantos.* It is possible that other sensibilities will give a different response to the poem. It is possible, that is, that the poem will indeed re-educate other wills without creating, in the process, abstractions perfectly recognizable, perfectly discutible. But until that happens—until, for a large body of readers, Pound's myth of language-as-it-ought-to-be coincides with the effects of language encountered in the actual poem—the following may perhaps be accepted as an account of what "happens" to a mind in contact with *The Cantos*. It is an account of being involved not only in time-binding but in abstractions; for, despite the embarrassments which Pound provides, language manages to behave in its wonted fashion—within the limits provided by the English language, at least. For that matter, one should remain skeptical that Chinese is as free from the evil process of abstracting as Pound supposes. The "machinery" of that language may not happen to produce words and locutions as obviously removed from sense experience as ours. But that is no indication that the human mind will not be up to its old *in*carnalities, even in Chinese. Such an assertion amounts to widening the argument, to saying that Pound strives against the structure of man's mind itself. There is a good deal of evidence that the human mind, beginning though it does with sense, cannot be restrained from hobbling on determinedly towards the abstractions that it usually manages badly, that it is very often deceived by. It is not irrelevant to note here what Chinese tell us about names like Cherry Blossom and Precious Wind, names that seem to us delicate and poetic and concrete. Such names arouse, in the Chinese breast, no more emotion than that which *we* feel when we hear a girl called Violet or Opal. In either language, any sensed metaphor has long since evaporated; both Precious Wind and Violet function as characterless tags—as, in a sense, words abstracted from concrete uses. So, one may suspect, with other elements in a language that, to Pound's taste, has a richness of sensual compulsion that English lacks. In any language, then—to take a dark view—the human mind staggers drunkenly after the potations that betray it. It does not cease systematizing impressions vivid and momentary. It is —in an earlier figure—not content with culling flowers only; it must press them.

We may be able to suppress a deviation into intellectual analysis when we look at Picasso's *Guernica;* but we cannot during the good many hours that *The Cantos* demand of us. Nor is this "failure" of ours *vis à vis The Cantos* our fault. Let us put the matter at its simplest, ignoring questions about what the psyche common to humanity may be. Mr. Pound and we, his readers, share a language. So long as he and we move within the confines of that language, we must submit to *its* coercion as well as to that of the ideogram. It is simply impossible to stop at the point where Pound would want us to stop, the point beyond which permissible and necessary time-binding degenerates into abstract thinking—even though we are aware of Pound's unclear caveat, "Thus far and no farther." We concede that Pound is no enemy of certain sorts of general statement, as many a passage in *Culture* shows. We know that what he really wishes to do is to discredit certain specific abstractions, bad abstractions that bully and stupefy mankind. To whatever degree we sympathize, we cannot keep from noting that what the poet of *The Cantos* really strives for is not to tear out all abstractions (his expressed programme) but to tear out of the mind and the will the evil abstractions and to implant there concepts no less generalized, even though they are approached obliquely by means of the ideogram. These beneficial concepts are seldom directly referred to in the poem; that is unnecessary since their presence is pervasive. The mode of their existence is indeed somewhat novel, but that must not deceive us as to what they are; they are concepts, and it is special pleading to ask that, because their existence has been "coerced" in the mind of the reader rather than explicitly conferred on them by the poet, they should receive, at our hands, treatment different from that which we allot to other concepts that we encounter more directly and simply. The end-product of the method of the ideogram is not different in kind from the end-products of poets who handle language in a way that does not confuse us at all.

The concepts which are created in our minds by a reading of *The Cantos* constitute two or three brief statements about civilization. Man has a large range of feeling which the relatively good society—Pound has no illusions about discovering or creating a society absolutely good—allows expression; a relatively bad society stifles the expression of the range of feeling. The problem of the immediate future is to undermine and destroy the economic order that supports usury, to set up an order which —like Italian fascism as Pound saw it—will inhibit full expression of emotions and talents as little as possible.

This set of ideas is what Pound's poem is "about." Since the poem urges on us participation in political and social action, since the approach proper to "pure" poetry is irrelevant, we should not hesitate to complete our analysis of Pound's concepts *as* concepts instead of offering up deep but mindless stirrings of the will which Pound chiefly wishes to produce by his poem.

We need not hesitate, then, to recognize—in Pound's ideas, in the relation to them of the ideogram blocks in his poem—the sort of over-simplification or, even, detachment from reality that Pound himself—and justly—perceives in the glosses nineteenth century poetry provided for the world. Indeed, the sins of over-simplification, of detachment from complexity, which we can observe in *The Cantos* or in the concepts it "coerces" us to form are just as sinful as the blemishes which Pound objects to in gross idealism. Pound, to be sure, would insist on this distinction: the professed idealist's balloon is bound to earth by no more than three or four cords (concepts from which everything else in a system is inferred); whereas, there are innumerable cords binding Pound's concepts to earth. If time-binding is a fair term for describing Pound's substitute for conventional methods of abstracting, then the cords binding Pound's concepts to the earth are quite beyond numbering. For time-binding, we are told, differs from abstracting in that each concept is linked with one sensory experience and one only. True, it may closely resemble other concepts similarly tethered; but a person who binds time never goes on to commit the idealistic sin of constituting an intellectual entity from concepts that resemble each other.

If it is true then that in the mind each valid concept is linked to only one percept, Pound's trouble in *The Cantos* is that the ropes get badly snarled; there is, in other terms, at least an effect of abstraction and rather naïve abstraction at that. What makes for this confusion? What makes *The Cantos* a less subtle poem than it ought, in some lights, to be? The answer is—Pound's guiding passions—his enmity to a certain economic system; his devotion (by now secondary) to certain human powers. This latter passion, the devotion to the "human," operates in the poem in an undiscriminating way. Pound would have no patience with the reader who preferred the concept that is linked with the "idea in action" that is John Adams to the concept connected with Malatesta. Both men are anti-usuristic. Is that not enough?

Enough, certainly, to reduce the real complexity of historical and present-day experience to a simple opposition that corresponds less to reality than to the rich contents of Pound's mind as he broods on reality, as he shapes his poem. Ironically, the trouble with the ideas that organize the poem, that are served by the method of the ideogram, is that they are too general; they tend to make the tension of the poem as much a matter of black-and-white opposition as that of heaven to hell-mouth in medieval drama. Consequently, the experience of good and evil that *The Cantos* forces upon our wills is one that we are constantly tempted to check or correct by our own fairly complex experience of social and cultural forms. The poem offers us an experience of good and evil inferior, for example, to experiences open to the reader of Dostoevski, where the opposition of the two forces exists even more strongly, but where brash schematization (by either author or reader) is difficult since the novels show at every turn how intimately the two forces interpenetrate in human experience. It is Pound's failure to do justice to the fact of interpenetration, of gradation, that creates (beneath the complex surface of his poem) an underlying effect of naïveté.

Pound's naïveté consists in taking a partial explanation—in many ways, a truthful one—for a complete explanation. No one can doubt that usury has contributed greatly to the inhumanity of the era in which we live; there are strong reasons for doubting that it is the only begetter of the evil which we know. We must draw back from sharing Pound's hope in its ultimate simplicity: that with the destruction of usury, we destroy the virus that is solely responsible for our sickness. There is, we suspect, much more that will have to be destroyed, nor will it be so easy to name and come at. And though we cannot doubt that a purification of language will contribute to the reconstruction of our society, we cannot hope that it will effect that reconstruction. Reconstruction, as understood by Pound, is almost exclusively a process of removing fetters, of freeing human beings from an enchanter's spell. In legend, once the spell is broken, the story is at an end; we have strong reasons for believing that, even with usury overthrown, our story would but be at a beginning. Pound, at this point, shows for a kind of Quietist, waiting for the descent of the Holy Spirit, expecting the painless emergence of a rich humanity in which we all shall share. Study of history suggests that the emergence of a full humanity in any period was a painful one, subject to chance, subject to the absence or presence of a variety of factors—certainly not made possible by the non-existence of one factor alone: usury.

But Pound, we know, is an indefatigable student of cultural history. But those studies—and *The Cantos*—have been invigorated by hatred rather than hope. Pound's hopes for humanity are various and not easily distinguished from each other. Only Pound's hatred is single; and it is as simplifying of reality as is the central tenet of a radically idealistic system. It is the power of the evil he attacks that gives Pound's poem focus. The "goods" that concern him are pluralistically conceived; it is a rank idealistic sin, in Pound's eyes, to try to relate one good to another. Thus, in his presentation of the good, the human objects and deeds, Pound suffers the fate that has dogged other pluralists; expression of widely scattered affections can never suggest a devotion that is either directed or intense.

A defender of Pound *in toto* might suggest that the poet of *The Cantos* does not pretend to be more than the leader of a section-crew that is making clear the track, that is removing the wreckage left on it by the nineteenth century and ours. Should one demand more? A little. There are, one might say, different ways of clearing wreckage from tracks. The single hate, the single ascription to capitalist-democracy of all our present evil, may prolong the delay of repairing past damage. It may, poetically speaking, keep the writer from rendering correctly the "idea in action"; he may, that is, finally prove inadequate to the single moment which *The Cantos* must present justly—fail because of the simplicity of vision we have just noted. And if the poet does not render the "idea in action" correctly, what chance is there that he will get far in the task of clearing the right of way?

Finally, cautious introspection presents to all of us the knowledge that no single moment, no "idea in action," really exists in itself, out of contact with vividly remembered moments. Nor does Pound deny this except when he gives conscious expression to the nominalist tendency bred in him by his revolt against hypocritical idealism or (worse) the verbal self-hypnosis of some poets. One does not need to say—with an accent of medieval "realism"—that man is the rational animal. If one says merely that man is a time-binding animal (perhaps a distinction without a difference), one says in effect that man is the animal that compares, that has the habit of ranking things according to the presence or absence of pleasure or intensity. So will any reader of *The Cantos* continue to approach the ideograms. Such procedure Pound in some moods would repudiate as a left-hand approach to idealism. It is as if his credo would run: man should hate usury and love a multitude of goods without inhibiting the spontaneous movements of the will by the acts of judging and arranging.

It is this hope, central to Pound's thought and his poem, the hope that modern man can be made so to hate and love, that we must regard as unrealistic. Our sensibilities, "conditioned" by unreflective life in a usurious world, are doubtless corrupt. But we find in ourselves and historical record a greater variety of hates than Pound reveals. Further, we find that mankind—from hope of survival as well as to gratify a thirst for systematizing—has always submitted to a need for arranging the good and evil which he perceives in successive moments.

By saying this, we do not fall into the simplification, the abstraction, which we can perceive in Pound's presentation of evil. We continue, rather, to be aware that men are just as curious about the interrelations of good and evil, of good and good, of evil and evil, as they are about the possible division between good and evil which is the intellectual capital on which Pound's poem draws. This continuing curiosity is as much a "fact" about mankind as each moment in itself, each "idea in action." It is a fact that Pound ignores, a taste that his poem is not designed to satisfy. His neglect is natural; complex, involved curiosity never sorts well with prophetic fervor, whether the fervor be Jeremiah's or Ezra Pound's. Yet this is the very play of curiosity that continues as we read *The Cantos,* a poem devoted to the celebration of a division; and Pound cannot legislate this curiosity out of existence. It contributes to the judgment one passes on the poem, as an imitation of reality, as a source of "renewing" reality.

If this analysis of the "effect" of reading *The Cantos* is just, what is that effect? One of freezing inertia. Shall we say that the will (much less the intelligence) is not moved on the terms that Pound permits and presents in his poem? What the poem presents us is a sharp perception of hate or the hateful balanced by no more than an omnibus, cultivated, eclectic perception of good. This good, upon acquaintance, becomes (for all the specificity with which it is revealed) as vague and unsatisfying as "The Good" in some nineteenth century systems. It may occur to us that Pound is expecting a great miracle indeed from his poem; for nowhere, to date, do we find a society that resisted evil, tramped it to earth, on the basis of an omnibus, undiscriminating perception of good. The most, in this sort, that we find to date is a poem, Ezra Pound's *The Cantos.*

It is a poem for which we should be grateful. It is the record of a negative criticism of our society that we should not ignore. It is the record of a real (if ultimately somewhat frustrated) struggle with the interrelated artistic and political problems which our period presented one poet. But not only one poet. For these same problems of renewing the techniques of poetry, of renewing the society which poetry serves, will become intimately ours the more we think of the mode of existence, of solution, they had when they were Pound's. However qualified our assent to the special answers Pound worked out, we know that Pound has a claim to great distinction—and not just because he has bent his vision on these problems and no others for a great many years. We may feel that an intransigent nominalist pose is more confining than Pound believed; we may think—possibly thanks to his negative demonstration—that making things new requires a more sensitive and various response to experience than *The Cantos* records. We may decide that at certain points Pound was self-deceived. But we cannot believe that central to his career is an intent to deceive us. We should see by now that the "truth" about Ezra Pound and *The Cantos* is—wholly or in part—the truth about matters that ought to be our first concern: the estate of poetry in our culture, the role of language in that culture, the sort of belief needful if that culture is to survive and unfold, the conditions under which belief of any sort is arrived at. This is the gift which Ezra Pound offers the country which he left; it should countervail much that is urged against him.

Pound, *Haiku*, and the Image

by Earl Miner

Ezra Pound's interest in Japanese poetry has long been acknowl-
edged, but only as an eccentric sort of literary relation which has little
understandable connection with his critical theory or his poetry. This
study of his interest in *haiku* aims at a partial explanation of his Japanese
studies, to show that they are not the poor cousins among his literary
relations, but rather enjoy a prominent place alongside Latin and Provençal poetry. Starting with a brief explanation of *haiku,* I hope to show
how this one form of Japanese poetry has influenced Pound's theories of
poetic imagery, and has offered him techniques which have exfoliated
into all his writing.

Haiku (alternatively called *hokku* and *haikai*) is a short Japanese poetic
form which developed about the middle of the seventeenth century. It
consists of seventeen syllables in three lines of five, seven, and five syllables
—the classical rhythm of Japanese poetry. Each *haiku* must concern
itself, preferably by implication, with a season of the year. Since the Japanese are intimately familiar with the flora and the fauna of each season,
and since each reference to a plum tree in blossom or to a crying pheasant
is bound up with centuries of religious symbolism and poetic practice,
this "rule" of *haiku* is anything but arbitrary and constraining. In order
to transcend the narrow limits of their form, Japanese poets have evolved
a style of condensation, ellipsis, suggestion, image and symbol, and echoing of well-known older poems, characteristics of style which present a
texture more tightly woven than the most eccentric metaphysical conceit.
The possibility of *haiku* being easily understood by someone unfamiliar
with the language and the culture is obviously remote, and yet if what
haiku was *thought* to be was imitated and promulgated, who may sneer?
No matter how many books may be filled with comment on Virgil or
Ovid misunderstood in the middle ages, or the metaphysicals and *haiku*
misapprehended in our own day, the point is that significant poetry has
often resulted from such partial understanding.

Since it may be true in a sense that *"haiku* misunderstood" is one key
to our understanding of Pound's theories regarding the image and to
some of his poetry, it may repay us to subject a typical *haiku* to close
analysis. I shall use one to which Pound refers, first translating it literally, then somewhat more freely, and then explaining how the poem expresses its meaning. The *haiku* in question is an early one which, in its
technique of word-play (or *kakekotaba*), retains vestiges of pre-*haiku* techniques. The poem was written by Moritake (1472-1549). We may read it:

Rakka-eda ni	To the branch of falling flowers
Kaeru to mireba:	Seems to return (a flower):
Kochō kana.	A small butterfly.

Or we may read it, again using English punctuation which does not exist
in the original:

Rakka eda ni	To the branch a fallen flower
Kaeru; to mireba	Returns; when I look,
Kochō kana.	It is a small butterfly.

The second reading depends upon our separating the compound, *rakka-
eda,* and our reading the syntax of the second line differently. Both readings must be understood:

> Petals return unto the branch
> Of falling flowers: returning I see
> A fluttering butterfly.

The flowers, that is, the cherry blossoms, are past their prime, and are
falling, but as the poet watches them flutter down it seems that some of
the petals are flying back to the branch. He discovers that he is watching
a butterfly. Cherry blossoms are the glory of spring and the symbol of
delicate natural beauty; it is pathetic that they must fall. However, they
are replaced in the natural order by the butterfly, which brings promises
of summer and other kinds of beauty. From the poet's delightful confusion of flower and butterfly we know that the cherry blossoms must be
white to be mistaken for a butterfly, and that the butterfly must indeed
be lovely if it can be mistaken for cherry blossoms, which are of such sur-
passing beauty that the *haiku* poet needs refer to them only as "flowers"
to be understood.

If we examine the symbols still further, we see that in a sense the poet
did see the flowers return to the bough. He has witnessed one of nature's
metamorphoses; the flowers fell, and arose, so to speak, in a new incarna-
tion. Beauty of one kind passes by changing into beauty of another form.

Fundamentally, then, this poem rests upon Buddhist assumptions concerning nature: all natural beauty is transitory and fleeting, but the
principle of beauty lives on in the everchanging, ever constant metamorphoses of the seasons. Moritake delineates both constancy and change;
for the Buddhist the two are polar principles which depend upon each
other for their existence.

The assonance and consonance of the poem are difficult to explain to
the reader who is unfamiliar with Japanese and who is used to reading
poetry based on accent or stress. However, what may strike the English
reader is what interested Pound, namely, the employment of the imagery.
We are presented first with the image of the petals returning to the branch,
and then we are suddenly asked to change the image to the little flight
of the butterfly. Having no understanding of the language, and little
knowledge of the culture, Pound's understanding of *haiku* was confined to
the imagistic technique, and to the condensation and suggestiveness which
are so much a part of the method of *haiku.*

There is no reason for thinking that Pound knew anything about Japanese poetry before he joined the Poet's Club of T. E. Hulme and F. S.
Flint just before the First World War. But once Hulme and Flint had
shown Pound the way, once they had shown him the value of the contemporary French poets and introduced him to *haiku,* Pound was soon a
more eager student than they, and he announced his "discovery" to the
readers of poetry on both sides of the Atlantic.

His interest in *haiku* was not clear immediately, because he was busy
at the time studying French poetry and criticism, but it is possible to re-
construct the development of his interest. He must have learned about
haiku from Hulme and Flint, who, with the other members of the Poet's
Club, were writing imitations of *haiku* and of *tanka,* the thirty-one syllable form. The degree of respect these men had for Japanese poetry can
be seen in Flint's account, "The History of Imagism," in *The Egoist* for
1 May 1915:

> I had been advocating in the course of a series of articles on recent books of
> verse a poetry in *vers libre,* akin in spirit to the Japanese.

But it was more than a spiritual kinship which the early Imagists desired,
for as Flint writes a little later in the article:

> We proposed at various times to replace [conventional verse] by pure *vers
> libre;* by the Japanese tanka and haikai.

Fortunately for our archaeological desires to dig up the sources and dates
of his discovery, it is true that in general French translators and critics
called *haiku, haikai,* while the English chose the other alternative term,

hokku. Since Pound talks of *hokku,* we may be reasonably sure that after
the introduction to Japanese poetry at the meetings of the Poet's Club,
he read about *haiku* in the writings of the English commentators and
translators.

The evidence suggests that Pound became interested in *haiku* about
1912. For one thing, the first issue of *Poetry* (October, 1912) carried as its
first specimen of the work of Ezra Pound a poem called, "To Whistler,
American." His homage to his fellow-expatriate's fame in introducing
Japanese art to England was overlooked at the time because of the attack
he made on American Philistinism. But he was too good a teacher not
to repeat an important point, and in his biography, "Edward Wadsworth,
Vorticist," in *The Egoist* for 1 June 1914, he repeated what he had said
in the poem, and this time there was little possibility of missing the point:

> I trust that the gentle reader is accustomed to take pleasure in "Whistler
> and the Japanese." Otherwise he had better stop reading my article until
> he has treated himself to some further draughts of education.
> From Whistler and the Japanese, or Chinese, the "world," that is to say,
> the fragment of the English-speaking world that spreads itself into print,
> learned to enjoy "arrangements" of colours and masses.

Ezra Pound would hardly have considered a taste for things Japanese to
be *that* necessary unless he had been immersed in Japanese art and poetry
for some time.

My phrase, "Japanese art and poetry," is important here. Europe was
excited about Japanese prints, lacquerware, and pottery long before it
knew anything about the poetry. Almost always the poet came to know
the prints before the poetry, and this priority meant that his ideas about
the nature of Japanese poetry were shaped, probably unconsciously, by
his previous impressions of the woodblock print. What this meant for
Pound and the other Imagists (except, perhaps, for H. D.) is that those
who formed their theories of Imagism by taking into account Japanese
art and poetry commonly regarded the image in a pictorial, or at least
in a visual sense. This usually ruled out a conception of the image as an
impression of any of the other senses, and also precluded using the term
to describe any merely metaphorical figure. Pound's interest in "Whistler
and the Japanese," in Wadsworth, in the sculptor Gaudier-Brzeska, and
indeed in the general state of European art suggests that his concept of
imagery is largely pictorial. This suggestion is strengthened by his writings on the image, and confirmed by the most important evidence, his
own poetry. Of course, other elements than the Japanese contributed to
the general interest in imagistic writing. However, I believe that the
available evidence, which we shall examine shortly, will show that

Pound, at least, used "Japanese art and poetry" as starting points and points of reference in developing his theories of the image.

We have Pound's own words to attest to his absorption in *haiku* about 1912. Writing of "Vorticism" in the 1 September 1914 issue of *The Fortnightly Review,* he told how *haiku* entered into the process of composition of one of his best known poems:

> Three years ago [1911] in Paris I got out of a "metro" train at La Concorde, and saw suddenly a beautiful face and another and another . . . and I tried all that day for words for what that had meant for me . . . And that evening . . . I found suddenly the expression . . . not in speech but in sudden splotches of colour. It was just that—a "pattern" or hardly a pattern if by pattern you mean something with a repeat in it. But it was a word, the beginning for me of a new language in colour. . . .
>
> I wrote a thirty-line poem and destroyed it because it was what we call work of the second intensity. Six months later I made a poem half that length; a year later [1912] I made the following hokku-like sentence.
>
> > The apparition of these faces in a crowd;
> > Petals on a wet, black bough.

This is not a "hokku-like sentence" because the poem is short, or because the image is vaguely Japanese. Pound's indebtedness to *haiku* is as definite as it is profound:

> The Japanese have had the same sense of exploration. They have understood the beauty of this sort of knowing [that is, "imagistic" as opposed to "lyric" writing] . . . The Japanese have evolved the form of the hokku.
>
> > The fallen blossom flies back to its branch:
> > A butterfly.

"That is the substance of a very well-known hokku," Pound adds. It is the one whose "substance" I have translated and explained earlier. He went on to define the technique which he had adopted:

> The "one image poem" is a form of super-position, that is to say it is one idea set on top of another. I found it useful for getting out of the impasse in which I had been left by my metro emotion. I wrote a thirty line poem, and destroyed it. . . .

This super-repository technique clearly evolved out of Pound's knowledge of Japanese poetry, for he thought that he was imitating or utilizing the technique of *haiku.* Actually he was using only one of the methods which *haiku* employs to overcome the limitations of its brevity. From one point of view, this leaves him open to the charge of inadequate understanding of Japanese poetry; however, if we are less pedantically inclined, we may be happy with one of the rare glimpses we have into the creative process, as the poet seizes upon his subject, shapes it according to a technique learned from another literature—a literature which ceases to be foreign because it has a sudden relevance to his poem—and then presents us with the finished object of art.

Apparently Pound's account of his writing of "In a Station at the Metro" and other such poems, and his advocacy of the "form of super-position" did not pass without comment from his fellow poets, for in the same article he wrote:

> I am often asked whether there can be a long imagiste or vorticist poem. The Japanese, who evolved the hokku, evolved also the Noh plays. In the best "Noh" the whole play may consist of one image. I mean it is gathered about one image. Its unity consists in one image, enforced by movement and music. I see nothing against a long vorticist poem.

The extraordinary thing about the programme or manifesto which he presents for Imagism ("Imagisme," he says, is the poetic branch of Vorticism) is that its techniques are "Japanese" and its justifications are the excellences of Japanese poetry. The question of the effect which Pound's study of the *Nō* had on his poetry, and later on the plays of William Butler Yeats, is not within the scope of this discussion. But the alerted reader may find the technique of the unifying image in the *Cantos,* and may also be interested in speculating on the relation which it bears to the concern of T. S. Eliot and other writers with finding adequate symbols or a "myth" to organize the refractory poetic materials presented by the modern world and to "inform" them with meaning.

Before turning to the question which is after all the most interesting and the most important, the question of Pound's use and modification of the technique of super-position in his poetry, we ought to consider a little further the role which *haiku* played in the formulation of his theories about Imagism. In the description of his experience in the "metro," he speaks of the loveliness of "that sudden emotion" and the later discovery of "the expression . . . not in speech but in sudden splotches of colour." This account may be compared with his famous definition of the image in *Poetry* for March, 1913 as

> an intellectual and emotional complex in an instant of time . . . It is the presentation of such an image which gives that sense of sudden liberation; that sense of freedom from time and space limits; that sense of sudden growth, which we experience in the presence of the greatest works of art.

If the chronology we have been following is correct, and if there is a justification for believing that this definition of the image is indebted to Japanese poetry, then the date of the definition in *Poetry* would come after his discovery of *haiku,* but before his coming into possession of the Japanese and Chinese manuscripts from Mrs. Ernest Fenollosa in early 1914. This is relevant because the definition of the image quoted above does not suggest the kind of image which he describes later as the unifying element in a long poem. That is, it seems likely that Pound's often quoted definition of the image is based upon his enthusiasm for *haiku,* and not upon other reading in Far Eastern poetry, and perhaps only secondarily upon the theories of the earlier Imagists—F. S. Flint, Richard Aldington, and H. D. We can also see the continuity of the development of Pound's theories concerning the image. The definition which was first stated in terms of an instantaneous perception transcending the boundaries of time and space (the *"haiku* image," as we may call it) is subsequently broadened to mean an image or metaphor about which the meaning of a longer poem might cohere (the *"Nō* image"). Also, given this modified meaning, we can see how ready his mind was to receive Fenollosa's theories concerning the ideogrammatic nature of the Chinese written character and its advantages for poetry. I feel strongly that the impression many people have of Pound's thought as a helter-skelter chasing after this or that interesting discovery distorts the continuous and essentially integrated quality of his artistic theory and his poetry. The development which we have noted here could probably be paralleled in a study of the uses he has made of the techniques of Browning or of the Provençal poets.

Lustra, which appeared in London in 1916, was the first volume to contain the results of Pound's discovery of the super-pository image technique. There are other techniques—many poems resemble those in *Ripostes* four years earlier, some are after H. D.'s manner, a few resemble Biblical forms—but the super-pository technique is very much in evidence, and we can see the first modifications which it was to undergo. "In a Station at the Metro" is duly included. So also are "L'Art, 1910"—

> Green arsenic smeared on an egg-white cloth,
> Crushed strawberries! Come, let us feast our eyes.

—and "Women Before a Shop"—

> The gew-gaws of false amber and false turquoise attract them.
> "Like to like nature": these agglutinous yellows!

—two poems which had appeared in the first issue of *BLAST* on 20 June 1914 as examples of Vorticist poetry.

We should note that "L'Art, 1910" has reversed the technique of "In a Station at the Metro" by putting the image *before* the non-imagistic invitation to feast our eyes. The technique of super-position is also slightly modified in "Woman Before a Shop." The last three words are superposed on the preceding, and, in a sense, the body of the poem is superposed on the title, which, like the title of many abstract paintings, is necessary to give us an idea of the meaning of the "picture" as a whole.

An example of the simpler use of the technique can be found in "April":

> Three spirits came to me
> And drew me apart
> To where the olive boughs
> Lay stripped upon the ground:
> Pale carnage beneath bright mist.

The technique is used even more strikingly, with the last line set off, in "Gentildonna":

> She passed and left no quiver in the veins, who now
> Moving among the trees, and clinging in the air
>   she severed,
> Fanning the grass she walked on then, endures:
> Grey olive leaves beneath a rain-cold sky.

And again, in the last line of "Dum Capitolium Scandet":

> How many will come after me singing as well as I sing,
>   none better:
> Telling the heart of their truth as I have taught
>   them to tell it;
> Fruit of my seed,
>   O my unnameable children.
> Know then that I loved you from afore-time,
> Clear speakers, naked in the sun, untrammeled.

"Alba" shows how the technique may be used at its simplest:

> As cool as the pale wet leaves of
>   lily-of-the-valley
> She lay beside me in the dawn.

> As a bath tub lined with white porcelain,
> When the hot water gives out or goes tepid,
> So is the slow cooling of our chivalrous passion,
> O my much praised but-not-altogether-satisfactory lady.

This short poem is all the more interesting for its humor, which seemingly parodies the super-pository image technique; for its elaborate Biblical simile which the Imagists were fond of using in their love poetry; and for the comic use of the language of Pound's Provençal love poetry.

"The Coming of War: Actaeon" shows how a longer poem might be written by inter-weaving the "expository" element with apposite images:

> An image of Lethe,
> and the fields
> Full of faint light
> but golden,
> Grey cliffs,
> and beneath them
> A sea
> Harsher than granite,
> unstill, never ceasing;
> High forms
> with the movement of gods,
> Perilous aspect;
> And one said:
> "This is Actaeon."
> Actaeon of golden greaves!
> Over fair meadows,
> Over the cool face of that field,
> Unstill, ever moving
> Hosts of an ancient people,
> The silent cortège.

Some of Ezra Pound's poems in the Chinese manner are composed in the same *haiku* technique. A very beautiful example (which also suggests "Gentildonna": I can suggest no priority) is the justly famous "Liu Ch'e":

> The rustling of the silk is discontinued,
> Dust drifts over the court-yard,

> There is no sound of foot-fall, and the leaves
> Scurry into heaps and lie still,
> And she the rejoicer of the heart is beneath them:
>
> A wet leaf that clings to the threshold.

Here Pound has outdone himself by super-posing on a series of delicately suggestive images a still more beautiful one.

Another "Chinese" poem which suggests the *haiku* technique is "Fan-Piece, for her Imperial Lord":

> O fan of white silk,
>   clear as frost on the grass-blade,
> You are also laid aside.

An analysis of this brief poem may be of some help if the earlier analysis of a *haiku* is borne in mind. The comparison of Pound's technique with that of the Japanese ought to show the nature of his use and his misunderstanding of Japanese techniques.

In the first place, it seems more than a coincidence that just as a *haiku* consists of seventeen syllables, this poem is made up of seventeen words, and these in the *haiku* pattern of five, seven, and five in three lines. Secondly, we have a modified version of Pound's "form of super-position" here. The "narrative," if explicit statement in so short a poem as this may be called that, is, "O fan of white silk . . . You are also laid aside." Besides this "narrative" we have a super-posed, or rather inter-posed, image of frost on a grass blade.

The title tells us that the poem is one sent as a message by a wife, concubine, or mistress to an Imperial Prince, her "Lord." The woman shows her tact and restraint by addressing the complaint to the fan instead of to her Master. The nature of her complaint is made clear only in the last line with the shock of the adverb: "You are *also* laid aside." We understand by the "also" that the woman has been deserted or forgotten.

We must not overlook the importance of the super-posed image to this theme. The resemblance of the silk of the fan to the frost on the grass is not one only of color. The point is that the clear frost melts quickly in the morning sun, that beautiful fans are used by imperial princes for only a short time, and that even a woman's beauty will serve as an attraction for only a season.

Certainly Pound has achieved a poetic success in short compass in this lament or complaint. Imagery, rhythms, and suggestion fuse to give a unified, moving poem. How then does this poem differ from *haiku*? First, *haiku* are nature poems, and exclude such topics as love complaints, which are considered the proper province of thirty-one syllable *waka*. Second, Pound's suggestion of the season (frost suggests autumn) lacks the over-riding importance of nature which is characteristic of *haiku*. He might have made his point of evanescence with the usual Buddhist symbol of dew. Had he done this (and had he been writing the poem in Japanese) such an image would have extended the meaning of the poem symbolically to the metaphysical realm where the transience of all earthly things is both deplored and scorned. This leads us to the third difference. The meaning of "Fan-Piece, for her Imperial Lord" is restricted to what might be called psychological and esthetic truth, while Moritake's poem about the cherry blossoms and the butterfly uses a religious symbolism which gives it a more profound universality. There are also differences in the use of language which may not be discussed here. What Pound's poem "lacks," and indeed what it does not pretend to have, is a centuries-old tradition of nature symbolism and a poetic practice to express it, as well as a language highly developed for brief, suggestive, and allusive poetry. But this is not surprising. What does amaze us is the degree to which Pound has emulated the techniques of *haiku* and the skill with which he has reproduced the tone of melancholy and restrained plaintiveness which is common in oriental poetry but rare in our own.

Besides these poems there are many other short poems which embody the same technique—"The Encounter," "Shop Girl," "Tame Cat," the concluding stanza of "Mauberley," "Fish and Shadow," etc.

However, we ought to turn away from the shorter poems and investigate Pound's use of the technique in longer efforts. T. S. Eliot thought that although much of "Near Perigord" echoed Browning, in the last seven lines only Pound's voice is audible.

> There shut up in his castle, Tairiran's,
> She who had nor ears nor tongue save in her hands,
> Gone—ah, gone—untouched, unreachable!
> She who could never live save through one person,
> She who could never speak save to one person,
> And all the rest of her a shifting change,
> A broken bundle of mirrors . . . !

It is the voice of Ezra Pound, certainly, but in his use in the last line of the super-pository technique to define the meaning of the poem in one distinct image there is what may be called a Japanese accent.

Like *The Waste Land,* to which they are comparable in many ways, the *Cantos* are made up of many diverse poetic elements. Our present concern is in the use which Pound made of *haiku* and of the super-pository image technique, although any full study of Pound's use of Japanese poetry would include an examination of elements of *Nō* which

are to be found in the poem. Generally speaking, Pound uses the super-
pository technique in two ways, either as a striking ending for a canto,
or, more commonly, within the canto to express with an image what has
gone before or what follows directly, a device we have noted in the
shorter poems. Most examples of the use of the technique which he
adapted from *haiku* are found in the early *Cantos,* before the prevailing
theme becomes the evil of usury and certain forms of government, or in
the more lyrical *Pisan Cantos.*

Since it is difficult to make very much sense of the cantos without quot-
ing a whole canto as context or without providing a great deal of explanation, I shall try to choose examples from passages which are relatively
clear. Pound uses the technique both within Canto XVII and, more
strikingly, to end it:

> Thither Borso, when they shot the barbed arrow at him,
> And Carmagnola between the two columns,
> Sigismundo, after that wreck in Dalmatia.
>   Sunset like the grasshopper flying.

The canto which makes most frequent use of the technique is probably
Canto IV. For example, the last line of this passage:

> The dogs leap on Actæon,
>   "Hither, hither, Actæon,"
> Spotted stag of the wood;
> Gold, gold, a sheaf of hair,
>   Thick like a wheat swath,
> Blaze, blaze in the sun,
>   The dogs leap on Actæon.
> Stumbling, stumbling along in the wood,
> Muttering, muttering Ovid:
> "Pergusa . . . pool . . . pool . . . Gargaphia,
> "Pool . . . pool of Salmacis."
>   The empty armour shakes as the cygnet moves.

Other examples are to be found in the succeeding sections of the same
canto:

> Thus the light rains, thus pours, *e lo soleils plovil*
> The liquid and rushing crystal
>   beneath the knees of the gods.
> *Ply over ply, thin glitter of water;*
> *Brook film bearing white petals.*
> The pines at Takasago

> grow with the pines of Isé!
> The water rolls up the bright pale sand in the
>   spring's mouth
> "Behold the Tree of the Visages!"
> Forked branch-tips, flaming as if with lotus.
>   Ply over ply
> The shallow eddying fluid,
>   beneath the knees of the gods.
>
> Torches melt in the glare
>   set flame of the corner cook-stall,
> Blue agate casing the sky (as at Gourdon that time)
>   the sputter of resin,
> Saffron sandal so petals the narrow foot: Hymenæus Io!
>   Hymen, Io Hymenæe! Aurunculeia!
> *A scarlet flower is cast on the blanch-white stone.*

The italicized (English) words show how the technique which began in a two-line poem has become adapted for a long poem.

For an example in a later canto, we might choose the following lines from Canto XLVII (the italics are mine):

> By this gate art thou measured
> Thy day is between a door and a door
> Two oxen are yoked for plowing
> Or six in the hill field
> *White bulk under olives,* a score for drawing down stone.

Earlier in the same canto (in the twenty-fifth line) there is the lovely super-pository image—

> But in the pale night the small lamps float seaward,

—which occurs in variation throughout the *Cantos*.

These examples ought to be sufficient to familiarize a reader of Pound's poetry with the technique. If it is possible to generalize, it might be said that this "form of super-position" has been most useful to him in poems and passages which are epigrammatic, elegiac, or lyric, although he seems also to have found it useful to gather together, as it were, several lines of narrative and exposition into one apposite image.

What these examples and Pound's criticism show is that *haiku* has made an important contribution to his theory and practice. It gave him material and examples for much of his theory concerning imagery, a programme or manifesto for poetry and art about the time of the First World War, and, finally, a flexible technique which he called the "form of super-position." It may also be assumed that he was attracted by the suggestive, allusive, condensed, and concrete qualities of Japanese poetry, or he would never have turned to it in the first place. This particular "influence" is so intangible, however, and might have come from such a variety of English and European sources besides Japanese poetry that it is more prudent to say that these qualities would have interested him only because they showed him that many of his own ideas could be embodied in poetry. In this sense, Japanese poetry confirmed what he was already thinking and advocating.

The super-pository image technique is not confined to the limits of the poetry of Ezra Pound, broad as these are. Examples may be found in the poetry of other Imagists over whom Pound had influence—notably Richard Aldington, Amy Lowell, and John Gould Fletcher. The extraordinary aspect of the story of the development and use of this technique is not perhaps the broadcast quality of it in the work of Pound and the other Imagists, but the clarity, the logic, and the assurance with which its author developed and promulgated it from a poetry written in a language he neither read nor spoke. Or perhaps it is still more remarkable that, in many instances, his uses of the technique do actually remind the informed reader of the original form from which the technique was taken, and in some poems there seems to be more of the spirit of Japanese poetry than in the deliberate imitations of *haiku* or *tanka* made by the other Imagists and by poets and poetasters who have been in Japan.

Ezra Pound and Music

by Murray Schafer

Pound has always been associated in one way or another with music. He has written much criticism including some extremely important remarks on harmony as well as perspicacious observations on the relationship of music to poetry. He is the author of an aesthetic known as *Great Bass* which, taking its roots in music, has multiple significance for all arts. He is also the composer of several pieces of music, including an opera, *Le Testament,* which, if better known, would have been one of the most controversial pieces of music of its epoch. And all these things have had incalculable influence on the poetry he has written, both in its sound and in its shape and structure.

We must realize that a poet's attitude to music will be conditioned by his profession. He will be coming at music through the word, through *melopoeia* as Pound has called it. He has distinguished three kinds of poetry: *logopoeia,* roughly poetry of ideas and precise expression; *phanopoeia,* poetry of images; and *melopoeia,* "wherein the words are charged over and above their plain meaning with some musical property, which directs the bearing or trend of that meaning." He remarks further that in *melopoeia* we find "a force tending often to lull or distract the reader from the exact sense of the language. It is poetry on the borders of music and music is perhaps the bridge between consciousness and the unthinking sentient or insentient universe." [1]

One does not really expect poets to get beyond seeing music as just one feature in the poetic universe. Their interest in *pure* music is generally limited, often non-existent. In this respect Pound is exceptional, for he has come to appreciate the value of much music which has nothing to do with poetry: Vivaldi's concerti, for instance, or the sonatas of Mozart. And in the case of Vivaldi's works it is not to our credit that he appreciated their value long before most musicians. This tolerance, however, probably came with the middle years, for he speaks of *pure* music

---

[1] Ezra Pound, *Literary Essays* (London: Faber, 1954), pp. 25-6.

"Ezra Pound and Music" by Murray Schafer. From *The Canadian Music Journal,* V (Summer 1961), 15-43. Copyright © 1961 by The Canadian Music Council. Revised by Murray Schafer for publication in this volume and reprinted by his permission and that of the editor of *The Canadian Music Journal.*

much more frequently in his *Guide to Kulchur* (1938) than in the earlier
critical writings. Previously he had been dedicated to the idea that, in
order to ensure the highest fruition of both arts, music and poetry must
in some way be wedded together.

There are two ways in which music may be seen in relationship to
poetry. It may be seen as an accompaniment to words, a means of giving
them delineation and vitality. Or it may be seen as an extension of
communication, an attempt to get beyond or under verbal language. Its
service is then mood painting, suggestive propaganda for the poetic idea.
These views are not compatible and it is natural that while the poet
clings to the former where the words control the situation, the musician
approaches the latter. The first tradition comes down as far as the troubadours and Minnesinger where, with occasional exceptions, it promptly
disappears. It was therefore to the perfect blending of *motz el son* which
was the troubadours' art that Pound's early inclinations drew him. It
occurred to him early in his career that poetry might benefit through
music. "It is not intelligent to ignore the fact," he has written, "that both
in Greece and Provence the poetry attained its highest rhythmic and
metrical brilliance at times when the arts of verse and music were most
closely knit together, when each thing done by the poet had some definite
musical urge or necessity bound up within it." [2] Elsewhere he remarked
that ". . . the divorce of the two arts had been to the advantage of
neither and that melodic invention declined simultaneously and progressively with their divergence. The rhythms of poetry grew stupider, and
they in turn affected or infected the musicians who set poems to music." [3]

Pound is probably right when he asserts that technical brilliance in
poetry stimulated invention in music, for the Provençal musicians, under
the spell of their richly varied texts, produced an equal variety of song
forms, standing in high contrast with the stereotyped forms of later
periods when composers were content with second-rate verse. In any case,
it is easy to lament the passing of that exquisite blending of *motz el son*
which was the troubadours' art, for nowhere since have we seen such an
unstrained and selfless tradition of artistic dependence and interplay.

But where it would have once been unthinkable to debate the pre-
eminence of the arts in collaboration, today there are divergent views,
depending on which art one belongs to. Pound has expressed his view of
the perfect song: "The perfect song occurs when the poetic rhythm is in
itself interesting, and when the musician augments, illuminates it, without breaking away from, or at least without going too far from the
dominant cadences and accents of the words; when ligatures illustrate

---

[2] *Ibid.*, p. 91.

[3] Ezra Pound, *Antheil and the Treatise on Harmony* (Paris: Three Mountains Press,
1924), p. 32.

the verbal qualities, and the little descants and prolongations fall in with the main movements of the poem." [4] There are few enough examples of successful songs of this kind today. Tagore's music to his *Gitanjali* is one and Pound's settings of Villon's words is another; both, therefore, by poets. Against this a composer looks at a poem as a stimulant for a discharge of lyrical music. If this is to be successful as music, many subtleties of the poetry will have to be overlooked. Many composers even deny poetry any importance in song except as an inspirational force for the composer. Schoenberg, for example, confessed that for many years he had not known, had not even been curious about the texts of his favorite Schubert songs—a perfect case of the view that music goes beyond verbal language. It is worth reminding ourselves how uneven the balance is in what is today taken to be the perfect song, for certainly no one will dispute that Schubert's melodies are more memorable than Müller's or Rellstab's or even Goethe's words.

This does not imply that the arts cannot, should not profit from interplay, and that an intimate understanding of another art will not benefit one in the execution of his own. Pound believes that the poet can learn from music. He puts it bluntly: "Poets who will not study music are defective." [5] He asserts that "poets should never be too long out of touch with musicians"; and this, to the credit of his poetry, Pound never was. In fact, since the breakdown of the arts probably no poet has profited so much from an intimate study of musical phrasing, forms, and rhythm, not metronomic rhythm, but the individual rhythm of masterpieces that adjusts itself according to the demands of the material which Pound was to call *absolute* and incorporate in his theory of *Great Bass*. Obviously other poets have been influenced by musical sounds, but none has been influenced by musical shapes to the extent Pound has. None has understood so well the real significance of musical form, especially that of the fugue, and the literary uses that might be made of it. As early as 1912 he had written that he was attempting "to compose in the sequence of the musical phrase." [6] During this period he was intimately involved with his Provençal studies. Provençal to Pound did not mean poetry alone, but rather poetry bound to music. Soon he was collaborating with Walter Morse Rummel in bringing out an edition of troubadour songs for which Pound not only provided the English translations, but actually located some of the manuscripts from which the music was drawn. This practice of working at poetry with music directly before him became an important exercise; it was by getting at the "sequence of the musical phrase" that he was led to develop the unusual verse techniques which were to release

[4] *Ibid.*, p. 84.
[5] *Literary Essays*, p. 437.
[6] *Ibid.*, p. 3.

English poetry from the cramped meters and forms that had imprisoned it for so long. Possibly no poet at any time has produced the abundance of technical innovations Pound has.

It is not surprising, therefore, that of all the troubadours Arnaut Daniel intrigued him the most. Had not Dante called him *il miglior fabbro*, praising his technical expertise? This same phrase Eliot in turn used on Pound in his dedication of *The Waste Land*. Daniel is not generally taken to be the greatest of the troubadours, at least not from the musical side though this may be due to lack of evidence, but the service he performed for *langue d'oc* by inventing new words and constructions in many ways parallels Pound's own achievements for English verse.

Pound learned the aesthetic of sounds from Daniel; clear sounds (l'aura amara), opaque sounds (sols sui qui sai lo sobrafan quem sortz), tintinnabulations (cadahus en son us); and the effects to which *shaggy* rhymes (letz, becs, mutz) might be put by muddying the anticipated sound to produce echo or antiphony. He learned the difference of legato phrasing and staccato and all that lies between. Not the least, he learned the function and effectiveness of rests. His translations of Daniel's canzone are matchless for their sound, the way they reproduce the notes of the original.

Pound studied Provençal for all it could teach him about cadence. He argued against a too rigorous acceptance of the rhythmic modes alleged to govern troubadour music, for surely the poetry shows no "hefty swat on alternate syllables." It was these studies too that made clear to him the way in which a poet might build up counterpoint, or a clever illusion of such, by playing on the memory and the residuum of sounds stored up in it through suspending, anticipating, or curtailing the expected. He speaks of this in relation to oriental music where the situation is analogous (and perhaps more than accidentally so, for the troubadours may well have gained some of the complexity of their versification from Arabic lyrics via the crusades or North Africa):

> In especial one notes the *extraordinary* length of the rhythm pattern units [in oriental music], comparable to the medieval rhyme-scheme of Provençal canzos, where, for example, one finds a rhyme pattern which begins its six-ply repeat after the seventeenth different terminal sound. In this Arabian music, as in the Provençal metrical schemes, the effect of the subtler repetitions only becomes apparent in the third or fourth strophe, and then culminates in the fifth or sixth, as a sort of horizontal instead of perpendicular chord. One might call it a *sort of* counterpoint; if one can conceive a counterpoint which plays not against a sound newly struck, but against the residuum and residua of sounds which hang in the auditory memory.[7]

What Pound's Provençal discoveries meant for his own verse is immediately discernible by turning to the early collections, *Personae,*

[7] *Antheil and the Treatise on Harmony*, p. 95.

Ripostes, and *Lustra.* Space does not permit the study one would like to make of the music in these early poems. Those interested are referred to Edith Sitwell's unique essay on the sound of Pound's early poetry. The celebrated *Na Audiart* is a particularly illuminating example of verbal counterpoint, for here a melodic echo is built up to be broken by rhythmic elaborations. The most abrupt change occurs at the end of the poem:

> Thou wert once she
> > Audiart, Audiart,
> For whose fairness one forgave
> > Audiart,
> Audiart
> > Que be-m vols mal.

The dull quiver of the last line, a dissonant arpeggio, is reminiscent of the Minnesinger whose song comes to premature end owing to a broken string.

> . . . nu hei!
> des videlaeres seite
> der ist enzwei!

Arnaut Daniel's dexterity with complex verse forms is especially evident in the sestina, a form invented by him. Here the six-ply scheme in which the terminal sounds are constantly re-shuffled to form new patterns creates an intensity which Pound has described as "a thin sheet of flame folding and infolding upon itself," adding that such a form can only be well judged when recited or sung. Pound has revived the form in his *Sestina: Altaforte.* Here a reader can gather the mood of the poem simply from the aura of the six terminal words: peace, music, clash, opposing, crimson, rejoicing. Their constantly shifting reiteration builds like an angry chord which comes to a crashing halt on the last word of the poem, the snarl *peace!*

Although Pound once passed an entire year writing a sonnet a day for practice, that form never became a favourite with him. He considered the sestina and the other forms used by the troubadours and Cavalcanti to be superior to the sonnet, and for musical reasons. "The sonnet occurred automatically when some chap got stuck in the effort to make a canzone." [8] He was seeking a tighter, more disciplined poetry. And after having spent so much time with Arnaut Daniel or Cavalcanti whose *Donna mi Prega* binds 52 out of every 154 syllables together into a

[8] *Literary Essays,* p. 168.

pattern, it is not surprising that he was impatient with anything as rhythmically relaxed as the sonnet.

It is important that Pound in revitalizing old forms should have empha-
sized their singability. He was familiar with many of the original melodies
of the Provençal lyrics he translated or adapted. One or two of his poems
like *Winter is icummen in* show that, like Goethe, he worked side by side
with music, following its meter and inflexion. If there is any contemporary poetry ready-made for retransposition into song, it is Pound's early
work; and it is both surprising and regrettable that it has not attracted
more attention from composers.

There is a kind of poetry which, though thoroughly musical, cannot
take song. To be set to music, verse must be versatile, for song attenuates
it and blunts its articulation. Song also imposes simplicity; complex ideas,
uncommon words, even the most deliberate devices of verbal music
including rhyme are largely wasted. A poem like Yeats's *Had I the
heavens' embroidered cloths* could not be subjected to the new time-law
music imposes, for its tempo is too well-defined in the music of words
alone.

By the time Pound had composed *Mauberley* he had reached a similar
stage, and from here on it becomes increasingly difficult to imagine his
verse in song (though naturally with the odd strong exception such as the
latter part of *Canto LXXXI*). In *Mauberley* Pound's language reaches
such precision and his motivating ideas are so elaborate that there is no
question of setting any part of it to music. The shapes defy attenuation
or readjustment; the intricate rhythms and rhymes—English against Greek
or Medieval French—would be quite lost in song. Hugh Kenner says that
Pound "asks for complex acts of discernment, not for immolation." [9]
Mauberley is the first poem of which this is wholly true. It is not a mood
piece, but a word-jewel cut clear and hard. Nothing in it wobbles; there
are no loose ends.

If most musical devices in poetry lose their point in song, the one
exception is rhythm. Every composer knows the value of a line in which
the arrangement of tensions and relaxations is so precise, so honest to the
ideas it expresses that it suggests its own music effortlessly. Pound's sense
of rhythm has been called his greatest gift and the service he did English
verse by uprooting iambic pentameter and offering innumerable alternatives has perhaps had an indirect significance for contemporary music.

It ought to be possible to show that verse meters and patterns have at
all times influenced the music of composers interested in song. Certainly
iambic pentameter was so much a part of the poetical mores of the
English-speaking peoples that it shaped not only the phrasing of sophisticated art songs, but even that of the blues! Just as certainly the con-

[9] Hugh Kenner, *The Poetry of Ezra Pound* (London: Faber, 1951), p. 20.

temporary composer's interest in asymmetrical texts, in order to attain freedom for his vocal line, may be largely traced back to the *vers libre* adventure in poetry.

It may take careful and repeated readings of Pound's early work to be persuaded that it is not merely an exhibition of brute force, and one can well understand why his early critics found Pound a disturbance; for while there was no denying the charm of a line like

> Eyes, dreams, lips and the night goes

they were confounded by its lawlessness. Pound has said he does not believe anyone could use to advantage rhythms more subtle than those he has used. Even when he works within the limits of the iamb, scarcely two lines measure alike.

Early critics of Pound were slow to realize that rhythm is not something that can be imposed on poetry, but rather something demanded by poetry in its material and situations. In instigating *vers libre* Pound forced this issue. To the old school *vers libre* was an escape from discipline; to the new it was an added discipline for it meant divining the precise meter and shape of each individual poetic thought. The shapes of his lines, their disposition on the page, the placing of punctuation and spaces, were all as much ubiquitous concerns with Pound as the craftsmanship of rhyming. When he breaks up the shape of verse, the impact is oral as well as visual. In the opening of *Provincia Deserta*

> At Rochecoart
> Where the hills part
> in three ways . . .

we have the outlines of the hills traced on the page, and any reader would instinctively make the appropriate divisions in the tempo of his reading as well.

And what would be the proper tempo for reciting the four-word poem *Papyrus* where we are left to invent on our own?

> Spring. . . . . . .
> Too long. . . . . .
> Gongula. . . . . .

If, as Stravinsky has suggested, there are two kinds of musical time, one running with the clock and one running counter to it or away from it, this is also true for poetry, and especially true for Pound's. One must turn to the later *Cantos* for the most accomplished examples of this.

> Here are lynxes   Here are lynxes,
> Is there a sound in the forest
>   of pard or of bassarid
> of crotale   or of leaves moving? [10]

This is no matter of fancy typography; it is the tempo of the breathing forest.

The freer spacing of contemporary poetry has its parallel in the preponderance of rests in contemporary music. It is perhaps not accidental that while Pound and his associates were investing English poetry with new rhythmic life (*c.* 1910) the same service was being performed for music by Igor Stravinsky. Perhaps Pound had him in mind when he defended *vers libre* with the following words:

> No one is so foolish as to suppose that a musician using "four-four" time is compelled to use always four quavers in each bar, or in "seven-eighths" time to use seven notes uniformly in each bar. He may use one half, one quarter and one eighth rest, or any combination as he may happen to choose or find fitting. To apply this musical truism to verse is to employ *vers libre*.[11]

Music played a strong part in convincing Pound of the necessity of the reforms he was initiating. He had made the acquaintance of Arnold Dolmetsch (the God Pan as he calls him), and Dolmetsch's book *The Interpretation of Music of the XVIIth and XVIIIth Centuries* made a profound impression on him. When opposition to *vers libre* was strong he found it to his advantage to draw on remarks made by Thomas Mace, Rousseau, and Couperin to support his point that verse ought to be composed in "the sequence of the musical phrase." The regular appearance of old music on paper was a deception commented on by all theorists. As Couperin put it: ". . . We write differently from what we play." And again ". . . I find that we confuse Time or Measure with what is called Cadence or Movement. Measure defines the quantity and equality of beats; Cadence is properly the spirit, the Soul that must be added." [12] Such remarks exposed the paradox of previous English verse techniques to the poet. Speech, which was of necessity unequal in stress and articulation, had in the highest form of poetry been constrained by arbitrary systems of quantitative meter. Music, on the other hand, which appeared equal on paper due to its awkward method of notation, came alive in performance, gaining its true freedom and *cadence*.

Thus, for Pound rhythm was not, could not be, a matter of mere

[10] Canto LXXIX.
[11] *Literary Essays*, p. 93.
[12] "Vers Libre and Arnold Dolmetsch," in *Literary Essays*, p. 439.

foot-stamping. He had frequently spoken of a kind of superior rhythm which he called *absolute,* a rhythm which was part of the poetic idea itself, not a discipline over which it was strung.

> I said in my Guido Cavalcanti that I believed in an absolute rhythm. I believe that every emotion and every phase of emotion has some toneless phrase, some rhythm-phrase to express it.[13]

James Joyce has defined rhythm too in a way which emphasizes the contribution of parts to an indivisible whole.

> Rhythm . . . is the first formal esthetic relation of any part to part in any esthetic whole or of an esthetic whole to its part or parts or of any part to the esthetic whole of which it is a part.[14]

Both poets are concerned with the function of rhythm in form; thus each has in turn been led to apotheosize music as the art in which rhythm is purest and assumes its greatest responsibility in building form. In fact, no poets of any period have shown such a keen interest in putting musical techniques to work for their own art as have Joyce and Pound, though, of course, each has achieved this in his own way.

Joyce's most concentrated attempt to utilize the formal techniques of music occurs in the "Sirens" chapter of *Ulysses.* Before the chapter opens two pages of fragments from what is to follow are given. Taken alone they are meaningless and have purely musical or sensory value:

> Bronze by gold heard the hoofirons, steelyringing . . .
>
> Imperthnthn thnthnthn . . .
>
> Jingle jingle jaunted jingling . . . .[15]

As the chapter unfolds each sound is given context and meaning. There are cross references and overlappings of the sixty-odd introductory fragments producing a polyphonic effect that makes for a vivid illustration of the kind of verbal counterpoint Pound has spoken of. Going a step further, Stuart Gilbert has called the "Sirens" episode a *fuga per canonem;* but I suspect Mr. Gilbert's otherwise excellent study of *Ulysses* has been

[13] Ezra Pound, *Gaudier-Brzeska: a memoir* (London: John Lane, 1916), p. 97. Hugh Kenner points out that the phrase *absolute rhythm* may have come to Pound from Rémy de Gourmont, who employs it in his *Le Latin Mystique* to describe the relationship of words to music in plainchant.

[14] James Joyce, *Portrait of the Artist as a Young Man* (New York: Modern Library, 1916), p. 241.

[15] James Joyce, *Ulysses* (London: The Bodley Head, 1937), p. 242 *et seq.*

betrayed here by his musical virginity. If we are to take the opening fragments as subjects and countersubjects we must then expect them to behave as normal fugal subjects and countersubjects do; that is, to exercise complete control over all the ensuing situations. As it is, Joyce's fragments contribute strongly to the flavour of the chapter, but no one could say that the important development in the "Sirens" is the clattering hooves of the vice-regal procession or the jingle of Blazes Boylan's jaunting car.

The problem resolves itself, I think, to this: is a fugal subject a heterogeneous collection of notes or is it an idea? If it is more than a collection of notes, then it must be the basic motivating power in everything that develops from it. Joyce undeniably creates the illusion of musical timbre and texture in the "Sirens" episode, but this should not be mistaken for musical form. No art has a monopoly over its terminology, but once defined by practice the meaning of terms should be respected by all who take them over. Too much literary criticism has been written in recent years in which musical terms have been used casually or inaccurately.

Pound himself claimed his *Cantos* would display the structure of a Bach fugue. He declared to Yeats that there was to be no plot to the *Cantos*, "no chronicle of events, no logic of discourse, but two themes, the descent into Hades from Homer, a metamorphosis from Ovid and mixed with these medieval or modern historical characters." [16] This means that when introduced the themes may have little significance, may in fact be as unassuming as many of Bach's fugue subjects, but that with each subsequent re-entry they would be progressively revealed until they stand consolidated at the end of the vast tapestry of events and reflections. It seems to me that Pound is more correct in applying the term *fugue* to his work, for despite the externalization of his themes, they themselves remain unchanged throughout the long poem. There are also subsidiary motifs, but they too remain intact: The usury motif for example or the lengthy stretches of the *Thrones* dominated by variants of the line

The temple is not for sale

enforced by its ideogram. These are truly like the subjects of Bach's fugues, ideas, not mere profusions of sound.

This is not to disparage Joyce's gifts of minstrelsy, but only to make clear the essential difference in the approach of each poet to music. Joyce's musicianship ran more to details, to isolated sounds. He is interested in the tinkle of words. He is like Helmholtz listening to his tuning fork. His gift was for charging individual words with an expansive power to hang on bell-like in the auditive memory. Although his musical devices were numberless, the majority had to do with single or pairs of words:

[16] W. B. Yeats, *A Packet for Ezra Pound* (Dublin: The Cuala Press, 1929), p. 17.

alliteration, assonances, onomatopoeia, neologisms, infixes, morphologies, spoonerisms, anagrams, palindromes, to name only a few of the most obvious, are all of this kind.

A lot has been made of Joyce's musicianship, so much, in fact, that it is sometimes supposed he was in reality a brilliant musician who strayed over into language. Actually, Joyce's musicial interests were elementary and got little beyond Puccini and John McCormack. If he composed a song or two, as he is said to have done, they must certainly have been of that rather bathetic Irish variety of parlor song.[17]

It is interesting to compare Joyce's musical tastes with Pound's, for the latter poet's are much more sophisticated. Jannequin, Vivaldi, Bach, Mozart, Dowland, Bartok, and Antheil rank among his enthusiasms. If we leave out the minstrels we see that all the others were great musical craftsmen, master builders of their art. As remarked earlier, such an advanced musical taste is rare among poets, but Pound had a special reason for paying close attention to the best in music. His theory of *absolute rhythm* governs the proportion of the elements of masterpieces. A second concept, that of *Great Bass*, links the elements into an indivisible whole.

Pound does not imply a bass in the present-day musical sense of the word, but rather a basis which exists like the keel line of a ship, exercising centripetal pull over everything above it. It too is a temporal not a formal concept, or more correctly, a temporal concept governing the form. Its rudiments were formulated as early as the preface to his Cavalcanti translations of 1910 where he had said: ". . . it should be possible to show that any given rhythm implies about it a complete form, fugue, sonata. I cannot say what form, but a form perfect, complete. Ergo, the rhythm set in a line of poetry connotes its symphony which, had we a little more skill we could score for orchestra." In the *Guide to Kulchur* Pound deals with *Great Bass* more comprehensively, this time stressing its musical roots.

> The wobbling about by deficient musicians, the attempt to give life to a piece by abundant rallentandos and speedings up, results in reduction of all music to one doughy mass and all compositions to the one statement of the performing executant, said wobbly time is due to their NOT divining the real pace of the segment. The 60, 72, or 84, or 120 per minute is a BASS, or basis. It is the bottom note of the harmony.[18]

Great Bass, therefore, is the exact tempo at which masterpieces must be performed or assimilated. It is not a tempo imposed on the elements; it is demanded by them. It is *Great Bass* that indicates to us the proper

---

[17] Padraic Colum writes me that Joyce did in fact make a setting of Yeats's poem "Who will go drive with Fergus now?" but that this appears to have been lost.

[18] *Guide to Kulchur* (London: Faber, 1938), p. 233.

tempo of Bach's unedited fugues. It is *Great Bass* too, that defines the
pace and form of Pound's Cantos, for these are not, it cannot be em-
phasized too strongly, two features, but are one and the same thing. This
can only be fully grasped by illustration. Examples are numerous and one
may go right to the beginning. *Cantos I* and *II* are enacted against a
backdrop of seascape. Its presence is ubiquitous and provides both the
movement and the shape of the expression. *Canto I* (a paraphrase of
Book XI of the Odyssey) suggests with its long lines a strong sweep of
waves breaking over a rugged shore. But as we are carried out to sea the
face of the water changes, and these changes are always audible whether
described or not. In *Canto II* the lines are shorter, often ending with one-
syllable words to mark the swifter pace. But at the conclusion a remarkable transformation comes over the water at dusk:

> Then quiet water,
> > quiet in the buff sands,
> Sea-fowl stretching wing-joints,
> > splashing in rock-hollows and sand-hollows
> In the wave-runs by the half-dune;
> Glass-glint of wave in the tide-rips against sunlight,
> > pallor of Hesperus,
> Grey peak of the wave,
> > wave, colour of grape's pulp,
>
> Olive grey in the near,
> > far, smoke grey of the rock-slide,
> Salmon-pink wings of the fish-hawk
> > cast grey shadows in water,
> The tower like a one-eyed goose
> > cranes up out of the olive-grove. . . .

The *Cantos* have aroused criticism. They are said to lack form. Perhaps
what they lack is the kind of form with which the literary critic is
familiar. I have suggested they might be better appreciated by measuring
them against musical forms, especially that of the fugue. This also clears
up another difficulty. It was once assumed there were going to be in the
nature of one hundred *Cantos;* Pound had forecast this early in his
career, but later changed his plans and has now well exceeded that number, throwing out the theories of his commentators that when complete
the poem would show a ternary division roughly corresponding to that
of Dante's *Divina Commedia* with a strong build-up to a definite conclusion. If one understands the nature of the fugue one will realize that
Pound's failure to supply the expected in no way diminishes the form of
the existing portion and that the *Cantos* though numerically incomplete

have, nevertheless, always been structurally complete. Ideally a fugue has no point of termination. It could continue its contrapuntal involutions without ever coming to a logical point of rest. Aside from shoving the dynamics and pitch up and down, what brings a fugue to end is no long chain of cadencing fireworks but a simple device which can be executed within as short a space as half a bar—the pedal point. When we have a pedal in a fugue we can be almost sure that the composer is getting tired and intends to stop. Thus, with the *Cantos* at their present state Pound might conclude them in a similarly tidy and economical way by means of a device just as unpretentious.

The fact that actual music does make an appearance in the *Cantos* should surprise no one. In the second of the *Pisan Cantos* Jannequin's celebrated motet *Les Oiseaux* is reproduced in an arrangement for violin. The circumstances should be kept in mind. The scene of the *Pisan Cantos* is Italy at the end of the war. The stench of war has just given way to the arrogance of the victors. Yet through it all comes the clear incisive voice of the poet.

> As a lone ant from a broken ant-hill
> from the wreckage of Europe, ego scriptor.

Then he is joined by another voice, then by many voices. It is the inextinguishable sound of Jannequin's birds. From the word we have been drawn over to music with a movement almost imperceptible.

Then a further slight stir and we are drawn over into the fascinating world of Pound's own music, but that is a story in itself.[19]

---

[19] The original version of this essay includes a discussion of Pound's opera, *The Testament of François Villon*. (W. S.)

Pound's *Homage to Propertius*:
The Structure of a Mask

by J. P. Sullivan

Creative translation is important to Ezra Pound because of the very nature of his poetry. Pound is a profoundly original poet inasmuch as he largely created the poetry of our time, and revolutionized its poetic diction and verse-forms. There are more *perfect* poets, but none responsible for more innovations. And the stress laid by critics on Pound's use of translation is important; his poetry is not to be separated from his translation, for the latter is part of it. This has led R. P. Blackmur, for example, to say that Pound is at his best when he is using what another poet has said to express his own feelings and ideas. But it would be more just to say that Pound often realized that what he wanted to express could *only* be expressed in that particular way.

The *Homage to Sextus Propertius* may be considered as translation, as part of a live tradition of an important art-form. But the *Homage,* like all similar examples of the genre, is also a poem in its own right, and one of the tasks of the critic is to explain why the poem is what it is and not any other thing. To understand the genesis of the *Homage* it is necessary to glance briefly at Pound's poetic theories.

Pound, like T. S. Eliot, sees literature, not as a succession of isolated, self-contained works of art, whose genesis is obscure and whose efficient cause is simple genius, but rather as the result of an interaction between the individual talent and tradition. This is a reaction against the canons of Romantic criticism and a reassertion of much older attitudes. The classic formulation of the view is of course in Eliot's *Tradition and the Individual Talent*:

. . . what happens when a new work of art is created is something that happens simultaneously to all the works of art which preceded it. The

"Pound's *Homage to Propertius:* The Structure of a Mask" by J. P. Sullivan. From *Essays in Criticism*, X (July 1960), 239-249. Copyright © 1960 by *Essays in Criticism*. Revised by J. P. Sullivan for publication in this volume and reprinted by his permission and that of the editor of *Essays in Criticism*.

existing monuments form an ideal order among themselves, which is modified by the introduction of the new (the really new) work of art among them. The existing order is complete before the new work arrives; for order to persist after the supervention of novelty, the *whole* existing order must be, if ever so slightly, altered. . . .[1]

This critical attitude has certain corollaries: great literature is seen as belonging to a vast *musée imaginaire,* which is not a tomb of *objets d'art* preserved out of curiosity but a place where everything worthwhile, when-ever and wherever written, is kept co-present and available for the use of the poet and the appreciation of the cultivated, and where each new addition changes the relations and aspects of all the pieces there. Pound's interest in such a wide range of literature, his critical "tipping" of such a diverse variety of merit, is partly why he has so affected twentieth cen-tury poetry. The influence of Pound on Eliot and Yeats, which enabled them to find their own individual voices, is well known; but less obvious effects are everywhere for the discerning: a poem like Robert Lowell's *The Ghost (After Sextus Propertius)* would have been impossible but for the *Homage.*[2] If Pound's influence on twentieth century poetry had to be summed up it would be that he had taught poets how to use other poets.

This belief in the whole range of literature as the source of poetic material underlies Pound's use of *personae,* masks of his poetic person-ality. The theory behind this has been explained by Pound himself.[3] Pound uses other poets to widen the range and deepen the effects of his own poetic personality. The method allows almost infinite nuances and shades of feeling, of irony and ambiguity, but above all an accuracy and a conciseness of expression for certain things he felt.

Although Pound has tried other ways of writing, he has given us a brief sketch of this poetic development into which the *Homage* fits:

> In the "search for oneself," in the search for "sincere self-expression," one gropes, one finds, for some seeming verity. One says "I am" this, that or the other, and with the words scarcely uttered one ceases to be that thing. . . . I began this search for the real in a book called *Personae,* casting off, as it were complete masks of the self in each poem. I continued in long series of translations, which were but more elaborate masks.[4]

[1] *Selected Essays,* p. 15.
[2] Mr. Eliot himself has kindly given me full information about Pound's deletions in *The Waste Land.* An example of Poundian techniques may be seen in Yeats's *A Thought from Propertius;* for his influence on Robert Lowell's translation of Propertius, see *The Paris Review,* XXV (1961), 80.
[3] A convenient summary of it may be found in Hugh Kenner, *The Poetry of Ezra Pound,* pp. 119-125.
[4] *Gaudier-Brzeska, A Memoir,* p. 98.

And he has fortunately given us a description of the mood, the self, which in 1917 made Propertius his mask; in a letter he said in defence of his poem:

> . . . I may perhaps avoid charges of further mystification and obscurity by saying that it [the *Homage*] presents certain emotions as vital to men faced with the infinite and ineffable imbecility of the British Empire as they were to Propertius some centuries earlier, when faced with the infinite and ineffable imbecility of the Roman Empire. These emotions are given largely, but not entirely, in Propertius' own terms. If the reader does not find relation to life defined in the poem, he may conclude that I have been unsuccessful in my endeavour. . . .[5]

It is hard to imagine now the atmosphere of those days, when the military stupidity of generals was equalled only by the militant stupidity of jingoists, when cultural internationalists like Pound were pressed to betray (in the national interest) values which had no connection with the aims of the warring powers. Pound's state of mind in a milieu which hysterically sentimentalized one of the most idiotic and tragic of human affairs, and which looked to Kipling for a new Tyrtaeus, is more clearly seen in *Mauberley* (in this sense at least *Mauberley* is a popularization of the *Homage*). However, it was the Roman poet who first became the mask through which Pound registered his protest at the monstrous state of society and culture in which he found himself living.

The general implications of this Pound *felt* as strongly as, say, Eliot, but his perception was not so sharp, nor could he realize its implications so broadly (*Mauberley*'s merits are more parochial than those of the *Waste Land*). It was entirely a matter of thinking and feeling, and not simply one of expression. Pound could express anything he felt and his expression of things seen is equally adequate, but neither his visual nor his mental conceptions are in general superlative. Herein lay the importance of Propertius: Pound's literary flair made him see in Propertius a structure from which he could evolve for his own feelings at the time an artistic *credo* and an expression of that creed. It was in the ability to absorb that part of Propertius' work and by means of some novel techniques make the Roman elegist his *persona* that Pound's originality in writing the *Homage* consists. *Mauberley* is a more complex expression of his feelings and it is more intensely charged with emotion, but it is a continuation of the Propertian themes, a clarification of their attitudes—in particular a change from an attitude of resignation and isolation to despair and disgust.

The change did not come entirely from within:

[5] *The Collected Letters of Ezra Pound,* edited by D. D. Paige (1951), pp. 310-311.

> Died some, pro patria,
>   non "dulce" non "et decor" . . .
> walked eye-deep in hell
> believing in old men's lies, then unbelieving
> came home, home to a lie,
> home to many deceits,
> home to old lies and new infamy;
> usury age-old and age-thick
> and liars in public places.

All of this naturally affected Pound's view of Propertius. Once he had seen in Propertius (rightly or wrongly) a kindred spirit, his aim was to enlist him as his mouthpiece. The whole structure and articulation of the *Homage* as a poem depends on Pound's view of Propertius as an *alter ego*.

Propertius for us is a love poet. Pound's choice of the opening of Propertius Book III to begin the *Homage* is therefore a critical one: Section I of the *Homage* discusses the nature of the art of Propertius and the expectations of the artist in a given society. "His true Penelope was Flaubert" is a mere modernization of:

> Shades of Callimachus, Coan ghosts of Philetas
> It is in your grove I would walk. . . .

This is the avowal of the artist's devotion to art and not to public propaganda, even though his audience is thereby limited to "young ladies of indeterminate character" and posterity. *Mauberley* puts it more savagely:

> The age demanded an image
> Of its accelerated grimace . . .
> Not, not certainly, the obscure reveries
> Of the inward gaze . . .

This is also the subject of Sections II and V in a rather different form. In Section II the poet seems about to attempt the very themes he has declared himself unwilling to attempt, but he is recalled from them by Apollo:

> Alba, your kings, and the realm your folk
>   have constructed with such industry
> Shall be yawned out on my lyre—with such industry. . . .
> And Phoebus looking upon me from the Castalian tree,

> Said then "You idiot! What are you doing with that
>   water:
> "Who has ordered a book about heroes? . . ."

Here Propertius himself serves the function of those characters in *Mauberley* such as Brennbaum or Mr. Nixon, who wished to conform to what "the age demanded." But Apollo, Propertius' conception of his own art and limitations, recalls him: like Pound himself or the minor poet Mauberley, Propertius, with the aid of Apollo, here finally makes the great refusal. In Section V he makes another assault on these themes, but the irony and doubt which pervade the first part of his section "If I have not the faculty, 'The bare attempt would be praiseworthy . . .' " is underlined by the juxtaposition of Part 2:

> Yet you ask on what account I write so many love-lyrics . . .
> my ventricles do not palpitate to Caesarial *ore rotundos*.

This stress on the relation of the artist to society, the vindication of private poetic morality against public compulsions, whether these be the demands of a government or promises of fame and fortune, is what Pound saw as the important element in Propertius and this is the critical burden of the *Homage*. It is interesting that Pound's choice of themes to represent Propertius' half-hearted attempts to conform, to write national epic, represents clearly certain elements in Propertius' work which reveal Propertius' own ambivalence towards the Augustan requirements. In the end Propertius made more concessions than did Pound or Mauberley.

Propertius' private themes, the centre of his art, are love, passion, and his mistress Cynthia; this was *his* "cultivation of Pierian roses." Here he differs from Pound in the *Homage*: Pound's prime concern is art and artistic freedom. Pound however offers a selection, reworked in a sophisticated manner, of some of the best of the Propertian love elegies. Although there are important other themes, these largely take up Sections III, VI, XI and part of XII, for the subject Propertius has chosen and vindicated against external grosser claims for his poetic allegiance is his love of Cynthia. Pound's allegiances which his *persona* in *Mauberley* vindicates against the temptations of Mr. Nixon are different, but he is at one with Propertius in the determination to cling to his chosen art. Consequently, although page for page we have more of Propertius' love poetry than his poetic *credo*, the significance of Propertius for Pound (which he clearly brings out in the ordering of the *Homage*) is the latter. It is for this that he serves Pound as a *persona*, not in his capacity as love poet. The two themes are woven together to produce variety, but the choice of theme for the opening and the close of the sequence makes Pound's critical intention clear.

Once the outline of the sequence is stated, one may turn to the subsidiary motifs present in the *Homage*. An attempt is made to define the
society (and thus the societies) from which the protest emerges. The
censor to which Harriet Monroe alluded in her letter to the Editor of
the *English Journal* (XX [1931], 86-87) was not a censor of sexual morals,
but a censor of thought.[6] There is nothing lewd in the *Homage,* but there
are elements which might be regarded as productive of "alarm and
despondency" in the political and cultural climate of the times. Although
in the *Homage* there is nothing like the bitterness and disillusion of
Mauberley, the general philosophy of the poem has much in common
with the later work. The recognition of failure, of the futile end of endeavour, most clearly represented in the person of Mauberley himself,[7]
is also present in the *Homage*. Propertius envisages a vindication by time,
Pound in *Mauberley* only a response in the sensitive reader:

> And I also among the later nephews of this city
> shall have my dog's day. . . .

is to be contrasted with

> . . . the case presents
> No adjunct to the Muses' diadem.

The hopelessness of poetic endeavour and the impossibility of contemporary recognition is brought out clearly in the *Homage*'s concern with
death, which reduces all things to one level:

> One raft on the veiled flood of Acheron.
> Marius and Jugurtha together.
> Nor at my funeral either will there be any long trail,
> bearing ancestral lares and images; . . .
> A small plebeian procession.
> Enough, enough and in plenty
> There will be three books at my obsequies
> Which I take, my not unworthy gift, to Persephone.

Yet even this note, the hope of posthumous recognition, has behind it
the tones of despair:

---

[6] Cf. "What America Has to Live Down," *The New Age,* XXVI (1920), 315: "He
[the intellectual] does not want his papers suppressed. He does not want a censorship
of literature and the arts placed in the hands of the ignorant and fanatics."

[7] See J. J. Espey, *Ezra Pound's* Mauberley, p. 15 ff.

> In vain, you call back the shade,
> In vain, Cynthia. Vain call to unanswering shadow,
> Small talk comes from small bones.

There is a failure implicit, "wrong from the start," which is deepened in *Mauberley*. Yet this is extracted from Propertius not by choosing elements which correspond to Pound's feeling of artistic futility and cultural death—for Propertius although fighting against the contemporary current of literature has a characteristic Roman confidence of his ultimate fame—but by utilizing Propertius' horror of death (which Pound himself does not have) to symbolize the artistic death for which Pound wrote in *Mauberley* the impressive poem—*E.P. Ode pour l'Election de son Sepulchre*. This feeling of horror, most clearly seen in Propertius IV. 7 (*Sunt aliquid Manes*)[8] is used by Pound to express his disgust at the passing of a cultural climate.

So although the bitterness of *Mauberley* is lacking (partly through the limitations of Propertius as a *persona*, partly through the conditions of the time, and partly because Pound could not see into the post-war future), the sequence springs from the same mood as *Mauberley*. Here and there, through the insistence on the claims of art itself, through the confidence of final vindication, a note of disillusioned indifference, almost of emptiness, shows itself. The allegedly important affairs of state are weighed in the balance and found wanting by comparison with a girl:

> And I also will sing war when this matter of a girl is
>   exhausted   (V. 1).

Yet even this subject cannot command full assent.

> Of all these young women
> not one has enquired the cause of the world . . .
> Nor anything else of importance

(XII—it is significant that this last line is an addition of Pound's). But such themes invite frivolity:

> Like a trained and performing tortoise,
> I would make verse in your fashion, if she should
>   command it . . .
> And even this infamy would not attract numerous readers
> Were there an erudite or violent passion,

---

[8] Robert Lowell's sensitive translation conveys the mood of this elegy very well. Lowell's own work of course shows a similar preoccupation with death.

For the nobleness of the populace brooks nothing below
    its own altitude.
One must have resonance, resonance and sonority . . .
    like a goose.

Pound, as always when he is infusing the verse with his deepest convictions, departs radically from the sense of the original. And the final passage of the poem does not alter this pessimism; the end is still a dying fall.

It should be clear then that the *Homage* emerges from and expresses the same attitudes and circumstances as *Mauberley*. It is less complex, of course, and lacks the range of that great poem; but *Mauberley* yields its secrets to the inspection it patently invites. The *Homage* is simpler in conception and feeling, but the local difficulties (which are many) and the constant misunderstanding of its aims as translation and as original poem, have stood in the way of a close study of the individual sections where much of the poetic action takes place. The whole sequence tends even now to be skimmed through for the striking themes, which are more obvious, limited, and repetitious than the subjects of the individual poems in *Mauberley*, which have always received due critical attention. Because of this too easy acceptance by the sympathetic and the too obtuse rejection by hostile critics, Pound felt obliged to call *Mauberley* a "popularization" of the *Homage,* even though it was also a deeper and subtler treatment of the whole subject. It was too easy and too hard for the understanding Pound had hoped for, and it attracted to itself too much irrelevant criticism.

Mauberley and the *Homage* are important documents for insight into Pound and a whole literary generation, indeed it would not be too much to say into a crisis of our time. They express much the same discontent as does *The Waste Land*. The difference between that poem and the two poems under discussions is significant. Pound and Eliot were in different ways immensely concerned for their civilization and its discontents. In Pound the concern is evinced by a care for intelligence, literature, and art and thus for the society from which these emerge. Eliot's temperament and insight, on the other hand, is other-worldly; he is a greater *thinker* (in poetic terms) and is less interested in technique than Pound is. Content and form are not separable and this comment is not to deny Eliot's technical gifts, but to indicate the difference of his poetic interests and his conception of his art. Eliot's diagnosis in *The Waste Land* implies a more universal criticism; it is concerned with spiritual and only then social malaise; art is not mentioned. Eliot's implied remedy is therefore a spiritual one.

This distinction makes it easier to understand Pound's movement further and further towards Fascism and such things as monetary reform.

Pound is not concerned with any deeper spiritual reality; his roots strike only into this world and this society and it is here he wishes reform to begin. The death of art in the modern world is attributable to social causes, to the venal vulgarities of the Arnold Bennetts, to certain classes and conspiracies, and ultimately to a certain form of government which brought about the betrayal, cultural and social, of a civilization.

> All men, in law, are equals.
> Free of Pisistratus,
> We choose a knave or an eunuch
> To rule over us.

In turn of course Pound insisted (*Polite Essays,* p. 164) that when the work of the "damned and despised *literati*" goes bad, "when their very medium, the very essence of their work, the application of word to thing goes rotten . . . the whole machinery of social and individual thought and order goes to pot."

The emphasis on art and intellect, the contempt for "a tawdry cheapness," the anti-democratic bias (not unreminiscent of an attitude to be found in some Latin poets—*Odi profanum vulgus et arceo*) produced, as we know and must deplore, a different personal solution from Eliot's, and the strong contrast between the poems each of them wrote after this period makes this plain. Their different roads led to strangely different places, but their ultimate destinations may be discerned in the earlier poems.

Nevertheless between the *Homage* and *Mauberley* important distinctions may be made. And although *Mauberley* is for me the greater poem, not all of its poetic attitudes are an advance on the *Homage.* There is one way at least in which the *Homage* because of the nature of its source is preferable to *Mauberley* as a criticism of life. The single-minded devotion of Pound to his craft is sometimes reminiscent of the art fancier's attitude to culture. Culture is seen as something *out there.* This externality perhaps springs from certain peculiar American conditions, the divorce of culture from a native tradition and from any solid grounding in the national life. It is the tourist's attitude to art, and it is not without significance that Ezra Pound himself is an American expatriate. One result of this is a simple-minded contrast between the idyllic past and the vulgar present, a mistake which the greater spiritual insight of Eliot did not allow him to make. *The Waste Land* offers a more timeless view of spiritual disease; its diagnosis is made *sub specie aeternitatis.* In *A Game of Chess* all vulgarity, Cleopatra's, Elizabeth's, and the modern lady's, is brought before us. Eliot is here subtler and more perceptive than Pound. Pound idealizes the past in *Mauberley:*

> Conduct, on the other hand, the soul
> "Which the highest cultures have nourished"
> To Fleet St. where
> Dr. Johnson flourished;
>
> Beside this thoroughfare
> The sale of half-hose has
> Long since superseded the cultivation
> Of Pierian Roses.

But Dr. Johnson himself can effectively "place" this idealization (and by implication the idealization of *"the mousseline of Cos"* and *"Sappho's barbitos"*). In *The Vanity of Human Wishes* we are told:

> Mark then what ills the scholar's life assail,
> Toil, envy, want, the patron and the jail.

In the *Homage* Pound is forced, despite himself, to adopt an historical view; the sentimentalization of the past becomes impossible because Propertius *is* the past. It is for this reason perhaps that the *Homage* has found at least one critic who rates it as a poem above *Mauberley*.

Poet of Many Voices

by George P. Elliott

Ezra Pound's poetry is most admired for the beauty of its sound, and anyone who has been able really to hear the poetry must know, in his own ear, why it is so admired. Indeed, it usually sounds so marvelous that the reader is often, as Eliot said, not much interested in what it means. This is a mercy: in most, though not in the best, of his poetry the meaning paraphrases out into one of three sad categories—private jabber, social analytics fluctuating from the obvious through the dubious to the vicious, or archaic platitudes of a Pre-Raphaelite cast. I'll begin by elaborating these three charges in turn.

Despite some lovely music in Canto 90 and a bar or two in Canto 105 ("Charles of the Suevi / a noose of light looped over his shoulder," which is excellent wherever it came from), the incoherence which troubled the *Cantos* from the very beginning back in the early '20's became progressively worse, until by the time *Thrones* was published nearly all the lovely music was so jammed that one could hear little more than the static thrown out by Pound's madness.

> "Should," said H. J., "for humanity's credit
> > feign their existence
> With the sun and moon on her shoulders,
> > the star-discs sewn on her coat
> > at Li Chiang, the snow range,
> > > a wide meadow
> and the ^{2} dto-^{1} mba's face (exorcist's)
> > > muy simpático
> > by the waters of Stone Drum,
> > > the two aces

Exegesis be damned. Those lines neither mean nor are, and the *Cantos* contain hundreds more like them. (Such private references as H. J., i.e.,

"Poet of Many Voices" by George P. Elliott. From *The Carleton Miscellany*, II (Summer 1961), 79-103. Copyright © 1961 by *The Carleton Miscellany*. Revised by George P. Elliott for publication in this volume and reprinted by his permission and that of the editor of *The Carleton Miscellany*.

Henry James, which abound in the *Cantos,* are cause only of obscurity of the parts, but not of incoherence of the whole.) Sane poets speak to themselves too, but in such a way that a reader can get pleasure from sharing in the imagined dialogue. In jabber like the above from Canto 101, it is a question whether Pound got through even to himself.

The most important of his social opinions concern economics and race. It is hard to take his proposed remedies for economic ills seriously, in themselves. His job as a poet was to make us take them seriously as a part of the poem at least, but he does this only in the case of uśury. His economic argument runs: money is the key economic creation of society; its abuse is at the root of the worst social evils; usury is its chief abuse; let us condemn usury. Well and good. But when the reader comes upon the splendid usury passages in the *Cantos,* that Latin *usura* sounds less like a socio-economic concept than like one of the universal human sins which prophets have been scourging men for for 5,000 years. It is Pound's prophetic zeal which makes *usura* important in the poem; there is nothing to make the other historical-economic opinions much more than curious. In the poem, his most important social opinions are on race. These, which derive a half-respectable support from Frobenius' racial theories, vary from the conventional prejudices of his Idaho-Pennsylvania Protestant middle-class upbringing—"whereas the sight of a good nigger is cheering / the bad 'uns wont look you straight" (Canto 79)—to statements of a sort which were being published only surreptitiously by 1948 when Canto 74 was published:

> The yidd is a stimulant, and the goyim are cattle
> in gt/ proportion and go to saleable slaughter
> with the maximum of docility.

The assumption behind this statement is that modern wars are caused by the bankers, who are controlled by international Jewry, that the Jew drives the Christians to slaughter because it is profitable. (Pound also thought Stalin was a pawn of the Jews, somehow.) When this was written, the Auschwitz ovens were scarcely cool.

Pound's earlier poems and much of the first 60 Cantos say something which can be understood, and understood without offense. Unfortunately one has usually heard it before a good many times, either from medieval literature or prettied up by the Victorian Romantics (whom Pound mostly scorns in his criticism but whose themes many of his themes resemble). Still, a poem which sounds marvelous and means something unexceptional is obviously preferable to one that sounds as good and means practically nothing or means something obnoxious. "Alba, from 'Langue d'Oc' " is absolutely pure of sound.

When the nightingale to his mate
Sings day-long and night late
My love and I keep state
In bower,
In flower,
Till the watchman on the tower
Cry:
    "Up! Thou rascal, Rise,
    I see the white
        Light
        And the night
           flies."

MAKE IT NEW! Pound is always shouting, but surely the idea, situation, sentiment in "Alba" is as venerable as *carpe diem,* nor is it newly adorned, nor, 300 years before, would the sound-patterning have astonished Thomas Campion a tenth as much as it would have delighted him. Reading a lot of Pound's verse generates the attitude that meaning doesn't much matter in poetry, lovely sound is enough. At such a pass, it is well to refer out from time to time to other and richer poetry, and so keep proportion; after a solid week of *Cantos* it is wise to turn back to "The Second Coming," say, for perspective. Read and reread "Alba" till you're swaying to it, but then turn to this poem of about the same size, a song by Josephine Miles, which is not only metrically masterful but says something hard to say, unparaphrasable, and her own—"new."

In friendship feeling quiet
I spent a time asleep,
And when I woke, the marrow
Out of my bones ran out
That you were the friend I dreamt for
But not the dream I woke for.
And so I put this down for
Doubt. For doubt.

Or, if it's unfair to compare "Alba" to a poem which means a good deal worth meaning, there's always "Full Fathom Five." It is about the same length and doesn't seem to mean much, but it has such magical and strange images that you can't *just* listen to it as you often can to Pound.

At this point let us admire the music of his poetry. I am also going to suggest that there is no such thing as the music of poetry.

At patterning verbal sounds, at metrics, Pound is one of the technical masters. It was not just out of courtesy or false humility that Eliot called him *il miglior fabbro,* the better craftsman, better at the carpentry and counterpoint of verse. (The phrase is applied by Guido Guinicelli to Arnaut Daniel in Canto XXVI of the *Purgatorio*. In life they were both excellent minor poets.) The special merits of Pound's craft, as of Spenser's, are more likely to be appreciated by other poets than by readers at large; this was especially true back in the wan Georgian days of the 1910's when he first made his mark. Eliot's praise is attributable not just to friendship and the gratitude of pupil to teacher but also to a genuine admiration for Pound's virtuosity. Pound's reputation will wane no doubt as Eliot's influence wanes, but I imagine that for a long time to come poets will be discovering Pound anew, swooning in the loveliness of his music, attending the meters of this master craftsman as they once listened to Spenser's.

> Compleynt, compleynt I hearde upon a day,
> Artemis singing, Artemis, Artemis
> Agaynst Pity lifted her wail:
> Pity causeth the forests to fail,
> Pity slayeth my nymphs,
> Pity spareth so many an evil thing.
> Pity befouleth April,
> Pity is the root and the spring.
> Now if no fayre creature followeth me
> It is on account of Pity,
> It is on account that Pity forbideth them slaye.
> All things are made foul in this season,
> This is the reason, none may seek purity
> Having for foulnesse pity
> And things grown awry;
> No more do my shaftes fly
> To slay. Nothing is now clean slayne
> But rotteth away.

The control of line in this passage from Canto 30 is perfect—both the modulations in length, from the conventional iambic pentameter with which it opens to the two-, three-, and four- as well as five-stress lines with which it continues, and also the line-endings, some on an iamb, some on a trochee, a few with most delicate spondees. Pound's prosody has not been adequately described. (Not that the prosody of many good poets in English has been adequately described. Has Bridges on Milton any peer?) But fortunately for Pound, his verse, being irregular, "free," resists even the inadequate description of schoolbook prosodozing [sic], which, by explaining so simply that it looks clear what is in fact a mystery of complexity, does more harm than good; and until his practice has been rationalized, even the initiate will have to keep on repeating with reverent perplexity: "What an ear." Meanwhile, the lines quoted above—and they mean something too, something harsh and worth hearing—should raise the hairs on any poetry reader's head.

Pater said, and Pound heeded, "All art constantly aspires towards the condition of music." Even if one accepts the gospel of art according to Walter, surely taking that saying literally is as absurd as the Jehovah's Witnesses' taking literally, "The meek shall inherit the earth." But Pound was a sort of fundamentalist in the religion of art: instead of speculating on, say, how realistic fiction and the cinema can be said to move towards the condition of music, and what "the condition of music" means anyhow, Pound set about writing lyrics which could be set to music and poems long or short which have as many of the qualities of music as he could devise. Yet there is surely a radical difference between the sound patterns of the words of even the most "musical" of lyrics and its actual musical accompaniment. "The music of poetry" remains intractably a metaphor, despite the fact that sound-patterning is of the essence of poetry as it is the essence of music. Poetry like music is composed of sound and structure; but, being made with words, both-ways-looking words, poetry unlike music is also composed of sense. Whatever "the condition of music" may be, meaningful words can aspire to it only as paint on canvas does, metaphorically. Take the last published Canto, 109: even if you have the languages, the erudition in Poundiana, and the patience to discover that it sounds fine, still it does not make enough coherent sense to be called poetry, and at the same time it too inescapably not-makes sense to be called music. It is a form of muttering, of muttery humming, with snarls.

Still, if his poetry sounds that good, and if the sense it makes is often inoffensive and sometimes good, then why is he so actively resisted?

An immediate reason that many people do not listen to Pound is resistance to high pressure from three chief sources: Pound's prose, his cultists, and T. S. Eliot. His prose, which not infrequently deals with ideas, events, persons, phrases that appear in his poetry, can turn you against these by its very techniques. After the mid 1920's, when the poetic rebellion had been accomplished, he gave up the exercise of power in the acceptable form of influencing poets and editors and turned to the writing of prose propaganda. He became a sort of highbrow literary Westbrook Pegler.

WHAT is the USE OF LANGUAGE? WHY STUDY LITERATURE?
LANGUAGE was obviously created, and is, obviously, USED for communication.

"Literature is news that STAYS news."

The best smith, as Dante called **Arnaut Daniel**, made the birds sing IN HIS WORDS; I don't mean that he merely referred to birds singing—

(from *The ABC of Reading*)

He so attacks and belabors the reader—bad poetry—America—England—the Jews—the bankers—Tennyson—anyone who doesn't think Confucius supplies *the* answer to social ills—U. S. publishers for not printing Martin Van Buren's autobiography until 1920—Milton—that before long the reader's resistance to that sheer propaganda extends to the poetry. The next source of pressure is from the E. P. cult, whose priests cannot be borne even when they are as erudite and intelligent as Hugh Kenner. In his book *The Poetry of Ezra Pound,* he sets out to justify, in the most arrogant tone, Pound's ways to man.

> Anyone can feel the play of silent cryptic finality in a Chinese ideogram, against adjacent fluidity or muddle or struggle after a word, without knowing what the ideogram means.

> Even when we can't read them [irreducible formulations such as "brododaktulos Eos"], their very inscrutability performs half their poetic function.

The trouble with statements like these two is not their intrinsic silliness, though this is indeed superb, but that they derive from a sustained determination to admit no weakness and to turn every fault into a virtue, which abuse of the intellect may not be tolerated. The prime source of irrational opposition to Pound's poetry has been T. S. Eliot himself, who abused his powers in the case of Pound, as in no other, by overinsistence. Eliot wrote in 1928 that Pound's "epistolary style is masterly"; you read Pound's letters and find they are quite fascinating, but if their style is masterly what just epithet is left for that of Rilke's letters? Proust's? Van Gogh's? Eliot insists that Pound is a great critic; you read Eliot's selection of Pound's literary essays, as well as *The Spirit of Romance.* It is true that studded through them there are brilliant illuminations; but it is also true that not one essay is a successful work of art in itself and that there is not a sufficient coherence among the ideas of the essays to make his criticism at all comparable in excellence to Eliot's own—this despite the fact that Pound planted a lot, perhaps most, of the ideas Eliot matured. The episode epitomizing Eliot's overpowering dictation in Pound matters is the famous Bollingen award in 1949. It is hard to imagine ten or twelve American literary gentiles, respectable enough to get appointed to a Library of Congress committee, who could—*could*—in the same room with T. S. Eliot have opposed his nomination of Ezra Pound.

Pound's been oversold. In his reputation, as in most things, he inspires superlatives, his detractors being no less intemperate than his cultists. A moderate opinion of Pound's poetry will be attacked from both sides. My contention is that a brief collection of his best early lyrics and of autonomous lyrical passages from the *Cantos*—New Directions' *Selected Poems of Ezra Pound* is an excellent compilation—encompasses all his durable poetry and that this poetry, viewed quite apart from the poet's historical importance, is exquisite and technically masterful, but slight in its impact.

"I scarcely know what to say of Pound's ear. Fifteen years of listening have not taught me that it is inferior to the ear of the author of *Twelfth Night*." So wrote John Berryman in *Partisan Review* for April 1949, making the biggest claim. Then he goes on to say of poets: "We write with our ears." It takes a man of brilliance and passion to push a figure of speech until it becomes wrong enough to illuminate the truth. *The Poet's Tongue* is the name Auden gave his first (and liveliest) anthology. Tongue is a metonym for speaking, ear for listening; and the poet is sayer not hearer. "We read with our ears, we write with our tongues"—that's as far as the trope will stretch.

Let the ear stand for the hearing. Let the tongue stand for the speaking. Let the voice stand for the person of the speaker and hearer. Greatness in poetry implies, above all, power, range, and steadiness of voice, and when Pound's voice possesses any of these qualities it is not his own. In any case, "great" and "major" are terms that ought to be used with discretion. Even if "major" is extended far enough to include Yeats, it cannot reach to Pound, who—hyperbolically speaking—scarcely knows as poet whose voice to call his own.

In his poetry there are audible the voices of quite literally scores of other writers of many and diverse ages and schools: in translation, adaptation, allusion, quotation, parody, imitation, borrowing, reference, by every conceivable literary device. One of the small interests in reading him is trying to define him by identifying those whom he is like: Swinburne, Browning, Byron, Waller, Josh Billings, hate-sheet hacks, Spenser, James, Whitman, Yeats, a dozen Ph.D's worth in foreign languages alone. Usually it helps define a poet to compare him to another: "Roethke's later work is like Yeats" implies a strong sense of who Roethke the poet is. But a strange thing happens with Pound: the more poets he is like, the less one is sure who Pound is. It becomes their voices as much as his that one hears: It is as though Pound were a medium most of the time, his head full of spirit voices, many of them exceedingly powerful and lovely, a few of them dull, some hideous; it is as though he were a verbal mimic hearing the words of his saying as he says them. Pound did not assume many voices, as Browning did or as any dramatist must, for strategic reasons but because he was arrogant and hollow. Eliot said of Pound that his hell was only for others; he neither supposed himself as being in hell nor hell as being in himself. Very arrogant and very hollow.

Consider a number of his best-known poems. In these famous lines, which he wrote while a prisoner, he preaches on a text from Ecclesiastes.

> "Master thyself, then others shall thee beare"
>> Pull down thy vanity
> Thou art a beaten dog beneath the hail,
> A swollen magpie in a fitful sun,
> Half black half white
> Nor knowst'ou wing from tail
> Pull down thy vanity
>> How mean thy hates
> Fostered in falsity,
>> Pull down thy vanity,
> Rathe to destroy, niggard in charity,
> Pull down thy vanity,
>> I say pull down.

I have heard a preacher in the Upper Lake Community Church in California who could work that handsome passage into his sermon any Sunday in Lent—except for "thee," "thy," " 'ou," "rathe," and "niggard"—and nobody in his congregation would turn a hair. Both he and they would assume that he would be speaking not in his own person but as a prophet of God's will. However, read with reference to Pound, it seems to work out this way: either it is the moral Pound chiding himself for his own vanity (and there is almost nothing else of this nature in his writings) or else it is Ezra in a prophet's mask commanding us who have imprisoned him to pull down our vanity for no better reason than that he says to (and surely his moral authority just after the war was hollow); at the most, forgetting who wrote the passage, it is the voice of a prophet without authority chiding all mankind, himself included, in large general terms. In "The River Merchant's Wife," an early poem celebrated for its poignance and the perfection of its delicacy, Pound assumed a young Chinese woman's voice, or rather, he assumed it in imitation of the way it had already been imagined in the eighth century by Rihaku (the Japanese name for Li Po). In most of the Mauberley poems he assumes the voice of a persona so closely parodying his own that the first poem of the sequence bears the title "E. P. Ode . . ." Admirable as most of these poems are, they invite comparison in form, tone, and theme with the satires, also in quatrains, which Eliot was writing at about the same time. Pound's meters are subtler, but surely Eliot's, in "The Hippopotamus" and "Sweeney Among the Nightingales" are stronger; in those two, Eliot's meaning is more available, his images more striking, and his ideas no less important. One can speak of *Hugh Selwyn Mauberley* as a single poem portraying a minor literary man ironically rendered; well enough; but the matter is excessively literary and recondite, and the image projected is neither as substantial nor as coherent as that of another unimportant, weak man, J. Alfred Prufrock. The masterpiece of the sequence and by general consent the little masterpiece of his short poems, is "Envoi."

> Go, dumb-born book
> Tell her that sang me once that song of Lawes:
> Hadst thou but song
> As thou hast subjects known,
> Then were there cause in thee that should condone
> Even my faults that heavy upon me lie,
> And build her glories their longevity.

It is the truest poetry: it makes comparisons odious. And this despite the almost incredible fact that to achieve this pure, small perfection, Pound assumed another man's voice—

> Goe lovely Rose
> Tell her that wastes her time and me,
> That now she knowes,
> When I resemble her to thee,
> How sweet and fair she seems to be—

and then sang in that voice better than Waller himself did. Pound knew better than Eliot how to hew *The Waste Land* out of a double bulk of Eliot's verses. The formula by which Yeats chose to praise one of Pound's poems, "The Return," was this: "It gives me better words than my own." The poet of many voices.

So here we are looking at the poet himself.

Most of those who are convinced of Pound's greatness say it is embodied in the *Cantos*. Let us look at them. The question raised by the *Cantos* is: What holds them together? It is a question asked by all who read the poem; it was asked by Yeats, whom Pound told to wait for Canto 100, when the *Cantos* would "display a structure like that of a Bach Fugue"; it has even been asked by Eliot. The cohesive force is not a narrative; it is not chronology or logical discourse; it is not steadiness of theme nor even consistency of verse form. If there is a quality which a long poem like any other work of art must possess to be called great, that quality is coherence. At every moment in the *Iliad*, whatever clear detail Homer may be directing your attention to, you are aware of a grand, realizable structure into which this detail, good or not so good in itself, belongs. Your secure awareness of this structure provides a kind of solidity of response which frees you, as life seldom leaves you free, to contemplate those ultimate matters with which the poem concerns itself, and such solidity is impossible in a poem which diverts attention to itself by the radical doubt, "Are these parts held together well enough?"

The aesthetic version of the question is: Do the *Cantos* have a true structure? Can the reader explain—no, that's too much: can he securely feel that in the *Cantos* there is a stable, rational structure such as the highest excellence always builds and is always built upon? I think not; at least, I am not able rationally to grasp that order either from studying the poem or any of the exegeses of it—a disability I share with all those with whom I have discussed the matter, including some whose critical assent only a madman would spurn. The justifiers, of whom Kenner is the most elaborate, assert that there is such a structure but that it is so novel as to elude or antagonize most contemporary readers, although, in time and with help, future readers will come to accept and appreciate it. This argument is too considerable to ignore.

First of all, one must agree that such a state of things is possible; there is precedent for it. Along the way, one must agree with Kenner that the antagonism toward Pound for his obscurity and private reference is no more legitimate than is such antagonism towards Dante, and that what he calls, after Eliot, "the poetry of surface" is indeed more difficult than the poetry of emotional depth. A willing reader can put up with a lot he does not understand and will consent to a good many footnotes, so long as he can feel—not can talk about intellectually but can feel—that the poem has a structure that gives meaning even to the parts of which he is ignorant. Kenner, agreeing, devotes his energies to persuading you that the *Cantos* do have such a structure, the main principle of which seems to be "the rhythms of recurrence." It is not only a host of subjects, public and private, which recur, but also contrasting sets of imagery, for example those of mud and light. These sub-elements are composed into "ideograms" or "vortices," which, according to Kenner, are the structural units of the poem. Such a unit "is not unlike the Joycean epiphany: a highly concentrated manifestation of a moral, cultural, or political quiddity." Granted that this statement means something, the recurrence of such elements cannot be called a structure. Recurrence regular enough to be called rhythmic (I fail to perceive any such regularity as Kenner suggests is there) could no doubt provide a sort of large "swaying" to the poem which would help hold it together. But behind recurrence there is the fundamental question: why the recurrence? Anybody can concoct ten dozen disparate themes, subjects, image-types, rhythms, attitudes, cultural quiddities, and keep popping them up one and another in patterns of varying complication and banality. This is merely technique; anyone who studied Kenner hard enough could do it. If the recurrences and juxtapositions of the *Cantos* are there for their own sake, the poem is elaborately trivial. Kenner fails to make clear what structurally valuable end these recurrences serve.

The last-ditch argument is that the *Cantos* are unified by the personality of their creator. Put in such a form as this, the argument cannot be flatly dismissed: "Because Pound is a master prosodist, is very learned, and is passionately concerned for the welfare of society, literature, and culture, he is permitted to write about anything whatever in any order he pleases. The *Cantos* are great because they express Pound." Roughly similar justifications could be presented for calling the assembled writings of Montaigne and Yeats great: they express great selves. A tenable position. Now suppose one were to grant of Pound that he was capable of insight as honest as Montaigne's or as deep as Yeats's, or that he possessed any autobiographic quality of comparable magnitude, yet the persona projected in his work must be, like theirs, coherent if the *Cantos* are to prove his greatness as a poet. If their unity is to derive from the person of their creator (and where else is one to look for it?), then we necessarily find ourselves contemplating Pound himself. That self is not integrated. The *Cantos* fall into bits because Pound is radically incoherent—not only the man-in-history certified insane, but also the maker as you come to know him by reading that large, occasionally splendid, disintegrating bundle of poetry and mutter.

Pound, Whitman, and the American Epic

by Roy Harvey Pearce

The place of the *Cantos* of Ezra Pound in the history of American aspirations toward an epic is established, of course, primarily because it is the kind of poem it is. But it is further established through the relationship which Pound has gradually discovered between himself and Whitman. In 1909 Pound said of Whitman:

"He *is* America. . . . He is disgusting. He is an exceedingly nauseating pill, but he accomplishes his mission. . . . He is a genius because he has a vision of what he is and of his function. . . . I am (in common with every educated man) an heir of the ages and I demand my birth-right. Yet if Whitman represented his time in language acceptable to one accustomed to my standard of intellectual-artistic living he would belie his time and nation. And yet I am but one of his ' "ages and ages" encrustations' or to be exact an encrustation of the next age. The vital part of my message, taken from the sap and fibre of America, is the same as his.

"Mentally I am a Walt Whitman who has learned to wear a collar and a dress shirt (although at times inimical to both)."

He put the matter more bluntly in *Patria Mia,* written sometime before 1913: "Whitman goes bail for the nation." As Pound's own views on poetry and poetics developed, he came to be even more critical of Whitman, even though he could write in 1913:

> I make a truce ["pact" in later editions] with you, Walt
>   Whitman—
> I have detested you long enough.
> I come to you as a grown child
> Who has had a pig-headed father;
> I am old enough now to make friends.
> It was you that broke the new wood,
> Now is a time for carving.

We have one sap and one root—
Let there be commerce between us.

By 1934 (in his *ABC of Reading*) Pound could accept Whitman by
splitting his meaning off from his manner: "Whitman's faults are superficial, he does convey an image of his time, he has written histoire morale,
as Montaigne wrote the history of his epoch. You can learn more of
19th century America from Whitman than from any of the writers who
either refrained from perceiving, or limited their record to what they had
been taught to consider suitable literary expression. The only way to
enjoy Whitman thoroughly is to concentrate on his fundamental meaning."

The latest evidence for the history of the truce/pact comes in Canto
82. Here Pound, at this point his own protagonist, writes out of the
murky depths of his prison camp experience:

> and the news is a long time moving
> a long time in arriving
>   thru the impenetrable
> crystalline, indestructable
>   ignorance of locality
> The news was quicker in Troy's time
> a match on Cnidos, a glow worm on Mitylene,
>   Till forty years since, Reithmuller indignant:
> "Fvy! in Tdaenmarck efen dh' beasantz gnow him,"
>   meaning Whitman, exotic, still suspect
>   four miles from Camden
>   "O troubled reflection
>   "O Throat, O throbbing heart"
> How drawn, O GEA TERRA,
>   what draws as thou drawest
>   till one sink into thee by an arm's width
>   embracing thee. Drawest,
>   truly thou drawest.
>   Wisdom lies next thee,
>   simply, past metaphor.
> Where I lie let the thyme rise
>   and basilicum
>   let the herbs rise in April abundant
> By Ferrara was buried naked, fu Nicolo
>   e di qua di la del Po,
> wind: 'ἐμὸν τὸν ἄνδρα
> lie into earth to the breast bone, to the left shoulder
>   Kipling suspected it

to the height of ten inches or over
man, earth : two halves of the tally
but I will come out of this knowing no one
neither they me
     connubium terrae ἔφατα πόσις ἐμός
            ΧΘΟΝΙΟΣ, mysterium

fluid ΧΘΟΝΟΣ o'erflowed me
 lay in the fluid ΧΘΟΝΟΣ;
   that lie
under the air's solidity
  drunk with ἸΧΩΡ of ΧΘΟΝΙΟΣ
    fluid ΧΘΟΝΟΣ, strong as the undertow
   of the wave receding
but that a man should live in that further terror, and live
 the loneliness of death came upon me
  (at 3 P.M., for an instant)   δακρύων
               ἐντεῦθεν

three solemn half notes
    their white downy chests black-rimmed
on the middle wire
    periplum

  The drift of the passage is clear enough, although even with the help of the Pound exegetes, all of its details cannot be resolved into the whole. The details consolidate ideogrammatically, as Pound would have it, into what he calls in the last line a "periplum"—his form of "periplus," a sea-journey into meaning, of which this is one of the stopping-points. The "news" here is knowledge in particular (Pound has been speaking of the impossibility of deciding whether or not a war is righteous) and in general. Then: "ignorance of locality" enforces a realization that men do not know themselves in terms of the very places which give them their culture. Pound first recalls Troy, where things were different, then "Out of the Cradle . . ."—the latter through a recollection of his instructor in German "forty years since," at the University of Pennsylvania, Richard Henry Riethmuller, who published in 1906 a study called *Walt Whitman and the Germans*. Riethmuller (Pound—forgetfully—transposes the initial vowels) is thus not necessarily just one of many Europeans interested in Whitman, as he has been taken to be. Recalling Riethmuller's (classroom?) statement, Pound fixes upon an image of a Whitman isolated by his genius from the very people to whom he addressed himself and his work; here Pound quotes directly from "Out of the Cradle. . . ." In the paean to Gea Terra which follows, he certainly echoes and imitates the same poem. He has properly identified Whitman's situation as poet with that of the protagonist in "Out of the Cradle. . . ." There is then a

passage on the burial (an earth-rite) of Nicolo d'Este in 1441—Nicolo
being one of the number of culture-creating Renaissance Italian figures
whom Pound places at the center of his understanding of history and
whose importance he indicates in the second line in Italian: "and on this
side and the other side of the Po." The significance of the Kipling line
has so far not yielded to exegesis, but what precedes it is clear enough:
Greek for "my man," a phrase from Theocritus II, which Pound quotes
more amply in Canto 81. Theocritus' poem is an incantation addressed to
the Moon Goddess by a woman who fears that her lover has turned to
someone new; we recall that the bird whose mate has disappeared likewise
addresses the moon; and we conclude that Pound would relate the inten-
tions of Whitman and Theocritus, so characteristically to get a double
perspective on his own situation. Then: "man, earth: two halves of the
tally" is a straightforward summation; and "tally" of course is Whitman's
word for a ritualistic summing-up. In the two lines which immediately
follow, Pound puts himself in Whitman's place: perhaps ironically, since
Whitman certainly thought that *he* knew and was known. The twelve
lines that follow these two ("connubium terrae . . . for an instant") offer
a precise account of death, burial, union with Gea Terra, and their meaning. The Greek "ἔφατα πόσις ἐμός offers some difficulty. It seems likely
that "ἔφατα" (usually elided to "ἔφατ' ") is a mistake for "ἔφατο"; and it
has been suggested that the source is at once Homer and Aeschylus, and
that the passage, which means "She said, 'My husband . . . ,' " recalls
Clytemnestra speaking about the Agamemnon whom she has killed; so
that it reinforces the whole possible meaning of that "connubium terrae"
on which the passage centers. The Greek which follows (forms of "earth")
makes insistent the ultimately earthly nature of the poet, who is even
"drunk with the earth's ichor," as strong in its pull as (in a Whitmanian
echo) "the undertow of the wave receding." This last seems to be Pound's
attempt to establish the earth as a force akin to the sea whose waves laved
softly all over the protagonist of "Out of the Cradle. . . ." This is
enough, he says, and all that man should bear, the primary "mysterium"
of locality. But beyond this there is a further (man-made?) terror (and
Pound pinpoints—3 p.m.—the moment of realization, to fix it in our
minds) of loneliness and isolation. The last two words in Greek mean
"weeping" and "thereupon"; and, placed upon the page so as to work as
stage-directions, they force our attention upon the song of the three birds
alight, like the notes on a staff, upon a wire. The shape of the notes (white
outlined by a circle) as we picture them, gives them a precisely ideogrammic function; they call to mind not only the birds in a similar passage
which immediately precedes this one in Canto 82, but also the birds
(two, but Whitman, participating in their agony, made them three) of
"Out of the Cradle. . . ." Even the technique here has its analogy to
Whitman's in "Out of the Cradle. . . ." For even as the place and his

recollections define Pound's situation and its meaning, so the Sea itself finally whispered (not whispered to) Whitman. Then: Periplum—it is finished; it is there once and for all. Pound is entirely himself, true enough; but the spirit and work of Whitman here are the crucial means whereby he would be (that is to say, for him, define) himself. This is an aspect of his drive toward CH'ING MING: Only call things by their right name, and they will exist for you and you will exist in them. We may note too how close Whitman's "vivification," cited above, is to Pound's "Make it new." And we may guess that it is more than coincidental that, even as Whitman (in *A Backward Glance* . . .) calls *Leaves of Grass* his "definitive *carte visite* to the coming generations of the New World," Pound has taken it upon himself to explain his life-work to an Italian audience in a pamphlet (published in 1942) he calls "Carta da Visita."

So the poet, in what he says have been his purgatorial years, makes the fullest (some would say, most arrogant) truce with Whitman, one of identification. Declaring that Whitman failed in everything except his aspirations, Pound would begin again and make a poem, a modern epic, which does what Whitman's really could not do. He would, as he has repeatedly insisted, write the kind of poem which would make of his reader a whole man, absolutely at home in his world. He wrote in an essay in *Poetry*, in February 1915: "Whitman is the best of it [American poetry], but he never pretended to have reached the goal. He knew himself, and proclaimed himself 'a start in the right direction.' He never said, 'American poetry is to stay where I left it'; he said it was to go on from where he started it."

Pound was one of those who would carry American poetry forward. He asked John Crowe Ransom in a letter of 1938: ". . . are you ready for a revival of American culture considering it as something specifically grown from the nucleus of the American Founders, present in the Adams, Jefferson correspondence; not limited to belles lettres and American or colonial imitation of European literary models, but active in all departments of thought, and tackling the problems which give life to epos and Elizabethan plays, without rendering either Homer or Bard of Avon dry doctrinaires?"

By this time, as references in the letter show, the *Cantos* were well started. The form and technique Pound evolved for them was indeed something new. But the driving force behind the *Cantos* is evident from the earliest stages of Pound's career. Thus in 1912 he had written to Harriet Monroe: "Any agonizing that tends to hurry what I believe in the end to be inevitable, our American Risorgimento, is dear to me. That awakening will make the Italian Renaissance look like a tempest in a teapot! The force we have, and the impulse, but the guiding sense, the discrimination in applying the force, we must wait and strive for."

The force was clearly Whitmanian. Pound accepted that fact then and has come to accept it again. In one of the later, "paradise" Cantos, 92, he writes, "Le Paradis n'est pas artificiel / but is jagged"—a motif repeated in Canto 93—and seems to be counterpointing a line from Baudelaire ("Le Paradis . . ."), already used in Cantos 74, 76, 77, and 93, with a pair of lines from the "paradise" phase of *Song of Myself,* in Section 52: "I depart as air, I shake my white locks at the runaway sun, / I effuse my flesh in eddies, and drift it in lacy jags." The guiding sense, the discrimination—his own unique contribution—he has ever since been trying to realize.

The principle of form and technique in the *Cantos* is so deliberately opposed to that in Whitman's poetry that the one is vitalized by the other, if only by virtue of a certain resistance. The opposition is between a poet who would infuse his world with a sense of self and then, and only then, accept it, and a poet who would infuse his self with a sense of his world. Where Whitman would include, Pound would discriminate. Where Whitman would energize so as to define, Pound would define so as to energize. *Song of Myself* is phased according to the movement of a creative, expressive sensibility; the *Cantos* are constellated according to the ordering of a precision-grinding, exacting sensibility. In Whitman it is too often impossible to distinguish expression from mere response; in Pound, expression from mere observation. The crux of the opposition lies in two conceptions of style. WHITMAN: "The greatest poet has less a marked style and is more the channel of thoughts and things without increase or diminution, and is the free channel of himself. He swears to his art, I will not be meddlesome, I will not have in my writing any elegance or effect or originality to hang in the way between me and the rest like curtains . . . [the elision is mine.] You shall stand by my side and look in the mirror with me." (Preface to *Leaves of Grass,* 1855) POUND: "STYLE, the attainment of a style consists in so knowing words that one will communicate the various parts of what one says with the various degrees and weights of importance which one wishes." (*Guide to Kulchur,* 1938)

It is, in essence, a matter of self-expression and decorum at all costs. Pound's belief in decorum ("knowing words") of this sort is at bottom the belief which would make possible his kind of epic: one in which degrees and weights would be so finely managed that communication (once the degrees and weights can be precisely measured and taken into account, a task for countless exegetes to come) would be exact and exacting knowledge. The end—its fusion of the artistic and the social and moral object—of the Poundian epic would be such knowledge: the new Paideuma which would, again, make the new man. Like Whitman, Pound would create, not confirm, the hero of his epic.

Here Pound's understanding of culture itself is all-important; for it gives his version of the American epic a substantiality which, despite its continual naming and cataloguing, Whitman's lacks. (By the same token, the substantiality of the *Cantos* is such as to drive out of it any properly controlling subjectivity—Pound's doctrine of multivalent, shifting *personae* to the contrary notwithstanding.) Pound's briefest and most adequate definition of culture is this one, from his *Guide to Kulchur:* "THE CULTURE OF AN AGE is what you can pick up and/or get in touch with, by talk [Pound seems in the *Cantos* to have transformed his reading into talking] with the most intelligent men of the period."

"Pick up and/or get in touch with"—much of the poetics which informs the *Cantos* derives from this notion. Allen Tate's pronouncement that the *Cantos* "are not about anything" is true, because the relationship is reversed: Pound tries to make them into the substantial center of culture, his Paideuma; everything—at least everything worthwhile—is about the *Cantos*.[1] He would make them into a convenient crossroads of the universe where everything (of importance to him, to be sure) is revealed and illumined in its total relatedness. It follows that the poet's great gift is to perceive, select, assemble, judge, evoke, refresh, make new. By Pound's time, the Whitmanian mode had spent its force—on the one hand in the *reductio ad absurdum* foolishnesses of the Fellowship, on the other hand in the maunderings of the imitators (which Pound so wonderfully parodied in *The Spirit of Romance* [1910]: "Lo, behold, I eat water melons . . ."). The sad end of such Whitmanianism, as Pound pointed out, marked the end of a great era in the history of the American imagination. In setting himself in opposition to outworn, because too directly imitative, Whitmanian modes of conception and expression, Pound was indeed taking up Whitman's burden. He too would go bail for the nation. But, even as Whitman, he could not carry the whole burden, and thus could not go the whole bail.

Halfway through Canto 85, in the midst of a passage of broken musings on the failure of the "understanding" in the nineteenth century, appear these sharply cadenced lines:

> No classics,
>> no American history,
>>> no centre, no general root,
> No *prezzo giusto* as core.

[1] On "Paideuma," see *Guide to Kulchur* (New York, 1938), p. 58: "When I said I wanted a new civilisation, I think I cd. have used Frobenius' term. . . . At any rate for my own use and for the duration of this treatise I shall use Paideuma for the gristly roots of ideas that are in action." See also Frobenius' *Das Paideuma, Erlebte Erdteile*, IV (Frankfurt, 1925); and Guy Davenport, "Pound and Frobenius," *Motive and Method in* The Cantos, ed. L. Leary (New York, 1953), pp. 33-59.

The *Cantos* are an attempt to remedy this radical defect. ("UBI JUS VAGUM," Pound writes in the line following the four quoted.) They supply, however, not a single center but a series—a constellation of exemplars of *prezzo giusto* and its contraries by means of which the center and the reader who will seek it may be defined. The *Cantos* consist of a complex of centers, the perception of which is ordered by the absolutely decorous management of "degrees and weights of importance." (I speak here as much of what the *Cantos* are intended to do as what they *do* do. No one, so far as I know, has yet reported on a mastery of them adequate enough to guarantee his interpretation of their substance and their theory.) In effect, they evoke not a single sensibility (writer-reader) which will make itself one with its world, but rather a group of sensibilities which will be the means whereby one sensibility (the writer) will teach another sensibility (the reader) how it may relate itself to its world and so know and control its destiny. What should emerge from the *Cantos* is a sense of propaedeutic control; the assemblage of centers that is the poem is, for Pound, the only proper Paideuma. It constitutes a rediscovery, a making new, of what are for Pound the noblest, truest, and surest elements in culture, a rediscovery so powerful in its stylistic precision that it will irresistibly reconstitute the sensibility, and thus the political morality,[2] of him who would give himself over to reading it—someone akin to the "cosmic man" whom Wyndham Lewis envisaged for America at the end of the forties. It is a brief but all comprehending encyclopedia which walks and talks like a man. "There is no mystery about the Cantos," Pound wrote in his *Guide to Kulchur,* ". . . they are the tale of the tribe—give Rudyard credit for his use of the phrase. No one has claimed that the Malatesta Cantos are obscure. They are openly volitionist, establishing, I think clearly, the effect of the factive [this would appear to be Pound's neologism for "fictive" and "factitive"] personality, Sigismundo, an entire man." In Pound's hands, the new tale of the tribe, the new epic, becomes openly volitionist and entirely factive—willing and making, through its collocation of centers (Sigismundo Malatesta, his corruption glossed over, is one such), a new Paideuma for a new world.

Defining even the gross structure of the *Cantos* is as difficult as defining the gross structure of *Song of Myself,* and for analogous reasons. This also is a poem which contrives rather than memorializes its hero—or rather, its series of heroes. They are persons whose sheer volitional and

---

[2] The relation between art and political-economic morality is made explicit in the well-known passage from Canto 45:

> with usura the line [of the painter] grows thick
> with usura is no clear demarcation
> and no man can find site for his dwelling.
> Stone cutter is kept from his stone
> weaver is kept from his loom

factive existence, decorously communicated, serves to create an ideal type, one who is out there, just beyond the confines of the latest *Canto:* believed in, aspired toward, sought after, perhaps to be imitated. There is no plot. There is no necessary beginning or end, except as Pound's perceptions make them necessary. Process is as central a concept for him as it was for Whitman: as it has to be in an epic which would make rather than commemorate. The process must be kept going, for the centers of reality which it would constellate are themselves in process. The core is a living core, to be understood in terms of effect, not of cause. Hence, it seems proper for Pound to say that Canto 100 will likely not be the end and that one cannot yet conceive of the "total organism." We have been given various attempts at assessing the total organism, from Yeats's celebrated account of the *Cantos* as fugue, through the emphasis on metamorphosis in Pound's letter to his father in 1927, to Pound's Dantesque statement to an exegete in 1953: "My *Paradiso* will have no St. Dominic or Augustine, but it will be a *Paradiso* just the same, moving toward final coherence. I'm getting at the building of the City, that whole tradition." In any case, we cannot be sure; and we might well extend the applications of some words from a 1939 letter of Pound: "God damn Yeats' bloody paragraph. Done more to prevent people reading Cantos for what is *on the page* than any other one smoke screen." In the same letter Pound concluded: "As to the *form* of the Cantos: All I can say or pray is: *wait* till it's there. I mean wait till I get 'em written and then if it don't show, I will start exegesis. I haven't an Aquinas-map; Aquinas *not* valid now."

Such exegesis as we can start—and likely such as we will conclude with—centers on the "ideogrammic method." In the history of Pound's career, movement toward the theory of the ideogram, as is well known, has proceeded thus: image > vortex > ideogram. That he successively refined his theory of the image and its functioning until he arrived at a stage where he felt that language itself could be made to work nondiscursively (or, as we have been recently urged to say, presentationally); that the crucial catalyst in this segment of the history of his thought is his discovery of the possibilities of Chinese as a language which still worked, to a significant measure, pre- (or infra-) discursively; that although his theories are wrong according to even the most charitable of sinologists, they nonetheless are right for the kind of poem he aspires toward—all these facts are by now well enough known and need only to be recalled here. They have recently been ordered, put in their proper setting, and analyzed and evaluated thus:

. . . the "dissociation of sensibility" . . . is an attempt to project upon the history of poetry a modern theory of the image. This theory owes something to Blake, and something to Coleridge; through the French symbolists it owes something to Schopenhauer, and through Hulme something to Bergson.

Before Mr. Eliot made his particular projection of it, it was familiar to
Yeats (who got it directly from Blake and indirectly through Symons) and
to Pound, who got it from Symons and de Gourmont and the French poets
themselves. Ultimately this image is the product of over a century of continuous anti-positivist poetic speculation, defining and defending the poet's
distinct and special way of knowing truth. It involves a theory of form which
excludes or strictly subordinates all intellectual speculation, and which finds
in music, and better still in the dance, an idea of what art should be: entirely free of discursive content, thinking in quite a different way from the
scientists. . . . Form and meaning are co-essential, and the image belongs
not to the mechanical world of intellect, but to the vital world of intuition;
it is the aesthetic monad of the Symbolists, the Image of the Imagists, the
Vortex of the Vorticists, and finally the ideogram of Pound.[3]

This is by now an authoritative statement. But one element needs to
be added properly to bring Pound's theory of the ideogram into the purview here set for us and at the same time to move it one step out of that
purview, into the world of the new Paideuma. "Knowing truth" must be
changed to something like "using truth and putting it into action," making it factive and volitional.

Pound has, of course, been quite explicit about his ideogrammic
method. He wrote in *Guide to Kulchur:*

> The ideogramic [sic] method consists in presenting one facet and then
> another until at some point one gets off the dead and desensitized surface
> of the reader's mind, onto a part that will register.
> The "new" angle being new to the reader who cannot always be the same
> reader. The newness of the angle being relative and the writer's aim, at least
> this writer's aim [,] being revelation, a just revelation irrespective of newness
> or oldness.

Such considerations as these led him to say, a little later in the *Guide:*
"The history of a culture is the history of ideas going into action." Ideas,
that is to say, as ideograms; for such ideas *are* culture and work on men
to cultivate them. " 'The character of the man is revealed in every brush-
stroke' (and this does not apply only to the [Chinese] ideogram)." The
Cantos, then, working ideogrammically, with a totally decorous attend-
ance to "degrees and weights of importance," reveal character, and revealing it, would make it new and so teach the new Paideuma.

The pedagogical task implied here is outlined quite straightforwardly
in a section of Pound's translation of the Confucian *Great Digest* (the
brackets in the quotation are Pound's):

[3] Frank Kermode, "Dissociation of Sensibility," *Kenyon Review*, xix (1957), pp. 180-
181. Mr. Kermode puts these matters into their largest context in his brilliant *Romantic
Image* (London, 1957).

4. The men of old wanting to clarify and diffuse throughout the empire that light which comes from looking straight into the heart and then acting, first set up good government in their own states; wanting good government in their states, they first established order in their own families; wanting order in the home, they first disciplined themselves; desiring self-discipline, they rectified their own hearts; and wanting to rectify their hearts, they sought precise verbal definitions of their inarticulate thoughts [the tones given off by the heart]; wishing to attain precise verbal definitions, they set to extend their knowledge to the utmost. This completion of knowledge is rooted in sorting things into organic categories.

5. When things had been classified in organic categories, knowledge moved toward fulfillment; given the extreme knowable points, the inarticulate thoughts were defined with precision, [the sun's lance coming to rest in the precise spot verbally]. Having attained this precise verbal definition [*aliter*, this sincerity], they then stabilized their hearts, they disciplined themselves; having attained self-discipline, they set their own houses in order; having order in their own homes, they brought good government to their own states: and when their states were well governed, the empire was brought into equilibrium.

6. From the Emperor, Son of Heaven, down to the common man singly and all together, this self-discipline is the root.

7. If the root be in confusion, nothing will be well governed.

In the end-product of some such process as this lie Pound's hopes for the *Cantos*, which are his hopes for his world. (The statement quoted is in fact paraphrased in Canto 13.) But he must also bring to bear in this process forces deriving from a plenitude of history far beyond that taken into account in the Confucian Paideuma. "An epic," he wrote Harriet Monroe in 1933, "includes history and history ain't all slush and babies' pink toes." He would, in short, lay bare the roots of heroic character through a rendering of universal history.

The character is that of a group of Pound's own heroes who have in common the fact that they went adventuring (in time and space, or in mind, or in both) and sought, in the step-by-step manner described in the Confucian passage quoted above, to bring their empires into equilibrium. All were bearers of the sun's lance. What they did and what they said—these are for Pound ideas in action. He would represent his heroes—Odysseus, Sigismundo Malatesta, Jefferson, Adams, Frobenius, Apollonius of Tyana, rulers out of the great periods of Chinese history, many artists—in such a way that their deeds and sayings are not values but modes of valuation. We are to be brought face to face with those deeds and sayings, are not to be allowed to have such perspective in them as will let us use them as mere counters. Biographical details, quotations from an ever-widening range of authorities, intruded estimations, translations, imitations, ideograms, and pictograms, and all the other *disjecta membra* set down in the *Cantos*—these are rendered and arranged so that we will soon give up hoping to put them back into their context in historical actuality; willy-nilly, we are to grant the poet's claim that in such contexts their meanings have come to be hopelessly tangled and confused. Our comprehension of them is to be controlled by the juxtapositions the poet makes and by the possibilities for metered progression which he discovers. We are to know them for what they *do*. They are propadeutic to our struggle to define ourselves anew.

History, in the broadest and most inclusive sense, becomes for the poet the only authentic language. But even that language has become corrupt; and the poet's obligation is to cleanse it by tearing it—but with loving care—out of its matrix in sheer factuality and by getting to the roots of its moments of truth. For him facts are true to the degree that, as we know them, they lead us to classify things in organic categories, so to attain in turn verbal precision, self-discipline, and social and political equilibrium. Such a criterion for truth not only directs Pound's choice of materials for the *Cantos* but his way of presenting them. Indeed, they appear to present themselves; a reader's only clue to their relevance in given places in the poem is his sudden, startled awareness that he is interested in them not for their value as "fact" but for the value as "truth"—truth as the poet would bid him conceive of it. Facts which are in this sense true are "ideas in action"—Pound's definition of history. Thus the concept of the "factive." It directs Pound to take into account only so much of his protagonists' deeds as will comport with his criterion for truth—not an actual Sigismundo Malatesta but a "true" one, not an actual Adams but a "true" one, not an actual Jew but a "true" one, perhaps not even an actual Pound but a "true" one. History, then, is not given to Pound; he takes it, and exclusively on his own terms. Either we accept the terms or decide that Pound has betrayed history, all the while claiming that it has betrayed him. In the *Cantos,* in either case, his is the last word. Its devices and techniques, however, are intended to be means of proving that the first word was history's and that the poet has only been echoing it in such a way as to recover it in its pristine state. Pound's mood is that of the Confucius who says in Canto 13, "'. . . even I can remember / A day when the historians left blanks in their writings, / But that time seems to be passing.'" The burden on the reader, if he would be drawn into the vortices of the *Cantos,* is not to abandon all hope as he enters there.

In the first seventy-one *Cantos,* ideograms (which lead to centers and cores of *prezzo giusto* and its contraries) are developed in rich and proliferating detail. Historical emphasis is on the achievements of Malatesta, and of early national American culture and Chinese culture—all counterpointed against the initial narrative of Odysseus' voyage. Again and again the matter of usury, with its alienating effect, turns up. Language shifts suddenly, even to Chinese ideograms themselves; historical records are quoted directly or are paraphrased; movement is freely back and forward in time. The total effect is vertiginously clear. One is often at a loss to relate one item to another, yet he is (whenever he can supply himself with the right learning and information) crystal-clear as to the specific quality of each item. (Pound himself furnishes a useful gloss to him who first looks into the *Cantos:* "Very well, I am not proceeding according to Aristotelian logic but according to the ideogramic method of first heaping together the necessary components of thought.") The movement of the poem is even more accelerated in Cantos 74 and following (72 and 73 have not been published). The *Pisan* section (74-84) centers on Pound himself as he pulls out of the world he has created material whereby he may comprehend his own destiny, and through his that of modern man. These are, in the perhaps Dantesque scheme of the poem, the purgatorial Cantos; it is here that Pound breaks through to the great statements he has (according to the scheme of the poem) earned the right to make—the passages that begin "nothing matters but the quality / of the affection—" (76) and the one that begins "The ant's a / centaur in his dragon world" (81).

The Pisan Cantos stabilize the whole, in preparation for the series of almost Mosaic pronouncements of the *Rock-Drill Cantos* (85-95). Here, as the working title indicates, Pound would drill holes for explosives, so as to move mountains and collect that part of them worth making new. These *Cantos* move with a rush of new insight; the ideogrammic mode achieves its fullest and richest and most literal use. Drawing from such widely disparate sources as the *Chou King,* a classic of Chinese history, from Thomas Hart Benton's *Thirty Years View,* and Philostratus' account of Apollonius of Tyana, marked by less of the extended personal, lyrical passages than is the Pisan group, these *Cantos* (so far as one can work his way into them) carry a sense of certitude and assurance that is at once apocalyptic and sublime. Their most important hero is Apollonius and a series of equivalents for him—all beneficent magician-creators, as Pound himself would now be.

Now at the edge of what he has called his paradise, in Canto 92, the poet looks back:

> And against usury
>   and the degradation of sacraments,
> For 40 years I have seen this,
>   now flood as the Yang tse
> also desensitization
>   25 hundred years desensitization
>   a thousand years, desensitization
> After Apollonius, desensitization
>   & a little light from the borders:
>   Erigena,
>   Avicenna, Richardus

He had first glimpsed manifestations of that little light in the heroes
of the earlier Cantos. Now he seeks heroes to whom the light not only
gives charismatic authority but those who have had direct access to it. His
paradise is yet to come; he would see the light too. Canto 90 ends: "UBI
AMOR IBI OCULUS EST." The question shifts from: How make it
new? to: In what light make it new? For what one sees in the light of this
truth one truly loves:

> Trees die & the dream remains
>> Not love but that love flows from it
>> ex animo
>> & cannot ergo delight in itself
>> but only in the love flowing from it.
> UBI AMOR IBI OCULUS EST.

Where love is, the poet would be. If history is ideas in action, the act is
one of love—by which the poet and his protagonists, out of some sublime
necessity, have been created. The distortions and perversions of historical
fact and the violence and hatred which so often emerge in the *Cantos*—
these demonstrate at the very least that the light can be blinding. Stum-
bling over the villainy of some of his heroes, Pound can yet pretend that
it has never existed—or at least, has existed to a good end—because he
cannot quite see it for what to the uninitiated it really seems to be.
Sensing that there are men and events just beyond his field of vision, he
can curse them for not being within it:

> *Democracies electing their sewage*
> *till there is no clear thought about holiness*
> *a dung flow from 1913*
> *and, in this, their kikery functioned, Marx, Freud*
>> *and the american beaneries,*
>>> *Maritain, Hutchins,*
> *or as Benda remarked: "La trahison"*

(91)

The question of who betrayed whom nonetheless remains an open one.
Perhaps Pound's achievement is to have forced it. Perhaps he will turn
out to have been the Ossian of the twentieth century. The important
point for the history of American aspirations toward an epic, for Pound's
search for a new Paideuma in which substance and the means to comprehend substance would be identical, is that betrayal has been a necessary condition for discovery of truth, hatred a necessary condition for
love. As Whitman's love for himself would drive him to transforming all

other selves into aspects of himself in order that he might love them, so Pound's love for himself would drive him to destroy all other selves whose existence his idea of love will prevent him from loving. Whitman's and Pound's means to making an American epic are thus diametrically opposed, but they have at least this in common: they ask that their poetry lead to a totally unifying sacramentalism. To know, is for Whitman, to become; for Pound, to become or be destroyed. Such propositions surely are urged or assented to in vain. But the fact is that they have been urged, assented to, and acted upon. In the process, Joel Barlow's earlier dream of winning a true passage to the heart of youth, of making the poem the means of creating an infinitude of American heroes, turns out to have been not entirely visionary; but, like most visions, it has always had its component of nightmare. Seeing what assenting to the vision has demanded of him, the American should not too much regret his lost youth. Yet the vision is such stuff as his life has been made on.

Chronology of Important Dates

1885	Ezra Loomis Pound born October 30 in Hailey, Idaho.
1901-05	Undergraduate at University of Pennsylvania and Hamilton College. Ph.B., Hamilton College, 1905.
1906	M.A. in Romanics, University of Pennsylvania. To Europe as a Harrison Fellow in Romanics.
1907	Instructor, for a half year, in French and Spanish at Wabash College, Crawfordsville, Indiana.
1908	To Italy. *A Lume Spento* published in Venice. To England: residence in London (until 1920).
1909	*Personae* and *Exultations*.
1910	*Provença. The Spirit of Romance.*
1911	*Canzoni.*
1912	*The Sonnets and Ballate of Guido Cavalcanti. Ripostes.*
1913	*Personae and Exultations* and *Canzoni and Ripostes*. Tenets of Imagism published in April issue of *Poetry: A Magazine of Verse*.
1914	Married Dorothy Shakespear. Edited *Des Imagistes*. "Vorticism" published in *Fortnightly Review*. Contributed to Wyndham Lewis' *Blast* (1914-15).
1915	*Cathay*. Edited *Catholic Anthology*. Began work on the *Cantos*.
1916	*Lustra. Gaudier-Brzeska*. Edited, from the notes of Ernest Fenollosa, *Noh—or, Accomplishment* and *Certain Noble Plays of Japan*.
1918	*Pavannes and Divisions.*
1919	*Quia Pauper Amavi*, including three "Cantos" and "Homage to Sextus Propertius."
1920	To France: residence in Paris (until 1924). *Hugh Selwyn Mauberley* and *Umbra. Instigations.*
1921	*Poems, 1918-21,* including Cantos IV-VII.
1923	*Indiscretions, or Une revue de deux mondes.*
1924	To Italy: settled in Rapallo by 1928. *Antheil and the Treatise on Harmony.*
1925	*A Draft of XVI Cantos.*
1926	Omar Shakespear Pound born September 10 in Paris. *Personae: The Collected Poems of Ezra Pound*, exclusive of the Cantos. Pound's opera, *The Testament of François Villon* performed in Paris. *The Natural Philosophy of Love*, by Rémy de Gourmont, translated with a postscript by Ezra Pound.
1928	*A Draft of Cantos 17-27. Selected Poems*, with an introduction by T. S. Eliot.
1930	*A Draft of XXX Cantos. Imaginary Letters.*
1931	*Guido Cavalcanti: Rime. How to Read.*

1932   Edited *Profile: An Anthology.*

1933   Edited *Active Anthology. ABC of Economics.*

1934   *Eleven New Cantos: XXXI-XLI. ABC of Reading. Make It New* published in London (American edition, 1935).

1935   *Alfred Venison's Poems. Jefferson and/or Mussolini. Social Credit: An Impact.*

1936   *The Chinese Written Character as a Medium for Poetry: An Ars Poetica* by Ernest Fenollosa, with a foreword and notes by Ezra Pound.

1937   *The Fifth Decad of Cantos. Polite Essays* published in London (American edition, 1940).

1938   *Guide to Kulchur* (American edition entitled *Culture*).

1939   First visit to the United States since 1910. Honorary D. Litt., Hamilton College.

1940   *Cantos LII-LXXI.* Began radio addresses in Rome, as personal propaganda in support of U. S. Constitution, as he saw it. Continued, after Pearl Harbor, speaking against the American war effort.

1943   Indicted for treason by the District Court of the United States for the District of Columbia.

1944   Arrested by U. S. Army in Genoa. To American military prison compound near Pisa: three weeks' solitary confinement in a steel cage.

1945   Flown to Washington, D.C., in November, to stand trial.

1946   Adjudged insane and remanded to St. Elizabeth's Hospital for the criminally insane.

1947   *The Unwobbling Pivot and the Great Digest* of Confucius, dated "D.T.C., Pisa; 5 October–5 November, 1945."

1948   *The Cantos of Ezra Pound,* collected edition including *The Pisan Cantos* (74-84).

1949   Bollingen Prize for Poetry for 1948 awarded Pound for *The Pisan Cantos.*

1950   *The Letters of Ezra Pound, 1907-1941,* edited by D. D. Paige. *Patria Mia. Money Pamphlets by £* (6 vols., 1950-52).

1953   *The Translations of Ezra Pound.*

1954   *Literary Essays of Ezra Pound, with an Introduction by T. S. Eliot.*

1955   *Shih Ching: The Classic Anthology, defined by Confucius.*

1956   *Section Rock Drill: 85-95 de los Cantares.* Sophocles' *Women of Trachis,* translated by Ezra Pound, published in London (American edition, 1957).

1958   Indictment for treason dismissed in U. S. District Court for the District of Columbia. To Italy: residence with daughter at Schloss Brunnenburg, near Merano.

1959   *Thrones: 96-109 de los Cantares.* 111th Canto completed by Christmas.

1960   *Impact: Essays on Ignorance and the Decline of American Civilization,* edited by Noel Stock.

Notes on the Editor and Authors

WALTER SUTTON, the editor of this volume, is Professor of English at Syracuse University. He is the author of *The Western Book Trade* and *Modern American Criticism* and co-editor (with Richard Foster) of *Modern Criticism—Theory and Practice.*

T. S. ELIOT, the poet and critic, still lives in London, where he was associated with Pound as a leader of the modernist movement in literature. He has edited Pound's *Selected Poems* and *Literary Essays of Ezra Pound.*

GEORGE P. ELLIOTT, the novelist and poet, teaches at St. Mary's College, California. He is the author of *Parktilden Village, David Knudsen, Among the Dangs,* and *Fever and Chills.*

DAVID W. EVANS of the University of Southern California is the author of numerous essays on modern poets, including Ezra Pound and T. S. Eliot.

W. M. FROHOCK, Professor of French at Harvard University, is the author of *The Novel of Violence in America, André Malraux and the Tragic Imagination,* and *Strangers to this Ground: Cultural Diversity in Contemporary American Writing.*

HUGH KENNER, Professor of English at the University of California at Santa Barbara, is the author of *The Invisible Poet: T. S. Eliot, The Poetry of Ezra Pound,* and *Wyndham Lewis.* He has edited the volume on T. S. Eliot in this series.

F. R. LEAVIS is Fellow of Downing College, Cambridge. He is the author of *New Bearings in English Poetry* and was the editor of *Scrutiny.*

EARL MINER, Associate Professor of English at the University of California at Los Angeles, is the author of *The Japanese Tradition in British and American Literature* and *Nihon o Utsusu Chisana Kagami,* co-author (with Robert H. Brower) of *Japanese Court Poetry,* and an editor of the California edition of the *Works of John Dryden.*

ROY HARVEY PEARCE, Professor of English at the Ohio State University, is the author of *The Savages of America* and *The Continuity of American Poetry.* He is also a general editor of the Centennial Edition of the works of Nathaniel Hawthorne and has edited the volume on Whitman in this series.

FORREST READ, Assistant Professor of English at Cornell University, is the author of several articles on Pound and an editor of *Epoch.* He is at present preparing an edition of Pound's letters to James Joyce.

M. L. ROSENTHAL, Professor of English at New York University, is the author of *A Primer of Ezra Pound* and *The Modern Poets.*

MURRAY SCHAFER, the Canadian composer and musicologist, is the author of *British Composers in Interview*. He has edited Pound's opera *The Testament of François Villon* for the B.B.C. Third Programme.

J. P. SULLIVAN, a British classicist now teaching at the University of Texas, has completed a study of Pound's *Homage to Sextus Propertius*. He is an editor of *Arion* and of two collections entitled *Critical Essays on Roman Literature* (1. *Elegy and Lyric*; 2. *Satire*).

HAROLD H. WATTS, Professor of English at Purdue University, is the author of *Ezra Pound and the Cantos* and *Hound and Quarry*.

WILLIAM CARLOS WILLIAMS of Rutherford, New Jersey, America's leading unexpatriated poet, has known Ezra Pound since both were students at the University of Pennsylvania.

WILLIAM BUTLER YEATS, the Irish poet, commemorated his friendship with the younger American poet in *A Packet for Ezra Pound*.

Selected Bibliography

Edwards, John H., and William Vasse. *Annotated Index to* The Cantos *of Ezra Pound*. Berkeley and Los Angeles: University of California Press, 1957. An extremely useful reference for the reader of the *Cantos*.

Emery, Clark M. *Ideas Into Action: A Study of Pound's* Cantos. Coral Gables, Fla.: University of Miami Press, 1958. A detailed commentary tracing the origins of the ideas expressed in the *Cantos*.

Espey, John J. *Ezra Pound's* Mauberley: *A Study in Composition*. Berkeley and Los Angeles: University of California Press, 1955. A critical application of the methods of traditional academic scholarship to a modern poem.

Fraser, G. S. *Ezra Pound*. Edinburgh: Oliver and Boyd Ltd., 1960; New York: Grove Press, 1961. A concise introduction to Pound's ideas, his verse and prose, and his critical reputation.

Kenner, Hugh. *The Poetry of Ezra Pound*. Norfolk, Conn.: New Directions, 1951; London: Faber & Faber Ltd., 1951. A sympathetic and detailed critical interpretation.

Leary, Lewis, ed. *Motive and Method in* The Cantos *of Ezra Pound*. New York: Columbia University Press, 1954. This collection of English Institute Essays includes—besides the reprinted essay by Forrest Read—"The Broken Mirrors and the Mirror of Memory," by Hugh Kenner; "Pound and Frobenius," by Guy Davenport; and "The Metamorphoses of Ezra Pound," by Sister M. Bernetta Quinn.

Norman, Charles. *Ezra Pound*. New York: The Macmillan Co., 1960. A biography providing the fullest documented account of Pound's career and literary associations.

O'Connor, William Van, and Edward Stone, eds. *A Casebook on Ezra Pound*. New York: Thomas Y. Crowell Company, 1959. A collection of essays and documents relating to Pound's mental and legal condition and to the Bollingen Prize controversy.

Rosenthal, M. L. *A Primer of Ezra Pound*. New York: The Macmillan Co., 1960. A useful brief introduction to Pound's poetry.

Russell, Peter, ed. *Ezra Pound: A Collection of Essays to be Presented to Ezra Pound on His Sixty-fifth Birthday*. London: Peter Nevill, 1950. Published in America as *An Examination of Ezra Pound*. Norfolk, Conn.: New Directions, 1950. A generous collection of personal tributes and critical essays by contributors including Edith Sitwell, Ernest Hemingway, Wyndham Lewis, and Ford Madox Ford.

Schlauch, Margaret. "The Anti-Humanism of Ezra Pound," *Science & Society*, XIII (Summer 1949), 258-269. A negative critique by an American Marxist critic.

Viereck, Peter. "Pure Poetry, Impure Politics, and Ezra Pound," *Commentary*, XII (April 1951), 340-346. An analysis of the Bollingen Prize controversy and its implications for literature and literary criticism.

Watts, Harold H. *Ezra Pound and* The Cantos. Chicago: Henry Regnery Co., 1952. A thoughtful discussion of *The Cantos* as the poet's response to a cultural crisis.

American Authors in the Twentieth Century Views Series

British Authors in the Twentieth Century Views Series